# Be That Teacher!

## BREAKING THE CYCLE
## FOR STRUGGLING READERS

# Be That Teacher!

## BREAKING THE CYCLE
## FOR STRUGGLING READERS

Victoria J. Risko
Doris Walker-Dalhouse

*Forewords by Richard L. Allington & Timothy V. Rasinski*

Teachers College, Columbia University
New York and London

The assessment forms used in Figure 3.5 is reprinted with permission from Dena G. McAllister.

The image used in Figure 8.5 is reprinted with permission from The C.S. Lewis Company Ltd. The image originally appeared in Robin Lawrie, *The Lion, The Witch and The Wardrobe: A Graphic Novel*. Copyright © C. S. Lewis Ptd. Ltd. 1995.

Published by Teachers College Press, 1234 Amsterdam Avenue, New York, NY 10027

*Library of Congress Cataloging-in-Publication Data*

Risko, Victoria.
    Be that teacher! : breaking the cycle for struggling readers / Victoria J. Risko, Doris Walker-Dalhouse ; Foreword by Richard Allington.
        p. cm.
    Includes bibliographical references and index.
    ISBN 978-0-8077-5322-4 (pbk.)
        1. Reading—Remedial teaching. 2. Reading disability. I. Walker-Dalhouse, Doris. II. Title.
    LB1050.5.R57  2012
    372.43—dc23                                                    2011045768

ISBN 978-0-8077-5322-4 (paper)

Printed on acid-free paper
Manufactured in the United States of America

19   18   17   16   15   14   13   12            8   7   6   5   4   3   2   1

# Contents

**Forewords** *by Richard L. Allington & Timothy V. Rasinski*     **ix**

**Preface**     **xi**

    Content and Organization     xii

    Our History     xiv

**Acknowledgments**     **xvii**

**1. Focusing on Strengths and Differences**     **1**

    Case Analysis: Colin     1

    Helping Each Student Make Connections     4

    Some Reasons for Reading Difficulties     5

    Summary     16

**2. Capitalizing on Students' Cultural and Linguistic Histories and Experiences**     **19**

    Case Analyses: Christine, Seth, and Erin     20

    Cultural and Linguistic Histories and Experiences     22

    Teaching Students Whose Languages Were Different from Their Own     27

    Culturally Responsive Reading Instruction     28

    Cultural Modeling     30

    Cultural Modeling Example     31

    Preparing Teachers for Diverse Teaching     35

    Summary     38

**3. Assessing What Matters for Students and Instruction**     **39**

    Case Analyses: Shakeela, Aslam, and Jenny     39

    Conceptualizing Assessment     41

    Planful and Useful Assessments     44

    Summary     66

**4. Using Anchors for Leveraging Problem Solving
   and Cross-Curricular Connections**                                                        **68**

   Case Analysis: Lenia                                                                      69

   Anchored Instruction                                                                      70

   Conceptualizing Instruction                                                               72

   Summary                                                                                   82

**5. Changing Strategies to Meet
   New Demands for Student Success**                                                         **84**

   Case Analysis: Maria                                                                      84

   Early Literacy Experiences                                                                87

   Conceptualizing Instruction                                                               89

   Beneficial Factors for Early Reading                                                      91

   Early Reading Instruction for Language Minority Students                                  93

   Summary                                                                                   95

**6. Contextualizing Word Learning and Word Identification**                                 **97**

   Case Analyses: Adam and Jeremy                                                            97

   Conceptualizing Instruction                                                               100

   Instructional Recommendations                                                             104

   Summary                                                                                   110

**7. Developing Concepts and Vocabulary
   Through Multiple Skills and Strategies**                                                   **111**

   Case Analysis: Catherine                                                                  111

   Vocabulary Instruction in Mrs. Schneider's Classroom                                      114

   Conceptualizing Instruction                                                               116

   Vocabulary Instruction for English Learners                                               124

   Summary                                                                                   127

**8. Enabling Students' Reading Comprehension and
   Access to Complicated Texts with Guided Instruction**                                      **129**

   Case Analysis: Colin Revisited                                                            130

   Conceptualizing Instruction                                                               130

   Maximizing the Benefits of Guided Text Instruction                                        139

   Reading to Deepen Comprehension                                                           143

   Summary                                                                                   151

**9. Capitalizing on Students' Families and Life Experiences**    **152**

    Case Analysis: William    152

    Parent Involvement    153

    Conceptualizing Involvement of
    Parents, Families, and Communities    155

    Starting with Preservice Teachers    159

    Involving Universities and Schools    161

    Summary    162

**10. Fostering Independence and Success in Reading**    **164**

**Appendix: Teacher Resources**    **167**

    Books    167

    Position Statements from National and
    International Professional Organizations    169

    Online Resources    169

**References**    **171**

    Children's Books Cited    193

**Index**    **195**

**About the Authors**    **206**

# Foreword

*Be That Teacher!* is a unique book. Unique because of the attention paid to the importance of creating culturally compatible curriculum and instruction in developing the literacy proficiencies of all students. Victoria Risko and Doris Walker-Dalhouse provide the reader with a clear portrayal of just how to adapt instruction to develop lessons that meet readers where they are and take them on to new learning.

Students in American schools reflect the diversity of our national society. This diversity can be found in the substantial differences in family incomes, in the family histories that children bring with them to schools, in the array of religious practices and beliefs, and it can be most easily observed in the children's different skin hues and in the different languages that families use at home.

The students in our schools today represent far greater diversity than I recall in those "country" schools I attended in the upper midwest 50 years ago. There was, even then, the income diversity, but basically I attended an all-White, all-Protestant one-room country school where all families spoke English at home. Which is not to say that diversity did not exist even then. Rather it is to suggest that today such classrooms have largely vanished, even in the upper Midwest, and in their place we commonly have classrooms populated with diverse students.

*Be That Teacher!* is an important as well as a readable book. It provides good advice on working with both children and their families. The authors assist the reader through the use of the stories of teachers, their students, and their students' families. Teaching to take advantage of the linguistic and cultural diversity present in your classroom makes it more likely that your students will become readers. It will also make you a more effective teacher. This book will assist you in achieving both goals.

—*Richard L. Allington*
University of Tennessee

# Foreword

It seems that every month we are reminded of the literacy crisis that faces this nation. The 2011 National Assessment of Educational Progress reported that nearly a third of all fourth grade students in the United States are reading at a level considered below basic. Moreover, this percentage has largely remained unchanged over the past decade despite major efforts at the national and state levels to improve student reading achievement. While acknowledging the importance of systemic efforts at the national, state, local, and school levels to help students become fully literate, it is also wise to consider how individual teachers in their own classrooms can change the literacy lives of their students—one student at a time. *Be That Teacher*! attempts to view effective instruction for struggling readers from the point of view of the classroom teacher. Vicki Risko and Doris Walker-Dalhouse challenge every teacher to consider what they can do, both through effective instruction and sensitivity to students' cultural environment, in order to move all students toward higher levels of literacy achievement.

Clearly, it is important to examine the macro issues that affect literacy achievement. At the same time, individual teachers must consider the micro issues that occur in their classrooms every day that can affect students' development as readers. I hope every teacher and every teacher-in-training has the opportunity to engage in thoughtful reading, discussion, and planned action related to content of this powerful volume. Literacy is a right for all people. To make literacy instruction effective it needs to be considered from all perspectives. Risko and Walker-Dalhouse make a major contribution to our field with this volume. The insights that they share can lead to more effective instruction that will surely lead to improved student achievement, especially among those students we view as most vulnerable.

—*Timothy V. Rasinski*
Kent State University

# Preface

It is time to break the cycle of reading failure for students who experience reading difficulties. For we all know students who return to school each year hoping that this is the year, that you are the teacher who will help them become successful learners, readers, and writers.

We advocate for instruction that is sensible, grounded in authentic reading and writing engagement, and designed to position students as successful learners. Richard Allington (2011b) argues that "sensible" instruction insures that students read something they like and understand every day, have opportunities to talk with peers and adults about their reading and writing, and receive instruction from expert classroom and reading teachers. In too many schools, students classified as struggling readers have little time to read connected texts, limited access to books, and few or no opportunities to choose what they are reading. And far too often these students receive instruction that does not address their strengths and needs.

Struggling readers are not a homogenous group; rather they vary in understandings, skills, and strategies they have acquired and those they need (S. W. Valencia, 2011). Yet across SES levels and different cultural and linguistic histories, struggling readers benefit from high-quality and differentiated instruction (Allington, 2006).

The disparities in reading achievement due to poverty and racial and ethnic differences are well documented (J. Lee, Grigg, & Donahue, 2007). Racial/ethnic and gender gaps in student performance for eighth-grade students and the dropout rate for Latino and African American students remain higher than the rate for White students (Planty et al., 2009). Students living in poverty and representing racial and ethnic differences are overrepresented in special education (Artiles & Kozleski, 2007), underrepresented in gifted education programs (Ford, 1998), and often positioned in classrooms as disabled (Collins, 2011). Despite a decade of major educational reforms aimed at closing the achievement gap and addressing reading difficulties, these problems persist. This is partly the case because schools emphasize the wrong things (Allington, 2011b; Collins, 2011; National Endowment of the Arts Annual Report, 2007). Skill drills, for example, replace authentic reading and writing opportunities. Consequently, the need to address gaps in reading achievement between and within various groups of students at the classroom and school level must continue to be a priority.

## CONTENT AND ORGANIZATION

This book is for classroom teachers and reading specialists and ultimately their students who may be experiencing reading difficulties, and for undergraduate and graduate students preparing to teach, to advance their understandings of literacy instruction, or coach those who teach.

This book focuses on changing the trajectory of struggling readers' learning in school and repositioning them as abled readers. We view good, sensible reading instruction as the vehicle that makes reading and writing work for each student. It builds on students' own curiosity, interests, prior knowledge, and cultural and linguistic experiences rather than denying them or treating them as deficits.

More specifically, our book is organized as follows. In Chapters 1–3 we attempt to put a face to the tens of thousands of struggling readers in today's schools. We begin, in Chapter 1, with a case study of Colin, a fifth-grade student in Ms. Schull's class, and consider possible reasons why Colin is experiencing reading difficulties. Like new and experienced teachers everywhere, it is important that we understand the reasons why students struggle in reading, as well as the type of instruction needed to accelerate their progress. In Chapter 2 we address this question: What cultural and linguistic considerations must we understand to provide the robust and responsive instruction that students like Colin need? In Chapter 3 we address assessments that are useful and usable in the classroom to pinpoint students' strengths, resources, and difficulties to assist teachers in providing robust and responsive instruction.

In Chapters 4–9 we introduce other primary and intermediate students whose struggles differ from Colin's yet whose instructional needs must be met. We analyze each student and instructional situation to identify directions for appropriate instruction. We provide specific instructional recommendations that can make a difference in the reading development of students in elementary and middle grades. These recommendations are grounded in research that occurred in real classrooms with real teachers and real students. Chapters 1 through 9 have a section entitled Case Analysis, where we analyze the students and instructional situations; starting with Chapter 4, another section, Conceptualizing

Instruction, focuses on our instructional recommendations. In Chapter 10, we provide a summary of instructional features that are powerful and robust for reducing student failure.

The cases we describe throughout this text are composites of students, teachers, and families who have impacted our thinking about reading instruction. No one case completely represents one student, one teacher, or one situation that has singularly or collectively influenced and extended our thinking about struggling readers. Descriptive information embedded in the case analysis sections of each chapter represents typical information shared by teachers and/or parents. We have gathered data across individuals and situations and organized these data thematically as individual cases to give voice to the multiple and representative instructional issues and dilemmas that we face as literacy educators. Pseudonyms are assigned to the teachers and students we describe.

Guided by the voices of many teachers and students who have influenced our thinking, we provide authentic examples of how instruction can be implemented and adjusted to accommodate students' individual differences—differences that are influenced by their school and instructional background, their cultural and linguistic histories, their interests and out-of-school activities, their reading and writing habits in and out of school, and their understandings and misunderstandings about texts, print, and digital media. We invite you to analyze and reflect about each case presented as you chart a course toward independence and success for the struggling readers in your classrooms and schools.

Each chapter begins with an overview of major chapter ideas and concludes with a summary and questions to guide reflection and analysis of issues we pose. Text highlights and figures provide explicit examples of teaching principles, materials, and instruction.

Our book differs from other texts addressing struggling readers in at least two ways. First, many texts addressing reading difficulties focus primarily on building students' motivation and positive attitudes, assessing students' skills and strategy knowledge and needs, and providing instruction that supports students' literacy development and targets students' needs. While these areas are central to the content of our book, we situate these areas in a consideration of students' lives. We take an ecological approach to our recommendations for instructing struggling readers as we consider the knowledge and experiences in multiple communities—home, neighborhood, peer group, church, and school—that influence students' identities as readers and writers and how their knowledge can be used as a resource for teaching skills and strategies and disciplinary knowledge.

We draw on research indicating that instruction of skills and strategies without considering the larger world in which students live and learn is highly ineffective, especially for students with diverse cultural and linguistic histories.

Second, the book differs from texts that challenge us to look at the larger issue of school improvement. We are firmly committed to the urgency of taking social actions needed to promote educational and social changes that will remove the inequities in school funding, resources, and achievement in high-poverty schools. Yet we believe that critical action must also occur at the classroom level. This is especially true for struggling readers who are found in all classrooms, but found in greater numbers in high-poverty schools. To initiate change at the classroom level for struggling readers, the needs of these students must be examined through the following six critical lenses: student-focused, motivational, sociocultural, constructivist, diagnostic/assessment, and instructional.

We apply these lenses to authentic classroom cases to promote critical thinking about the individual nature of the students who struggle in reading. We address factors affecting student motivation in reading and explore ways to increase intrinsic motivation to read. We analyze the sociocultural factors that affect student learning and explore ways to change trajectories in reading achievement. Ultimately, we want to explore how teachers can use students' individual and cultural backgrounds, as well as the results of diagnostic/assessment measures, to provide the type of differentiated instruction that struggling readers need. We invite you to consider our instructional recommendations in an effort to provide forms of instruction that matters the most for students who continue to fail in reading.

## OUR HISTORY

We have been interested in students' reading problems since we began teaching. Vicki's first teaching assignment was first grade in an urban school in a small industrial town in western Pennsylvania. Doris's first teaching assignment was in a first-grade classroom in an urban school district located in a mid-sized city in central Kentucky. Starting with those first teaching assignments and in subsequent years when we taught in the fourth to sixth grades, and continuing in our years as teacher educators when we collaborated with many teachers and reading specialists, we have learned valuable lessons about students who experience reading difficulties. We've learned that our students responded favorably to some aspects of our literacy instruction and had difficulty with others. Some were inter-ested in the daily reading and writing activities of our classrooms, and oth-ers were far more interested in activities that they created for our classroom (e.g., the fourth graders who wrote plays during lunch for all to perform or the first graders who found books in the school library for us to read aloud) or that occurred out of school. Mostly, we have learned that our students have many capabilities that often are not realized or developed fully during reading and writing instruction, and that students often are thought to be less than capable or sorted into groups or special placements that designate them as having disabilities. Too often school situations and high-stakes as-sessments lead to quick (and often negative) judgments about students' capabilities, and students are sorted into groups of being either "able" or "unable"—labels that often negate the importance of a more comprehen-sive understanding of students' capabilities and instructional needs.

# Acknowledgments

It is true that none of the things that we accomplish in life are realized without the encouragement, guidance, and care of others. We want to express our gratitude to the teachers, students, colleagues, and friends who have contributed in a multiplicity of ways to inform our thinking and to encourage our efforts.

We sincerely appreciate and have enjoyed the opportunity to work with Regina Ward at Teachers College Press in bringing the project to fruition. The careful editing and editorial advice from Daniel Richcreek, Lori Tate, Karl Nyberg, and Jennifer Baker, and Meg Hartmann's support in promoting our book is greatly appreciated. We extend our special thanks to Karen Gaard, who willingly and skillfully provided the technical assistance needed during the development of the manuscript.

*Vicki:* I am grateful for the special people in my life. My parents, Evelyn and Michael Risko, who taught me that everyone has special talents that can be realized with caring and supportive others. For them, these caring others included teachers who work tirelessly to make connections to their students. My husband, Dr. Marino C. Alvarez, who is my mentor, my colleague, and my best friend, encourages me to live life fully. I thank him for listening to my ideas (over and over again) and offering critique and enthusiasm, mostly enthusiasm for taking on new projects. Christopher Alvarez, our son, who constantly reminds me that students will succeed when you believe they can and when they take the lead in their own learning and goal setting.

*Doris:* I am indebted to those people in my life who have played a significant role in my accomplishments. First, I want to thank my parents, Mr. and Mrs. John David Walker III, who instilled in me a passion for learning and the confidence to persevere in the pursuit of my goals. My sister, Dr. Sharon A. Walker, for helping me realize through our childhood play of being teachers that teaching was to be my life's passion. Most importantly, I want to whole-heartedly thank my husband, Dr. A. Derick Dalhouse, and my children, Yanick and Jean-Pierre, for their love and support, which keep me grounded in both my life and work.

# CHAPTER 1

# Focusing on Strengths and Differences

Fundamental to this text is the belief that all students in our classrooms can be successful readers. Yet achieving this goal requires instruction that engages students' interest, experiences, and knowledge, and choice of texts that students can and want to read. It requires instruction that is thoughtful and specific in addressing students' needs.

Some practices, such as requiring a common text for the whole classroom to read, can be motivational for some students or hotly contested by others. Reading a common text typically benefits those students who see themselves in the text and/or those who are committed to its content for various reasons (e.g., interested in fantasy regardless of text difficulty). Those with little background knowledge of the content or interest typically do all that they can to avoid engagement. Such is the situation for Colin, a fifth-grade student who has no interest in the Narnia series that engages some of his classmates. There are multiple reasons that can explain this lack of engagement.

## CASE ANALYSIS: COLIN

The case we describe here is situated in a K–6 elementary school located in an urban area of a countywide school district. There are 350 students enrolled in this school and approximately 45% of them receive free or reduced lunch. The school building is modern, and classrooms have round tables and chairs (instead of individual desks) for students to work in small groups. The building and classrooms have multiple windows and walls are brightly painted and used to display students' work. Technology access, however, is limited to computers located in one computer lab or media center.

The school principal meets with the teachers to guide curriculum development and implementation. Two reading specialists collaboratively teach students identified with reading difficulties. This instruction is provided either in the classroom or in an alternate setting; occasionally a reading specialist will team teach with the classroom teacher during the reading and language arts class period.

Our case is located in Ms. Schull's classroom. She is a first-year teacher in this school, having taught 3 years in another school district in the state. The students in her fifth-grade classroom are 55% White, 40% African American, and 5% English learners (all of whom speak Spanish as their first language). Colin, the case developed in this chapter and revisited in Chapter 8, is African American. Some students walk to school while others are bused there from other communities in the county.

Ms. Schull teaches all subjects to her students, including reading and language arts. She teaches reading with a literature anthology textbook, which has excerpts of classical and popular literature. It is part of her school district's core reading program. Ms. Schull conducts whole-class instruction for reading.

When we entered her room, we noticed that students were seated in groups of four around tables. Ms. Schull began by reading aloud the first three paragraphs of a passage entitled *The Island*, written for the literature text and representing information from the C. S. Lewis Narnia series. She then asked her students to predict what may happen in the story. To start the predictions, she said, "Let's predict what happens when the children are left alone at the train junction." Answers came from Carey, Teneka, and Byron: "They will be afraid!" "They will fall asleep and miss the train!" "They will go back to Narnia!" Eight of the 28 students made predictions that Ms. Schull wrote on the board. She asked the students to refer to these as they continued to read the text, confirming or changing their predictions. The students then took turns reading the text aloud.

After class Ms. Schull told us that she is concerned about the reading skills of several of her students. One of these students is Colin. She said that Colin had difficulty reading passages with expression. When we heard Colin read aloud during class, we noticed that he read softly and haltingly and missed several words. And we noticed that once he completed his reading, he put his head down on the desk and seemed uninterested in the story while other students took turns reading aloud. He did not participate in generating or confirming predictions about story events, and he didn't answer Ms. Schull's questions about the meaning of words in the story.

We share the above vignette to illustrate one of the greatest challenges we face as classroom teachers and reading specialists: how to provide instruction in ways that best support all students, especially those who may be experiencing reading problems. Reading problems are associated with multiple contributing factors.

There is no one approach that is appropriate for all students to accommodate the range of factors contributing to reading difficulties.

> Differential paths leading to reading difficulties require differentiated instructional responses.

Among the several students experiencing reading difficulties in Ms. Schull's class are African Americans, English learners, and students who move frequently when their parents are unemployed. Ms. Schull was interested in knowing more about all her students, especially the students whose cultures seemed to be different from her own. She seemed to be well aware that students from minorities or nondominant groups representing multiple cultural and linguistic heritages are disproportionately identified as having reading problems and placed in remedial reading or special education programs as compared to students whose heritage more closely matches mainstream school practices and curricula (Gutiérrez & Lee, 2009). We consider how instruction itself (e.g., round robin reading as used by Ms. Schull that allows students to retreat) can contribute to students' reading problems and distance nondominant groups of students from succeeding in school literacy programs.

We define *nondominant students* broadly to include students who may be marginalized by school practices and who, consequently, are identified as struggling readers. Among students who may be represented in our definition of minority or nondominant students are those who find little relevance between the school curriculum and their life experiences or the real-world problems that interest them (Mueller, 2001). They may be recent immigrants and fluent (and literate) in a language other than English who find few, if any connections, to their home language in school, as identified by Orellana, Reynolds, and Martinez (2011). They may be students who are homeless (Noll & Watkins, 2003) or live in poverty (Portes & Salas, 2009) and may not have access to resources that will support their success in schools. Or they may be students whose home and community cultural life stories are not represented in school textbooks or classroom discourse, as described by Nieto (2000) and others.

Additionally, the students we discuss as struggling readers may be White and represent dominant cultures, yet their reading trajectory has not progressed as expected. Thus we approach the study of who may be identified as experiencing reading problems broadly and inclusively, and with the dual goal of scrutinizing potential reasons that students are positioned as failures with reading disability labels and identifying educational solutions that will reposition them as successful readers and writers.

CASE QUESTIONS

1.   What are possible reasons that Colin seems disinterested in the Narnia text?
2.   How can prior knowledge of the Narnia series (e.g., having read another book in the series or seen a Narnia movie) impact students' engagement and understanding while reading a new Narnia text?
3.   What actions can teachers like Ms. Schull take to begin transferring their concern about struggling readers, like Colin, into engaging classroom practices?

## HELPING EACH STUDENT MAKE CONNECTIONS

We draw on sociocultural and constructivist perspectives for our interpretation of students' reading problems and for forming directions for assessment and instruction. These theories are grounded in research that positions "learners as competent" (Gutiérrez & Lee, 2009), a perspective that is particularly important for countering low expectations that are commonly associated with students who are experiencing reading problems (Bass, Dasinger, Elish-Piper, Matthews, & Risko, 2008; Nocon & Cole, 2009). Researchers influenced by these two theoretical perspectives consistently demonstrate two central principles to transform instruction in ways that enable, rather than disable, students' reading development.

> All students bring rich sources of information that can be used as a resource for teaching and learning.

First, all students across ethnic and cultural heritage and life experiences bring rich knowledge that can be used as a resource when teaching literacy skills and strategies and disciplinary knowledge (Cummins, 2007; Moll, 2003). Too often schools fail to use and build on students' capabilities and prior knowledge even though researchers are reporting how such an approach can diminish risk factors, such as poverty (Griffin & Case, 1997) or a history of failing in school (Mueller, 2001). Other researchers, such as C. D. Lee (2005, 2008); Moll, Saez, and Dworin (2001); and Tellez and Waxman (2006) report on how academic achievement and literacy development are enhanced when using students' home language and community knowledge, called funds of knowledge by Moll and Greenberg (1990).

Second, learning new information involves making connections between previously learned information and the new concepts under study and applying this new knowledge as tools for in-depth learning, acquiring new literacy skills and strategies, problem-solving, and using disciplinary knowledge in real-world applications (Bransford, Brown, & Cocking, 1999). Wolf (2007) reminds us that "comprehension is affected by everything the reader brings to the text" (p. 160) and that comprehension is a dynamic process. Thus there is this simultaneous exchange occurring—students' life experiences influence what is understood and taken from the text while also changing how students understand their world and their experiences. Defining texts broadly to include digital, print, pictorial texts, and more, theorists and researchers evoke a vision of how schools can work proactively to "take up the multiple and diverse [text] literacies that children bring with them" (Portes & Salas, 2009, p. 99) and provide access to disciplinary knowledge and to higher order thinking required for school achievement and to succeed in the world.

> Learning involves making connections between prior knowledge and new information.

## SOME REASONS FOR READING DIFFICULTIES

Many reasons are associated with reading difficulties and sometimes several occur in combination to affect students' progress. For example, the major problem confronting Ms. Schull, described above, is that her instruction is not benefitting all students in her classroom. Some students are highly engaged in the class discussions and are able to make connections between their interests, their knowledge and cultural experiences, and their previous reading experiences; they seem to be skillful and strategic. It is likely that they have a history of successful performance in school and that they expect they will succeed in this classroom. Conversely, other students are not engaged and seem to be having difficulty making connections to the texts they are reading in class. Several students told Ms. Schull that they had never read the Narnia books and didn't know anything about them. Colin and other students often misread words during the reading and seemed unconcerned about the changes their mistakes made to the text. This suggests that they were not reading for meaning or were not using strategies to help them self-correct. There may be many reasons for these actions: They may not have specific "Narnia" knowledge to help them make sense of an unfamiliar text; they may have a history of instruction that did not address their particular strengths or needs; and/or they may be uncomfortable reading aloud in front of the whole class.

In a related example, Mueller (2001) describes a student, Kayla, who liked reading books in the early grades but had difficulty transitioning to more complicated texts in middle school because she was not taught skills and strategies to help her identify unknown, content-specific words. By sixth grade she hated reading because she could not read "three hundred plus pages in like five weeks" (p. 21) and she learned to skip words that she did not know, a strategy that contributed to her comprehension problems. But by ninth grade Kayla considered herself a reader, and she explained that this came about through her own persistence and hard work. She listened (really listened) to her mom read to her and her brother (a long-standing home activity), used time on the school bus for reading, chose her own books and read four or five a week, learned how to identify chunks of longer words that helped her pronounce the words, and sometimes pictured herself in the book to make sense of it and the (longer) words. And even though she made great progress, she was disappointed that no teacher had taken enough time with her to help her solve her word-learning problems and make sure she was making sense of the text. This vivid description of Kayla's insights reminds us how hard students will work if they have some clues about how to succeed. And we notice that Kayla's independent reading increased her volume of reading, another positive outcome associated with increased achievement (Guthrie, 2004; Wigfield & Guthrie, 1997).

Often it is difficult to identify when a reading problem began or why it occurred. And sometimes, as in the Kayla example above, students and/or their parents are the best resources for identifying causes or the nature of their problems. Kayla described her difficulty with longer words and texts with unfamiliar content. Students may identify other areas that are troubling for them, such as "I can remember the facts but I never learned how to find main ideas" or "I don't like to read because the books are about topics that are unimportant to me." Students' perceptions of their own reading problems can be quite accurate. After weeks of independent assessments, teachers often draw the same conclusions that students propose. Thus students' perceptions are often starting points for teachers and students to work together to plan a pathway that leads to successful reading. We have learned that students are quite concerned about their reading abilities; they often evaluate themselves by their personal achievements or disappointments as readers. And we have never met a student who didn't want to learn to read.

All students have strengths and needs, both of which should be addressed if they are to become successful readers and writers and independent learners. As classroom and reading teachers, we need to make visible what students know and can do, and plan instruction that honors that knowledge as a resource. Thus the study of possible factors associated with reading difficulties is important for understanding the instruction we will describe throughout this text. Often conditions can be enabling or disabling depending on the students' cultural and linguistic history, prior experiences and knowledge, *and* whether or not instruction takes advantages of these experiences and knowledge. We refer to our brief description of Ms. Schull and Colin at the beginning of this chapter to discuss some possible reasons for reading difficulties. We begin with the area of students' interest and engagement in reading.

## Interest and Engagement

Interest and engagement are areas that can either support students' literacy development or hinder their progress. It may be difficult to determine cause and effect relationships between reading comprehension and engagement and self-directed learning as they are mutually enabling of successful learning. Yet high interest in the topic and active engagement in pursuing additional information can be the catalyst for deepening reading comprehension and increasing the chances to become self-directed and independent readers. This finding seems to hold true for students across income levels and across comparisons of international student performance (Guthrie, 2004). Relatedly, low interest and engagement is often associated with reading problems. Why might this be the case?

> Interest and engagement can be mutually enabling or disabling or hinder literacy development.

Let's think about our observations of Colin during the reading of the Narnia passage. Putting his head down on the desk while other students took turns reading and staying quiet during the text discussion may have been indicators of disinterest in the passage and/or a lack of confidence. We would want to examine these possibilities further, however, to confirm this since we have observed that many students can appear to be unengaged and disinterested when just the opposite is occurring.

## Skills and Strategy Development

While each student has many skills and knowledge areas to draw on for instruction, there are others yet to be developed if the student is going to be successful in academic settings (from pre-K all the way through the grades) and as independent learners and problem solvers. Thus skill and strategy strengths and needs is one area that we want to investigate as we learn about our students' literacy development. We also need to know about students' previous instruction. Specifically, were there possible limitations that may have diverted students' progress?

In the case of Colin, we noticed that he had difficulty reading some of the words in the Narnia passage including: *wardrobe, railroad junction,* and *fascination.* We inquired further to learn more about how new vocabulary words are taught in this classroom and whether or not they are taught to support the reading of new texts. We noticed that he often read the beginnings of the words he misread and sometimes the endings, but passed over the middle syllables or parts of words. This led us to questions about his previous instruction in identifying words, whether or not he knew the meanings of these words, and whether or not he had interest in learning these words. All three of these questions impact instructional decisions for helping him gain strategies for identifying unknown words.

## A Mindset for Identifying Problems, Labeling Students, and Predicting Failure

We learned from Ms. Schull that about half of the students in her class seem to be successful students. They perform at the average or above average levels on the state's achievement tests, they pass her quizzes and tests, they complete in-class work and homework assignments, and they participate in class discussions. About half of the students, however, worry her. They have a history of performing poorly on the state tests, they often seem to have little connections or understanding of texts they are reading, their performance on class work and homework is marginal, and many do not participate in class.

She indicated that her principal, relying solely on state test data, has identified these students as "at risk" for failing fifth grade for there are many skills and concepts that they have not learned. This mindset for predicting their failure based on one assessment may be part of the problem these students face.

> A mindset for predicting failure based on limited information can be part of the problem.

McDermott, Goldman, and Varenne (2006) argue that school and legislative policy, and sometimes educators, have a cultural inclination to focus on what students can't do rather than identifying the skills and strategies they have developed already. More specifically, they advise us to observe students carefully when they work in groups and independently to identify the knowledge and the skills and strategies they may use spontaneously to solve problems or complete class assignments. For example, they observed middle school students who were described as "at risk" for failing math who were highly engaged in math problem solving when they could convert abstract concepts to real-world applications. They were asked to use modeling software to design a research station for scientists in Antarctica. Hector, described by McDermott and his colleagues as a student who had learned to hide his capabilities in the classroom, led his team to a successful design. Noting that scale was off on the simulated model produced on the computer screen, he searched for a measuring stick and mapped out the dimensions in real space in the classroom, setting real objects in place to represent actual use of space. He then mapped these dimensions onto the simulated version of the design. With his guidance and constant reworking of the applications, the small group of at-risk students often took on the role as math experts leading other students described as "smart" in math. Overall, they were observed to be persistent in monitoring their comprehension, revisiting problems to make sense of the data, and self-correcting inaccuracies. These attributes may have been overlooked without careful observations of their problem-solving strategies.

Literacy researchers describe similar findings. Situated within events that encourage them to use their knowledge, students described as struggling readers are highly engaged and successful in building meaning and connections to complicated texts. For example, when observing English learners, Gutiérrez, Baquedano-López, and Álvarez (2001) and Iddings, Risko, and Rampulla (2009) described how students translated English text into their first language (i.e., Spanish) to facilitate reading comprehension. Further, their discussions with peers, using both English and Spanish, helped them to clarify misconceptions and facilitated their active participation during guided reading lessons. Perez (2004) found that when students read texts that more closely represented their community and home discourse, students were viewed as "competent" in their literacy development. And Zentalla (1997), who examined the literacy learning of 19 Puerto Rican high school students in New York, reported that the most successful students were those who were fluent in both their first language and English and those who also received instruction that encouraged the use of both languages to make sense of their reading and writing. Similarly, Delpit (1992, 1995) and Delpit and Dowdy (2002) described high engagement in classroom and text discussions that invited students' natural switching from African American and standard English languages. A respect for students' knowledge about and use of different languages is associated with students' active participation in their own learning and enabling, rather than disabling, supports for their literacy development.

## Lack of Appropriate and Timely Instruction

Colin is not participating in the class activities, has minimal actual text reading, and instruction is not designed to build on his strengths and knowledge or focus specifically on his learning needs. This should not be the case. Across 60 in-class observations, Allington (2011b) reported only three instances of instruction specifically designed to support students' reading needs. Others, such as Pease-Alvarez (2006), describe similar findings with an overall lack of instruction that is designed specifically to address reading difficulties.

Colin is not interested in the Narnia series and the class anthology may be too difficult for him to read independently. And Colin is not reading the text (except when called on to read small segments aloud in class). Yet researchers argue that students, especially struggling readers, need to read and write every day. Students need access to texts that they can and want to read every day (Allington, 2011b); reading practice is of primary importance for producing readers. Guthrie (2004) called for a substantial increase in daily reading opportunities for struggling readers, advocating for up to "200–500% increase in their engaged reading" (p. 19) to achieve meaningful progress.

More specifically, students need to read a variety of texts daily that includes those on instructional and independent reading levels and across content areas (Allington, 2007; Blachowicz & Ogle, 2008). Use of authentic texts (e.g., newspapers, magazines, historical artifacts, digital texts) to encourage engagement and real-world applications is associated with increased comprehension (Purcell-Gates, Duke, & Martineau, 2007). And optimally, teachers should meet with small groups of students for guided instruction with texts on students' instructional levels and those that are more challenging. Guided instruction involves teacher modeling and demonstrations, coaching, and explanations (Bransford, Brown, & Cocking, 1999; Morrow, Tracey, Woo, & Pressley, 1999; B. M. Taylor, Pearson, Clark, & Walpole, 2000) to help address misconceptions, to teach novel concepts and vocabulary, and to deepen comprehension.

## Lack of Instruction That Is Responsive to Students' Cultural Knowledge

We noticed in Ms. Schull's classroom that several students who were active participants in the discussion of the Narnia passage were quite familiar with this series of texts. Several students indicated that they saw the movie and read some of the books, and Byron explained, "I saw the movie, a play, and read all the books!" Thus these students brought rich information to their readings and consequently could "picture in their minds" the *railroad junction* where the Narnia students waited for their train to take them back to school and the *wardrobe* that provided the doorway to enter the land of Narnia.

In contrast, it is highly probable that students unfamiliar with the story line had little information to help them make connections to the characters or the story problems. We didn't interview Colin, but he may have been uninterested in this text because of unfamiliarity with the story and content-specific vocabulary and concepts.

> It is highly probable that students unfamiliar with the story had little information to aid their comprehension.

Researchers associate high levels of learning and literacy achievement with instruction that is culturally responsive. According to Moll (1997), such instruction is based on the knowledge and strategies students use in their everyday family and community lives, and unfortunately, these knowledge areas and strategies may not be readily apparent to teachers. As we discussed earlier, too often the culture of students of nondominant groups is not represented in the school curriculum (Nocon & Cole, 2009); rather, curriculum represents White, English-speaking, middle-class cultures (Rogoff, 2003). Consequently, students have difficulty making connections between their prior knowledge and experiences and those represented in school texts or discourse. And Moll, Saez, and Dworin (2001) found that some students will hide from teachers what they do know, such as linguistic skills and strategies (e.g., word translation skills, changes in verb tense) they learned with their home language, because they believe they will be ridiculed by their teachers or other students.

Researchers discuss instructional supports to address this issue. For example, McCarthy (2002), Compton-Lilly (2007), and Torres-Guzman (1992) describe how teacher interviews with students can lead to increased teacher understandings about student interests and home and community experiences that might be used for connections to school assignments. McCarthy and Moje (2002) describe a teacher who learned that one of her students, Ella, who resisted writing in class had a history of fictional writing at home, an avocation that was supported by her mother, who was a proofreader in a publishing company, and her father, who was a university professor. During individual conferences, the teacher and student negotiated a method for completing the required expository writing assignments with added fictional sections, thus optimizing Ella's rich writing history while supporting her development of expository writing skills and strategies. Compton-Lilly (2007) describes how choice of topics and inclusion of popular media genres, including teen magazines, helped a student use her knowledge to write adventure books that were required by the school curriculum. Torres-Guzman (1992) describes the high engagement of inner-city, linguistically diverse, high school students who studied and wrote about the toxic waste in their New York City neighborhood. These students became known as the Toxic Avengers and their project led to a cleanup of polluted property and a citizen award for their contributions to their neighborhood. And these students enhanced their high-order comprehension and analytical thinking skills in the process.

Students often don't see the relevance of school assignments or how to use their life experiences or world knowledge to help them succeed in school. Teachers can help by setting up learning environments that engage them in authentic projects as a method for inviting students' use of their world knowledge and their interest in solving real-world problems.

A significantly greater percentage of African American, Latino, and Native American students and those living in poverty are classified as mentally retarded and placed in EBD (emotional and behavioral disorder) and SLD (specific learning disability programs) (Artiles & Trent, 1994; Oswald, Coutinho, Best, & Singh, 1999; Parrish, 2002). Our inability to respect differences and respond to cultural issues while teaching academic knowledge in ways that are culturally relevant to our students has produced serious and negative consequences, such as resistance to school activities and eventual dropping out of school. Students and their learning must be viewed from a cultural lens if trajectories of underachievement are to be altered significantly for minority students (International Reading Association [IRA], 2002). Teacher acknowledgment of differences in students' knowledge, especially academic knowledge, and school achievement resulting from childhood poverty is a starting point for understanding and providing the type of instruction that students need (McLoyd & Purtell, 2008).

## Inattention to Equity and Pluralism

Understanding reading difficulties involves several issues that relate to questions about equity and diversity: Are students receiving instruction that is fair? Is the instruction using students' own cultural experiences and knowledge as resources for teaching? Are students able to use their first language to support their learning in English? Is instruction appropriate for students' reading skills and strategy strengths and weaknesses? In Ms.

Schull's classroom, every student is receiving the same instruction. Following a schoolwide decision, Ms. Schull uses a core text, the basal English anthology, for all students regardless of whether students can actually read the text or have interest and background knowledge that would enable their success. Ms. Schull explained that she knows round robin reading is not the best way to read a new text, but many students would find the text too difficult to read on their own. Well-intended instructional decisions can, unfortunately, have a negative impact for the students requiring the most instructional support, as with Colin. And the issues of text difficulty and providing opportunities for reading are not considered.

## Parents and Reading

A higher proportion of children in low-income families are at greater risk for low levels of reading achievement when compared to other socioeconomic groups (Ramey & Ramey, 1998). This finding tends to be consistent across generations in families (Snow, Barnes, Chandler, Goodman, & Hemphill, 1991), which may seem to be an insurmountable obstacle in changing the reading trajectory of low-income, struggling readers. However, it does point to a greater need to determine the funds of knowledge of all families and to build upon them in working with these children in the classroom and in teaching parents to promote literacy engagement at home (Moll, Velez Ibanez, & Greenberg, 1990; Ordonez-Jasis & Ortiz, 2006).

Seeking opportunities to interact with families during community or school events can help teachers analyze their assumptions and negative stereotypes of families (e.g., no access to books at home, little interest in children's reading and writing development) and learn how a myriad of home and community experiences (e.g., clapping rhymes, rap songs, cartoon theme songs, video gaming) support literacy development (Compton-Lilly, 2009; R. Valencia & Black, 2002).

> Taking time to talk with families during school events or in the community facilitates communication and helps break down negative feelings and stereotypes.

## Gender Differences

Reading disabilities affect both boys and girls (Shaywitz, Shaywitz, Fletcher, & Escobar, 1990) with both boys and girls exhibiting deficiencies in writing and reading (Berninger, Nielsen, Abbott, Wijsman, & Raskind, 2008).

Gender differences in the severity of writing and reading disabilities in children have also been investigated. In a study of families that involved 122 children and 200 adults, boys were found to be more impaired in handwriting and composing than were girls, but they were not more impaired than girls in accuracy and rate of reading connected text. Berninger et al. (2008) recommend early screening and interventions in writing to reduce these differences in writing achievement.

> Gender differences in achievement and motivation continue to exist.

Girls show more positive patterns in reading and language arts than boys. Girls' perceptions of their skills in reading and language arts and boys' perceptions of their skills in math and science emerge during their early years of development and persist throughout their school experiences (Meece, Glienke, & Burg, 2006). Gaps in reading achievement of boys versus girls living in poverty have been attributed to differences in the ways that teachers and parents respond to them. For example, Entwisle, Alexander, and Olson (2007) found that teachers rate boys lower in classroom behavior and reading achievement, and parents living in poverty display lower parental expectations of boys.

## Issues of Reading Motivation

Self-concept about reading is related to reading achievement. Less proficient readers have lower self-concepts when compared to more proficient readers (Allington & McGill-Franzen, 2003; Chapman, Tunmer, & Prochnow, 2000). When students develop negative beliefs about their competence, or self-efficacy, they lose an internal desire to read (Wigfield & Guthrie, 1997), which has a serious impact on their reading achievement (Shanahan & Barr, 1995). Consequently, motivation is a factor that must be addressed to improve struggling readers' ability to comprehend text (Guthrie & Wigfield, 2000).

Struggling students' attitudes toward recreational and academic reading become increasingly negative as they advance from the first to the sixth grade, and their interest in reading declines (McKenna, Kear, & Ellsworth, 1995). It is essential that teachers provide classroom environments that create engaged readers. *Engaged readers* are readers who are motivated to read a variety of material and are skilled in using a variety of decoding and comprehension strategies. They are also skilled in regulating and monitoring their reading, and are knowledgeable and socially interactive, sharing and communicating meaningfully with others (Guthrie, McGough, Bennett, & Rice, 1996).

## Text Considerations for Student Improvement

Characteristics of text, such as author's writing style, organizational patterns, and density of concepts, can challenge and intrude on students' reading comprehension. These characteristics of text should be considered with text selection. Access to text and matching readers to text are factors to be considered in meeting the needs of struggling readers (Ganske, Monroe, & Strickland, 2003). It is important that children have the opportunity to choose at least some of the reading materials for instruction, including texts that they want to read and are interested in talking about with others (Oldfather, 1995).

Planned instruction in comprehension and fluency, as well as matching readers to texts is vital for choosing texts that are used for independent reading by students (Graves, 2004). *Leveled texts* are reading materials that reflect a progression from varying degrees of simplicity to increasingly greater degrees of complexity and challenge, which allow teachers to more effectively match readers with text. Leveling text involves considering text and print features, sentence difficulty, vocabulary, text structure, content, language and literacy aspects, themes, and ideas presented in the text (Brabham & Villaume, 2002). Leveled texts, available at all levels of reading across elementary and middle grades, can be used to supplement basal readers and other school textbooks to provide wider reading on the topics and to differentiate instruction instead of requiring the same level text for all students.

For students reading at early reading levels, repetitive texts (with reoccurring words, phrases, and ideas) may be useful since they offer opportunities to expose students to words with consistent and frequently encountered word patterns (J. R. Jenkins, Peyton, Sanders, & Vadasy, 2004). However, teachers of struggling readers must be cautious in their use of repetitive texts and of overrelying on publishers' assigned levels of texts. For example, the simplicity and lack of density of ideas in easier leveled and repetitive texts does not provide struggling readers with opportunities to apply good strategies for comprehending text (Ganske et al., 2003). Conversely, simpler words can be used to represent quite complicated concepts, and students may learn to read the words without attending to their deeper and intended meanings. Hiebert (2011) cautions against the use of too complicated texts for young and struggling readers.

> Students need to be able to read the material of instruction and be able to choose at least some of their reading materials if we expect engagement and comprehension.

At all levels, instruction needs to support students in ways that they can read and comprehend the text. Simply assigning students to independent or instructional-level texts, however, does not obviate the need to consider reader factors such as interest, motivation, and the opportunity to develop and use strategies in word recognition and comprehension (Brabham & Villaume, 2002). It is important that teachers are knowledgeable about the features of text needed to support beginning and struggling readers and that explicit teaching is used to help students to handle these materials (Hiebert & Sailors, 2009). Using decodable and leveled texts can reinforce students' understanding of word features while supplementing the text provided in the anthologies of core programs (Hiebert, 2009). Similarly, informational texts that have repetitive formats and features (i.e., related themes, topics, and authors; definitions of words; and illustrative graphics) can support readers' comprehension, making these texts less challenging (Duke & Billman, 2009).

High-interest, easy-reading books are useful resource materials for developing the fluency, comprehension, and motivation to read of young, struggling readers because of the organization of the narrative text, familiarity of the content, limited background knowledge required for comprehension of text, and the appropriateness for the targeted grade-level audience. However the quality of and enthusiasm for this form of writing, if overused, may be limited. Use of such texts exclusively prevents struggling readers from being exposed to excellent models of writing and literature that can promote intellectual and emotional connections (Graves & Philippot, 2002). Thus a combination of text genre, writers' style, formats, and levels of reading are required.

## SUMMARY

Colin is not succeeding in Ms. Schull's classroom. Despite Ms. Schull's efforts to create shared and meaningful learning activities around a common text, Colin is disinterested and unengaged. He does not read for meaning and the round robin oral reading activity displays his discomfort and difficulties with the text. We elaborated on Colin's situation by discussing some issues that are associated with reading problems. These issues range from a mismatch between students' cultural knowledge and knowledge required to understand targeted texts, to gender considerations, to inadequate preparation for tackling complicated and dense texts, and to a lack of congruence between school reading requirements and real-world problems. The issues are complicated but can be addressed with appropriate instruction. In the remaining chapters we will identify specific instruction intended to break cycles of student failure. This instruction can accommodate the issues we discussed in responsive and robust ways.

We advocate for instruction that is conceptual, productive, responsive, and empowering. What do we mean by the descriptor, *conceptual instruction*? Conceptual instruction has both long-term and short-term goals for the students. These goals address curricular expectations—often stated as standards—that include goals for teaching skills, strategies, and content, and they address the social-affective dimensions of learning and engagement. Conceptual instruction works toward integrating the skills, strategies, and content into a balanced whole—it builds on students' capabilities while teaching skills and strategies and content that is needed for further development.

Instruction should be productive, responsive, and empowering—students are not just listening or taking in information but actively involved in their own learning and producing evidence of their learning in multiple ways. Instruction should be responsive—responding to students' differences including their skill and strategy development (what can they do already and what do they need to learn), their language and cultural differences, and their experiential differences. The ultimate goal for instruction is empowerment—students believe they are capable and instruction demonstrates that they are.

Following are characteristics of the instruction we recommend. We ask teachers to examine how these characteristics are embedded in their own teaching practices.

- *Knowledge acquisition* is at the heart of instruction aimed at insuring that students are developing disciplinary and world knowledge. Instruction should build new knowledge by providing access to more complicated texts, concepts that are novel, and content across the curriculum.
- *Skills and strategies* students have already acquired provide the starting point for instruction and for making connections to skills and strategies that students need. Instruction should teach students the multiple skills and strategies they will need as successful and independent readers and learners, and those that build on their capabilities and needs.

- *Imagination and creativity* often provide the conceptual glue that supports reasoning and transfer of novel ideas to understanding real-world problems.
- *Active engagement and production* are on display consistently throughout instruction—with students generating their own questions and purposes for learning and to demonstrate their authentic uses of reading and writing tools.
- *Cultural and linguistic histories and experiences*, once known by teachers, provide the centerpiece for making connections with developing knowledge and independent applications of knowledge for solving problems.
- *Multiple texts* afford reading power—thus instruction should include a range of texts, including those that are sometimes described as "just right texts" (appropriate for students' comfort and instructional levels), texts that students choose to read in addition to those assigned in school, texts of increasingly difficult levels, and texts with different styles (e.g., magazines, video texts, graphic novels) that students may be reading out of school and are not part of the classroom library.

## REFLECTION QUESTIONS

1. Examine your own reading history to identify factors that contributed to your reading success, or factors that made reading difficult for you. Derive implications for your teaching.
2. Interview two or three children, adolescents, or adults to learn about their reading habits and preferences. For example, you can ask them about their independent reading and how they choose texts to read and why they may read books written by the same author. Or you may ask them to name what aids their reading comprehension or to explain why they may start but not finish some books that they choose. Consider what you learned from them and its implications for teaching.
3. Choose one of the areas associated with reading difficulties (e.g., living in poverty or lack of interest) and read some additional writings on this topic. What did you learn and what information will you share with parents, teachers, literacy coaches, and/or instructional leaders?

# CHAPTER 2

# Capitalizing on Students' Cultural and Linguistic Histories and Experiences

In *Notes of a Native Son* (1955) author James Baldwin wrote, "People are trapped in history, and history is trapped in them" (p. 163). If that statement is true, then trapped inside each student are cultural and language backgrounds and histories that may be either valued in schools or perceived as incompatible with school or societal norms. In both cases culture and language background define students as individuals: If valued, they can serve as a resource for promoting reading engagement and providing differentiated learning through appropriate materials, experiences, and instructional practices; if devalued, they can produce impediments to these things.

In the case study of Colin, Ms. Schull, his teacher, did not know Colin's cultural and linguistic history nor that of the other struggling readers in her classroom. She failed to realize that literacy and identity are powerfully entwined. According to literacy scholar Jerry Harste, "reading is identity," and the type of reader that readers perceive themselves to be influences their self-perceptions (Harste, 2009). Thus teachers must understand that children's identities as readers are created and changed in conjunction with their literacy teaching (Compton-Lily, 2006). Their identities are socially constructed (Spencer, 2009; Triplett, 2007) with power acting as a major force in determining the way that students' identities are developed and the way in which students are perceived in relation to others (McCarthey & Moje, 2002). Thus the socially constructed label of being a struggling reader impacts the social relationships, instruction, and motivation of these learners, and the social cultural dimensions of their lives are often ignored in literacy instruction (Risko, Walker-Dalhouse, & Arragones, 2011).

In this chapter we describe three teachers on journeys to understand the cultural and linguistic diversity within their classroom and to apply their knowledge in ways that attempt to promote student learning.

## CASE ANALYSES: CHRISTINE, SETH, AND ERIN

### Christine, a First-Year Teacher

I (Doris) first met Christine, a preservice teacher, in the hallway of the building where I work. We engaged in small talk that led to longer conversations about her and her preparation as an elementary education major with a specialty in preprimary education. Whenever we met, Christine would share her interest and experiences in working in a southern state where her boyfriend lived, as well as her plans to make the area her home. Later she became a student in my foundations of literacy class where our conversations about diversity and her planned interest in teaching in the South continued. The fact that I was the only African American faculty in the unit at the university, along with my experiences living and teaching for 10 years in the deep South, might have identified me as a kindred spirit who understood diversity firsthand.

Christine is a bright, curious, and friendly individual. She asked questions and made connections to observations that she made about diversity, based on her experiences when she visited with her boyfriend in Alabama.

Christine grew up in a small town of approximately 1,400 people. She described her family as one that valued others and encouraged her to be open to learning about people of different races and cultures. In describing her mother, she indicated that she believed her mother might have been "African American in another life." In recounting details of her early education, Christine noted that there were only about a total of 40 students in her elementary school. Her family later moved to a larger rural environment where she had four African American children in her class.

Two of the four students had been adopted by White families. The other two children were biracial and lived with White families. Despite her limited educational experiences with racially and ethnically diverse students, Christine expressed a positive disposition toward diversity. Her family's openness toward diversity was instrumental in forming her own attitudes about social justice and diversity.

Christine requested to do her student teaching in Alabama believing that "the experience of teaching in a southern state and in a high-poverty rural school will give me an opportunity to get acquainted and familiar with differences in southern culture, school systems, and teaching criteria when compared to what I will experience here in Minnesota."

She learned a lot about herself and the children during that experience. While some lessons that she learned about the impact of her literacy history and cultural background on her teaching were difficult, it did not dampen her desire to make the necessary connections with her students. "After all," as she said, "I just want to see all of my students succeed. I think I can begin to make that happen." Consequently, she readily accepted a position as a fourth-grade teacher at a predominantly African American, high-poverty school in rural Alabama.

This is where the story of Christine's journey as a first-year teacher in a fourth-grade classroom began and continued as she strived to understand and recognize the value of students' cultures and diversity in her classroom.

## Seth and Erin, Classroom Teachers of English Learners

In the past decade, I (Vicki) collaborated with classroom teachers, reading specialists, doctoral students, and university faculty colleagues to plan and implement reading instruction for English learners (ELs). Often the ELs in our classrooms were recent immigrants to the United States or were in the early years of acquiring English as a new language. Early in our work we questioned how teachers who are mostly English-speaking and monolingual hold text discussions when they don't speak the same language as their ELs or share a similar cultural history.

We address that question in our discussion of the teaching experiences of middle school teachers Seth and Erin. Seth, a native English speaker, was teaching a small group of students who were new immigrants from Mexico and new to this classroom where most of the other students were native English speakers. Our description of Seth is influenced by our previous analysis of Seth's teaching and his students' participation in text discussions (Iddings et al., 2009). The students were Alicia, Pedro, and Gonzalo. Erin Bridges, who coauthored a paper with us on text structure and comprehension (Risko, Walker-Dalhouse, Bridges & Wilson, 2011), also a native English speaker, taught a small group of new immigrants who were receiving reading instruction within a school-based English as a Second Language program.

A major learning for us was the advantage of using students' home or first language as a resource for enabling text discussions among students, advancing conceptual learning and reading comprehension, and supporting active engagement.

CASE QUESTIONS

1. What understandings should teachers have about their students' culture, language history, families, and communities?
2. How can teachers gain an understanding of their students' cultures and languages?

3.  How can teachers use this knowledge to develop curriculum in literacy that meets English language arts standards?

## CULTURAL AND LINGUISTIC HISTORIES AND EXPERIENCES

Regardless of the degree of language proficiency (i.e., dual language, limited English, or English dominant) of language minority (LM) learners who come from homes where languages other than English are spoken, they lag behind native English-speaking students in reading achievement (August & Hakuta, 1997; August & Shanahan, 2006). However, Kieffer (2008) found that LM students who enter kindergarten with limited oral proficiency in English had lower reading growth trajectories from kindergarten through fifth grade than LM kindergartners who were proficient in English. Kieffer also found that there were greater differences in the growth trajectories of kindergartners with limited oral English proficiency in comparison to those of native English speakers.

> Students' language history is part of their identity.

In addition, dialectal differences such as those between Standard American English (SAE) and African American English (AAE) speakers have been considered to be responsible for lower teacher expectation and/or reading achievement of African American students (Cecil, 1988; Wolfram, Adger, & Christian, 1999). Conversely, students with greater proficiency in the use of Standard American English or who use more SAE forms have been found to have higher reading achievement (Charity, Scarborough, & Griffin, 2004; Connor & Craig, 2006; Craig & Washington, 2004). Nevertheless, LM students and speakers of African American English have a language history created in the cultural context of their homes and/or communities and these language histories are not referenced optimally to support learning.

All students possess cultural capital; however, not all cultural capital is valued equally in school settings. This creates a disparity between home and school (Garas-York, 2010). *Cultural capital* is based upon social class and includes the cultural background, knowledge, and skills that are transmitted from generation to generation (Bourdieu, 1986). Consequently, ethnically and racially diverse children from impoverished homes are perceived to lack the background knowledge, experience, and language needed for literacy instruction. Yet, when this knowledge is recognized, it can be valuable for reading instruction. Moll, Amanti, Neff, and Gonzalez (1992) found that by building upon the home and community resources of children or their funds of knowledge, teachers are able to organize classroom instruction that is of a higher quality than classroom instruction without these considerations. Understanding the cultural and social values and language of their families is integral to responding to children's development and learning (Tadesse, Hoot, & Watson-Thompson, 2009).

## Foundations for Instruction

Literacy needs to be connected to the lives of students and provide opportunities for social engagement (Alvermann, 2005). The International Reading Association (IRA, 2010) recognizes this need and has identified diversity as a standard that must be included in teacher preparation in their *Standards for Reading Professionals—Revised 2010*. Standard 4 of this document, Diversity, states that "teacher candidates must be able to create and engage their students in literacy practices that develop awareness, understanding, respect, and valuing of differences in our society" (p. 12). This includes attention to student differences in race, ethnicity, class, gender, religion, and language. Recognizing that students' life experiences are shaped by these factors is essential to understanding how to engage, instruct, and respond to students' academic, social, and emotional needs.

Schools involve worlds through shared journeys (Van Sluys & Reiner, 2006). This involves understanding and transforming the world of teachers and their students during the course of daily instruction. It means realizing that teachers bring their cultural norms into the classroom (Hollins, 1996) and that their cultural norms may differ to varying degrees from those of their students. Sometimes this results in a mismatch between school and home cultures, cultural discontinuity, which can be a major obstacle to learning (Au, 1993; Sanacore, 2000). To combat this problem, teachers must assess their cultural values and be willing to be transformed by their experiences with their students.

> Highly successful teachers teach to their students' cultural knowledge and experiences.

## Creating a Context for Learning

Understanding and being sensitive to students' culture and linguistic differences represents genuine caring. *Genuine caring* involves responding to students' needs (e.g., academic, social, emotional, and language) and developing trusting relationships with others (Thayer-Bacon, 1993;

Thayer-Bacon & Bacon, 1997). We believe that genuine caring is necessary to create a learning environment that accommodates the learning needs of students. Sanacore (2004) believes that demonstrating genuine caring can improve the academic success of African American students. For example, teachers can use their knowledge of African American culture to structure the classroom environment so that students have greater opportunities for interaction and collaboration, movement, lively discussions, and creativity in expression (e.g., drama and language) in learning.

Teaching to students' cultural and linguistic history also has academic benefits. For example, when students use codeswitching to draw on their first language to help them learn a new language (e.g., associating words that have same or similar meanings in the two languages), they advance their knowledge of linguistic elements in both languages (Kenner, 2004; Lantolf, 2000). Researchers, such as Bauer and Manyak (2008) and Orellana and Reynolds (2008), associate text paraphrasing and translating activities, moving back and forth across their languages, with increased comprehension of texts.

*A New Teacher.* When Christine met her class of 20 African American fourth graders during her first year of teaching, she decided that she wanted them to know about her and her life in Minnesota. She asked them to tell about life in Alabama as if they were selling it to someone like her— someone new to the state. Christine was surprised and pleased about what they had to share. Because Christine had shared that she had just recently graduated from college, some of the students also said that they wanted to go to college someday. Having graduated from a teacher education program that emphasized social justice, Christine told them that she wanted all of them to go to college. She decided to call them all her "college-bound students" to affirm her belief in the academic ability of her students and to set high standards for achievement in spite of the fact that half of her students were reading below grade level.

Christine made a concerted effort to make cultural connections with her students and to use these connections to motivate them to read. She began each day reading selections from *The Children's Book of Virtues* (Bennett, 1995) to provide the students with stories and sayings appropriate for self-control and motivation. Proverbs were also written on the board daily and students were asked to record the proverbs in their journals and to write what they meant to them. Here are two examples of proverbs used in this activity:"He who conquers others is strong; he who conquers himself is mighty" (Lau-Tsze, 1868/2004, p. 26); and "We must all learn to live together as brothers or we will all perish as fools" (King, 1986, p. 209).

This was followed by class sharing and discussion. Proverbs such as "Great works are performed not by strength, but by perseverance" (S. Johnson, 1977, p. 96) were used to motivate students as they struggled with school tasks. Another proverb, "To come to be you must have a vision of being—a dream, a purpose, a principle. You will become what your vision is" (*Vision: Quote/Unquote*, 2002, p. 20), was also effective in reminding students who were not attentive during class to get back on task.

The seven principles of Kwanzaa (Riley, 1995) were also used to motivate students. Christine felt that it would foster ethnic awareness and pride in her students and create cultural and ethnic awareness in the entire school. The principles were also used because they conveyed high expectations for success and emphasize the uniqueness, worth, and intelligence of each child. The principles of Kwanzaa were used as proverbs to teach and motivate students to achieve and to assume responsibility for their lives and behaviors. Kwanzaa, derived from the African celebration of the harvest, is the only original African American holiday that celebrates culture and the joy of being a family. The Kwanzaa principles were posted in the classroom as principles that could be applied to guide students in their daily lives:

1. *Umoja* (oo-MO-jah), *Unity*. We help each other.
2. *Kujichagulia* (Koo-jee-cha-goo-Lee-ah), *Self-determination*. We decide things for ourselves.
3. *Ujima* (oo-JEE-mah), *Collective work and responsibility*. We work together to make life better.
4. *Ujamma* (oo-jah-MAH), *Cooperative economics*. We build and support our own businesses.
5. *Nia* (NEE-ah), *Purpose*. We have a reason for living.
6. *Kuumba* (koo-OOM-bah), *Creativity*. We use our minds and hands to make things.
7. *Imani* (ee-MAH-nee), *Faith*. We believe in ourselves, our ancestors, and our future.

Students recited the principles each week and references were made to the principles in reflections about content learned or in analyzing individual and class behaviors or actions. They memorized the principles of

Kwanzaa quickly, and they became increasingly able to recite them and talk about character actions, classroom behavior, and life events in terms of the principles.

Christine's school had a 3-hour period for literacy instruction. Christine decided to teach reading using a workshop format with a minilesson about reading and writing concepts, skills, and strategies; opportunities for independent reading and writing; and reading conferences.

The proverbs introduced each day were used in a whole-class writing experience at the beginning of the literacy instructional period in which students were asked to connect the meaning of the poem to their lives and to their world. She required students to learn and recite chorally poems like "On the Pulse of Morning" by Maya Angelou (Angelou, 1993) and "I, Too" by Langston Hughes (Hughes, 1990). The underlying message of making new beginnings in Angelou's poem and preparing oneself for a future characterized by equity between Black and White Americans were class favorites.

> Family and cultural texts are the springboards for reading and writing productions and instruction.

In addition to their basal or core reading program, Christine's students read multiethnic books and continued reading and responding to proverbs and books read in literature circles and read-alouds. Biographies of key African/African American contemporary and historical figures (i.e., Nelson Mandela, George Washington Carver, and Martin Luther King, Jr.) were used to extend the themes from her core reading program. Students wrote different types of poems including list poems, diamante poems, rhymed and unrhymed verse, and connected them to music and issues with which they were familiar. Students wrote friendly and business letters to story characters about issues associated with story events. They applied these same skills in writing about a homeless family in their community. In this way her classroom was much like other classrooms. The difference was that Christine incorporated community issues (i.e., demolition of the local housing project; homelessness) and made cultural connections whenever she could to the students' home literacies. She encouraged Davon's fascination with video games and used it to help him add rich descriptions of characters in his writing and to broaden his reading to include fantasy. While Christine worked hard to help Franklin see himself as a successful African American male despite his difficulties in word identification and comprehension, she realized that her journey to achieving this was not to be an easy one. This is where we begin to think about how to help Christine, ourselves, and our colleagues to make meaningful next steps in making cultural connections to students.

## TEACHING STUDENTS WHOSE LANGUAGES WERE DIFFERENT FROM THEIR OWN

### Seth

When Seth began teaching his third-grade students, he decided to choose a book series, the Curious George (Rey & Rey, 1969) set of books. These are books that he enjoyed and he hoped that repeated story plots and problems, vocabulary, and characters and characterization, once understood, would lead to deeper comprehension. As he predicted, revisiting common text elements across the book series did aid reading comprehension and students began to acquire vocabulary in English, including those words for which they knew Spanish equivalents (e.g., George and *Jorge*, problem and *problema*) and English grammatical structures (e.g., the man in the yellow hat). He learned also that preteaching central concepts (e.g., George had a problem, the man in the yellow hat often rescued George from danger) and linking these to story details during the discussions were important for advancing comprehension.

His focus on key concepts was important to students' participation and learning—they begin to anticipate and predict similar occurrences (e.g., that George would have a problem to be solved) as they read subsequent texts and to clarify their understanding of the plot and characters' actions.

Throughout the text discussions, Seth noticed that students were deliberate about helping each other understand story information. Students switched frequently from English to Spanish and back again to English to explain to Seth what they were discussing. Even though Seth could not completely understand what the students discussed, he noticed that the interactions in Spanish were often lengthy, that Alicia (a native Spanish speaker) at times asked questions in Spanish, and that a common goal was to explain content to Pedro, who was just beginning to use and understand English. For example, Alicia asked Gonzalo to tell her the word for ship (i.e., *Como se dice* "ship"? How do you say "ship"?). She and Gonzales then explained to Pedro that George was traveling in *un barco* (a boat) (Iddings et al., 2009, p. 56). Noting the importance of these opportunities for peer support, Seth provided spaces and time during text conversations for peer-shared language learning and knowledge building.

### Erin

Erin taught a group of fifth-grade ELs by selecting texts that were relevant to their experiences and knowledge. For example, she chose Shaun

Tan's *The Arrival* (2007) for her group of English learners. *The Arrival* is a wordless graphic novel about a man who leaves his family to move to a new country. The story is developed through black, white, and sepia-tone images, with dark shadings representing the fears and uncertainty associated with moving to a new country and arriving in a strange, new place.

Erin's students examined the illustrations making connections to their own feelings when they arrived in their new city to live, comparing their experiences with those of the main character of *The Arrival*. Students worked in small groups to discuss their experiences, usually in their first language, putting words and ideas to the text, developing their own version of *The Arrival*. For example, the two students from Burundi developed their story ideas in Kirundi, their home language, and the three students from Mexico developed their story in Spanish. The group then came back together to share their ideas, translating what they had discussed to English and dictating a jointly created story for Erin to record. They described the immigrant's arrival to a new country (e.g., The man sees the new town. He got out of the boat. He took his suitcase.) and his first experiences off the boat (The man stands in line. The doctor checks his ears. The man meets new friends.). The students discussed each of the happenings as they composed the story and revisited these words and ideas when they wrote a sentence in their journals, laying a foundation for additional writings.

> Use of a first language can facilitate comprehension of another language.

## CULTURALLY RESPONSIVE READING INSTRUCTION

Educators must "see culture as a prerequisite for culturally responsive teaching" (Allen & Hermann-Wilmarth, 2010, p. 214). Culturally responsive teaching is built upon academic indicators of achievement, cultural competence, and sociopolitical consciousness (Ladson-Billings, 2001). Among the indicators of academic achievement are a teacher's belief in the capacity of all children to learn (high expectations); knowledge of content, their students, and how to teach the content; and encouragement of academic achievement as multidimensional in nature. Cultural competence includes teachers' understanding of culture and how it influences education and learning about students and their communities. Sociopolitical indicators include teachers' knowledge of political contexts within schools, community, and at the national and international levels, and the use of this information to make connections to their students and promote their understanding of the larger social world (Ladson-Billings, 2001).

Thus culturally responsive teaching demands eliciting critical thinking from students, reflects real-language usage, and provides opportunities for students to provide and gain meaning and work toward understanding community problems (Delpit, 2006). It is predicated more on a way of being as opposed to specific teaching practices (Ladson-Billings, 2006). The ways of being are reflected in the practices of teachers who build and demonstrate cultural competence through their efforts to understand the realities and identities of their students. Although the current culture of education (standardized testing) makes it difficult to engage in culturally responsive teaching, teachers can connect their teaching to social justice themes in an effort to foster culturally responsive teaching in their classrooms (Morrison, Robbins, & Rose, 2008).

> Culturally responsive teaching is dynamic; it invites critical thinking and authentic language activity.

Milner's (2011) case study of Mr. Hall, a White middle school science teacher teaching in a diverse urban classroom, provides insights into this developmental process. Mr. Hall began his journey of becoming a culturally responsive teacher by recognizing the importance of building strong relationships with his students that was based on knowing who they were, both in and outside of school. He listened to them as they shared information about themselves and asked questions that engaged them in conversations about their interests and experiences. In turn, Mr. Hall shared personal narratives about his life and family by talking about his personal history and cultural background. The mutual sharing helped him develop his cultural knowledge of his multiple identities as a father, teacher, and husband, and recognize and understand his students' multiple and varied identities. The information gained helped Mr. Hall incorporate the content, instruction, and management strategies needed to engage the students in his classroom. The high expectation that Mr. Hall set for students' leaning and the many opportunities he provided for them to be successful in learning helped students develop knowledge about themselves and the larger community. In the process, Mr. Hall learned about himself as a teacher and cultural being, which helped him in adapting the curriculum and his teaching to the needs of his students (Milner, 2011).

Teachers must assume a critical stance about content and issues as part of culturally relevant teaching (Morrison et al., 2008). An example of a teacher incorporating culture into the classroom and engaging in culturally relevant teaching and literacy instruction is found in research by May (2011). This research specifically explored the use of animated text talk about multicultural informational texts during interactive read-alouds.

Animated talking involves interpreting, paraphrasing, and/or modeling the meaning of text. In the study of a European American teacher and her class of ethnically and culturally diverse upper-elementary students, May (2011) found that the teacher was effective in using and engaging students in animated talk about culturally relevant informational texts with social justice themes that focused on culture. This talk required her to use skills in summarizing and paraphrasing the authors' words, restating students' words, and explaining the positions or views of other people about the content or topic. In the process, the teacher assumed three socially constructed positions during the reading and discussion of the chapter books shared: (a) cultural advocate for social groups identified with the topics studied and for the communities represented by her students; (b) facilitator of class discussions about the content of the books; and (c) teacher of reading by modeling reading and teaching students to comprehend the features of informational text and the content of the books using comprehension skills such as making connections and inferencing. May (2011) concluded that the content and organization of teacher talk is important. It is also essential for teachers to provide increased opportunities for student talk as part of culturally relevant teaching. May also emphasized the importance of teachers examining the multicultural literature used as cultural resources in the classroom to ensure that it reflects the complexity of life experiences of the "cultural insiders" or students in their class.

## CULTURAL MODELING

Another method for teaching struggling readers that builds on the tenets of culturally responsive teaching is cultural modeling. Cultural modeling recognizes the knowledge developed by students within family, community, and peer social events, and makes conscious connections between this knowledge and instruction and learning in urban school classrooms. The analytic instructional framework used in cultural modeling begins with analyzing four things: (a) the content (e.g., U.S. History) that will be taught; (b) the generative tasks (e.g., interpretation of symbolism, inferring motives and actions) that are required for learning information in that subject matter; (c) the routine literacy practices (e.g., listening to music, writing poetry) of the students—literacy actions that are routine to them out of school, concepts embedded in the target content that they may know or misunderstand; and (d) ways that the students engage in conversations with peers that may be brought into classroom instructional conversations

(C. D. Lee, Rosenfeld, Mendenhall, Rivers, & Tynes, 2004; Risko & Walker-Dalhouse, 2007). Thus the practical application of cultural modeling aligns Common Core Standards or district language arts standards with subject area standards to engage students in problem solving and higher level thinking skills. It also involves encouraging students' use of oral and written language in interpreting and responding to literature that builds upon the cultural data sets of knowledge and experiences that students bring to the learning task (Risko & Walker-Dalhouse, 2007). The following guidelines provide directions for engaging in cultural modeling. They specify that teachers should do the following:

1. Identify content to be taught
2. Identify problems embedded in the content that require higher level thinking
3. Identify language arts skills and strategies you want your students to learn
4. Identify students' prior knowledge about the culture including patterns of language used in their community, at home, and with peers
5. Select multiple texts that represent the cultural data sets of culturally diverse students to supplement school texts. (Risko & Walker-Dalhouse, 2007)

> Cultural modeling is an instructional bridge to relevancy and authenticity for students; connections are made to students' routine and real-life literacy actions.

We provide below an example of a specific instructional application of cultural modeling applied to elementary language arts instruction.

## CULTURAL MODELING EXAMPLE

### 1. Content to Be Taught

- *Topic:* Immigration/refugees
- *Grade:* 4

### 2. Problems Embedded in the Content

Teachers might begin by examining Common Core Standards in content areas for the grade level identified. Potential problems are embedded in the following standards:

**Social Studies Standard**

*Identify the historical background and meaning of important political values such as freedom, democracy, and justice.*

One problem might involve identifying the adjustments associated with a new culture and relocating to a new country. Another problem might involve comparing and contrasting the similarities and differences in the political problems and social conditions that prompt refugees to leave their home countries. The language arts standard below focuses on this skill.

**Language Standards**

*Explain the meaning of simple similes and metaphors.*

### 3. Prior Knowledge of Students

Teachers might begin by helping students distinguish between immigrants and refugees. While immigrants leave their country for another country voluntarily, refugees leave their country due to life-threatening circumstances in their home country. Teachers might interview the parents of ELs in their classroom, the EL instructor in their school, and/or refugee families in the community to learn about the issue. Some guiding questions associated with the topic of immigration/refugees might be:

- Do you know any refugees?
- What do you know about the lives of refugees in their home country?
- What do you know about their experiences since resettling in the United States?
- In what way do you think the lives of refugees are similar to or different from the lives of immigrants?

### 4. Multiple Text Sets for Building Students' Cultural Data Sets

The two books described below can be used as core texts for reading and engaging students in a discussion about the topic. These books are about refugees seeking asylum in another country due to political situations sparked by wars in Guatemala and Sudan.

Pellegrino, M. (2009). *Journey of dreams*. London, England: Frances Lincoln Children's Books.

*Journey of Dreams* is a story told through the voice of Tomasa, the main character, about her family's escape from Guatemala. Tensions mount when the mother is forced to leave the area with her oldest son to protect him from being forced to join the army. The family is forced to seek asylum in the United States when the Guatemalan army initiates a scorched earth campaign in which it burns their home and kills several people in their village. The book chronicles the dangerous journey of the father and the three children as they travel north searching for the mother and older brother—and safety.

Coates, J. L. (2010). *A hare in the elephant's trunk*. Markham, Ontario: Red Deer Press.

*A Hare in the Elephant's Trunk* focuses on the experiences of a southern Sudanese boy named Jacob, who along with his young uncle and friend are forced to flee their village when it is invaded by soldiers from northern Sudan. Their village is destroyed, their families are killed, and the children are forced to seek refuge in Ethiopia. They join other boys as they travel by foot for months across dangerous terrain. They encounter death, destruction, and danger while the war between northern and southern Sudan rages. The story describes the journey and experiences of the boys and their lives in refugee camps in Sudan. The story is based upon the experiences of thousands of Sudanese children and youth who later became known as the "Lost Boys of Sudan."

Additional resources that might be used to supplement the core texts are listed here. Picture books and biographies about refugee children are types of literature that can broaden struggling readers' understanding of the lives and experiences of refugees.

Tan, S. (2007). *The arrival*. New York: Arthur Levine Books/Scholastic.

A graphic novel that can be used with older students to examine the experiences of an immigrant and compare them with those of refugees.

Williams, M. (2001). *Brothers in hope: The story of the lost boys of Sudan* (G. Christie, Illus.). New York: Lee & Low.

A picture book that can inform younger children about the journey of children from Sudan.

> Hoffman, M. (2002). *The color of home* (K. Littlewood, Illus.). New York: Phyllis Fogelman Books.

A picture book about a Somali refugee.

> Cha, D. (1996). *Dia's story cloth* (C. & N. Thao Cha, Illus.). New York: Lee & Low.

A picture book about Hmong refugees.

> Lombard, J. (2006). *Drita, my homegirl*. New York: Penguin.

A story of a refugee girl from Kosovo.

> Williams, K. L., & Mohammad, K. (2007). *Four feet, two sandals*. Grand Rapids, MI: Eerdmans Books for Young Readers.

A picture book about two Afghan girls in a refugee camp in Pakistan who share a pair of sandals.

> Bradman, T. (2007). *Give me shelter: Stories about children who seek asylum*. London: Frances Lincoln Children's Books.

A book that is appropriate for students in Grades 3 and above that features stories of children and families seeking asylum in other countries.

## 5. Instructional Sequence and Connection to Cultural Data Sets

The teacher selects examples of text from each book to teach the concept of similes and metaphors. We have identified two examples from the core texts that can be used:

### Journey of Dreams

> "I asked another soldier if he would check for my son, who must have been mistaken for someone older. That soldier called, 'Carlos!' Young men on the truck stood back and Hector and Carlos came out to where I could see them both," Papa says. "'I don't want to feed all these worms,' the soldier told me. 'He's too skinny, anyway,' he said, pointing to Carlos. (p. 28)

Carlos and Hector, two Guatemalan friends, are kidnapped by the Guatemalan army on their way home from town. The soldiers intend to force them to join their fight despite the fact that the boys are only 14 years old. In his search for the boys, Carlos's father asks the soldiers if they have taken them.

In this quote, the boys, Carlos and Hector, are being compared by the soldiers to worms. The metaphor might cause students to draw upon the data set of comparing human beings to worms using expressions like "they are just small potatoes" or " they are just like a bunch of fleas" or "they are a bunch of parasites."

## A Hare in the Elephant's Trunk

"Why should they kill so many of our people?" Willy asked innocently. "The militia are like wild animals, lions in the skin of men." Monyroor spat out the words. "They have no respect for our traditions and customs. They hope that by killing our cattle, the Dinka people will not be able to exist. Then Southern Sudan will belong to the North." (p. 153)

The simile compares the Sudanese People Liberation Army (SPLA), or the Southern Sudanese Army, formed to defend Southern Sudan from Northern Sudan, with wild lions. As Majok and the group of boys continue on their journey to Ethiopia, one of the boys, Jacob, sees the bones of many cattle killed by the SPLA. He questions why they killed the cattle, which are sacred to the Dinka people of Southern Sudan. Willie, another of the boys in the group, wants to know why the SPLA, formed to protect Dinkas, kill so many of the Dinka people.

In this quote a simile is used to compare the Sudanese army with wild animals. The SPLA is perceived as fierce and uncontrollable in their actions by killing and taking advantage of the people and land that they were organized to protect. The cultural data set that students might bring to this quote is to identify someone in their community as "a snake in the grass" or a "wolf in sheep's clothing" to demonstrate their understanding of the quote.

## PREPARING TEACHERS FOR DIVERSE TEACHING

Teacher quality is a critical factor in student learning and in educational equity (Darling-Hammond, 1987; Ingersoll, 2002). Teachers must not only be competent but must be culturally aware and sensitive to students' needs if they are to be effective in instructing linguistically and culturally diverse learners (Kea & Utley, 1998; R. W. Taylor, 2010). Teachers must understand the relationship between students' cultural backgrounds and literacy learning.

Graduate and undergraduate courses in literacy methods and theory can provide opportunities to examine issues related to diversity in culture, language, race, and class. For example, McIntyre, Hulan, and Maher (2010) examined the beliefs and attitudes of graduate students enrolled in a course focused on literacy learning and cultural differences. Preassessment of students' beliefs revealed deficient views (parental and familial) and difference (disparate financial resources, classism, and racism) of diverse students. Changes in reported dispositions were noted at the end of the course, but McIntyre, Hulan, and Maher (2010) cautioned interpreting students' responses as necessarily indicative of true changes in their actions or beliefs.

Consequently, the question that needs to be asked is whether or not preservice teachers feel prepared to teach diverse students. According to the National Comprehensive Center for Teacher Quality and Public Agenda (2008), preservice teachers feel unprepared to teach poor, urban, and ethnically diverse students, as well as students with special needs. In a survey of first-year teachers' opinions about teacher preparation, professional development, and retention, new teachers, in contrast to preservice teachers, expressed generally positive beliefs about their preparation and their ability to cope with special needs and racially and ethnically diverse students in classroom situations. Seventy-six percent of the teachers surveyed indicated that their teacher preparation taught them strategies for teaching racially and ethnically diverse students. However, of this percentage, only 39% indicated that their preparation had helped them a lot with teaching in racially and ethnically diverse classrooms compared to 52% who felt that it had only helped them a little (National Comprehensive Center for Teacher Quality & Public Agenda, 2008). Consequently, R. W. Taylor (2010) believes that teacher education programs have a moral and ethical responsibility to rethink how their programs are preparing students to be culturally competent teachers.

> A place to start is with teacher education and professional development.

To begin the needed dialogue about improving teacher education programs, teacher education faculty must first realize and examine our own cultural influences. Allen and Hermann-Wilmarth (2010), maintain that teacher education faculty can successfully engage in a process of learning about themselves as cultural beings through writing, photography, and talking with family.

We must keep in mind what Labov (2003) said: "Because education is the chief avenue of social mobility in the United States, this massive failure to read reinforces and intensifies social inequality" (p. 129).

Teachers must increase their understanding of students' cultural and linguistic differences and prepare themselves to use this knowledge to improve reading instruction for the struggling readers in their classrooms. Some of the options that they might choose to pursue are listed here:

- Explore their life history to determine their feelings about and preparation for teaching for equity and social justice (A. S. Johnson, 2007).
- Construct memoirs to better understand their literacy and language histories (Allen & Hermann-Wilmarth, 2010).
- Interview parents to determine their strengths and areas where they can provide support when needed (Risko & Walker-Dalhouse, 2009).
- Complete a cultural and community inventory of students' communities. Use the information obtained for individual professional development to begin the process of thinking about linking cultural resources with instructional reading themes, content, or materials.

The literature in this area also provides several useful recommendations for helping preservice teachers examine their cultural and linguistic identities. Labbo (2007) designed three class assignments using Schmidt's (1998) ABCs of cultural understanding framework. Labbo used these assignments to prepare her preservice teachers for the reality of working in a classroom of multiethnic and multilingual students. Two of these follow and we add an additional activity.

- Write a self-narrative or autobiography in which educators describe and examine their lives as cultural beings and language learners.
- Construct biographies of elementary students from diverse cultures to better understand students with whom they work in classrooms, practicum, or field-based experiences teaching or working with children.
- Use multicultural children's literature to explore other cultures and languages and to make connections to information learned from constructing individual autobiographies and student biographies.

## SUMMARY

Culture and language influence who students are and who they will become. The social dynamics in classrooms affect children's reading development and identities. For example, English learners who do not have the English language proficiency or the dominant cultural knowledge needed to succeed in classrooms are often marginalized and see themselves as poor readers (Christian & Bloome, 2004).

Classroom teachers must examine their attitudes, beliefs, and instructional practices related to culture and language because they position students for success or failure by influencing students' self-perception as readers. Jerry Harste (2009) challenges teachers to develop students' identities as readers. According to Harste, "We want readers to see themselves as having agency, not only in terms of making meaning, but also in terms of critiquing what they read, and in terms of positioning themselves more capably and powerfully in the world" (p. 7). Teachers can meet this challenge by changing the way they see struggling readers in their classrooms because ultimately this influences the way struggling readers see themselves.

### REFLECTION QUESTIONS

1. What barriers interfere with teachers' and/or school efforts to incorporate the cultures and languages of their students into the curriculum, their instruction, and classroom management? How might these challenges be addressed at the classroom and/or school level?
2. How responsive are struggling readers to instruction that is reflective of their cultural and language background? What effect does it have on the perceptions of themselves as readers and of their positioning within the social environment within the classroom?
3. How do teachers who consider students' cultural backgrounds differentiate curriculum and instruction in urban school settings? In rural school settings?

# CHAPTER 3

# Assessing What Matters for Students and Instruction

Teachers administer a wide array of assessments and only some of these are helpful for informing instruction. For example, teachers administer tests to meet federal, state, and school-district requirements. Among these are standardized, norm-referenced tests that provide achievement data for district leaders, and curriculum-based assessments to determine progress on curricular goals often aligned with state standards. Both forms of assessments can be narrow in scope, underrepresenting reading as a broad array of abilities and activities (Afflerbach, 2007).

If assessments are narrowly conceived, it is quite possible that what is measured underrepresents what students know and do as readers (Bracey, 2001). This chapter focuses on assessments that provide a more elaborate and precise understanding of students' reading performance. These assessments can be credible, providing information that can be trusted to represent students' range of capabilities and needs, and they are useful for planning instruction that is student-centered and aligned with curriculum and/or district goals (Risko & Walker-Dalhouse, 2010).

To be most useful for instructional planning, assessments should be

- Situated in the students' perspective
- Situated in authentic reading activities
- Focused on more than single skills and/or strategies simultaneously
- Both formative and summative
- Multimodal
- Doable in the real life of classrooms

## CASE ANALYSES: SHAKEELA, ASLAM, AND JENNY

Three student cases are described here to situate our discussion of assessment and to illustrate how assessment tools may be used in practice and to accommodate student differences.

## Shakeela

Shakeela, who is African American, is a second-grade student. She is in a first-grade/second-grade split classroom and this is her 2nd year with her teacher, Ms. Isaac. Ms. Isaac teaches reading with children's literature. She has students meet in different groups depending on purpose, such as discussing a favorite text. She teaches skills and strategies through small-group instruction. Students write daily about texts they are reading or on topics that come from book discussions with Ms. Isaac. Ms. Isaac describes Shakeela as a student who "has come into her own" this year. She indicates that she has made great progress since first grade. In first grade, Shakeela loved reading predictable books, such as *Why Mosquitoes Buzz in People's Ears* (Aardema, 1975). She read with expression, knew the words of most predictable books both in and out of context, and comprehended the information. She had difficulty transitioning to more complicated texts and ones that have less of a predictable structure. Following first grade, she told Ms. Isaac that she had read "all summer." In second grade, she is reading "ever increasingly difficult texts." Her self-concept as a reader is positive, she says that she loves coming to school, and she tells her friends that she wants to be a teacher.

## Aslam

Aslam is in fifth grade. His family immigrated to the United States from Pakistan when he was 5 years old, and he has attended school in the United States since kindergarten. He is bilingual and biliterate although he seems to have more experience reading and writing in English both in and out of school. His parents are fluent English speakers and English is the primary language of the home. He attends a religious class where he reads texts in his home language—Urdu. Aslam seemed to make good progress in reading instruction during the primary grade levels. In particular, his scores on annual achievement tests through Grade 3 indicated strong word identification, fluency, and literal comprehension. His teacher, Ms. Callan, reported that Aslam is expected to read literature, social studies, and science textbooks in fifth grade and that his comprehension of these texts is limited, noting particular problems understanding important text concepts and complicated story plots. Instruction in the subject areas, including reading, requires independent reading of the assigned text followed by whole-class discussions. The discussions are typically led by teacher questions, and small-group projects are assigned and completed in class. Skills (e.g., grammar rules, dictionary use to define vocabulary) and strategies (e.g., inferring characters' motives) are taught during whole-class instruction.

## Jenny

Jenny is White. She is a second-grade student who has had difficulty with reading since first grade. She did not attend kindergarten and she has changed schools 11 times since beginning first grade. Her parents are itinerant farmers who move frequently to earn money to support their family. Her teacher, Mr. Marlin, reported that Jenny has acquired a basic sight vocabulary and can read books that have picture clues and repeated phrases such as in *I See* and *I Can* books. Mr. Marlin teaches with shared reading activities for the whole class and guided reading groups using children's literature. He conferences with students regularly and provides instruction for individuals as needed. He also guides students' writing in a workshop format and engages students in numerous language arts activities, such as puppetry, dramatization, and writing to publish personal stories.

Taken together, we have three students in different places in their reading development. Shakeela is reported to be making good progress in second grade, Aslam is challenged by the texts he is reading in middle school, and Jenny is a second-grade student who is viewed as a "beginning reader." For all three, assessments should provide additional information and direction for instruction.

### CASE QUESTIONS

1. According to her teacher, Shakeela is making good progress as a reader. What assessments would be useful for informing instruction that builds on and supports Shakeela's continued development?
2. What assessments will be useful for planning instruction that will improve Aslam's comprehension of the school's literacy, social studies, and science textbooks?
3. What assessments will be useful for identifying Jenny's reading abilities and areas of need to accelerate her early reading progress?

## CONCEPTUALIZING ASSESSMENT

The assessments we discuss in this chapter are those that can be administered by the classroom teacher and/or reading specialist who is collaborating with the classroom teacher to identify possible reasons for students' reading difficulties. They are administered individually to students during teacher-student conferences and/or small-group settings.

We approach assessment from an ecological perspective with the goal of capturing the educative events and contexts that are most supportive of students' learning; what students understand about reading, writing, and learning; the skills they have acquired and the strategies that guide their active engagement; their interests and world knowledge; their out of school and family activities; and their cultural and linguistic history.

As part of the process, we want to know how students feel about themselves as learners and as readers. We want to know their reading interests as they relate to what they choose to read. Their choice of reading materials might include video texts, such as video games or digital stories; signs and written material read in the community; magazines and newspapers; and Internet texts.

> Texts for assessments should be authentic to students' reading experiences and preferences.

When we examine their performance on assessments, such as oral reading assessments, we want to understand the stance students take (i.e., how the student defines the reading event, and the goals they have for the task) and the students' identity (e.g., do they take the stance of a struggling reader with few attempts at self-corrections, or do they take the stance of the author and thus act out parts of the text as they read or project different voices for the different characters) (Bloome & Dail, 1997).

We also choose reading assessments that capture what students know about reading and what they do as readers. For example, assessments should help teachers answer questions, such as the following:

- Do students know that there are several strategies that can help them identify unknown words?
- Do students know that their prior experiences can aid their comprehension (what readers know)?
- Do students use several strategies to fix mispronunciations when reading aloud?
- Do students cross-reference several texts they have read to help them interpret new information (what readers do)?

We describe assessment as a support for instruction, and thus for this chapter, the audience is the teacher and reading specialists or other teacher leaders. The assessments inform instruction by providing information

*Figure 3.1. Ecological Assessment*

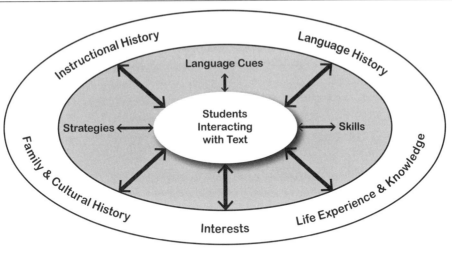

about students' strengths and capabilities, instructional needs, interests, cultural and linguistic history, specific instructional history, and instructional conditions that seem to best support students' performance.

Pellegrino, Chudowsky, and Glaser (2001) indicate that usable reading assessments address three features: First is the feature of cognition, as described above, focusing on what students do as they read. Second are conditions of testing that are carefully considered for they affect outcomes. For example, are students asked to identify vowel sounds when shown vowel letters in a list or are students asked to read written text to determine if vowel sounds are read accurately? Ability to read vowels in isolated words has different demands than applying vowel knowledge to text reading. Third is interpretation. Teachers need sufficient data, such as using more than one assessment or more frequent samplings of performance, to construct an explanation of students' performance, and possible reasons, such as interest in task or background experience, may have a positive influence on performance. Interpretations come from observing individuals and the instructional conditions that impact students (Johnston, 1997; Johnston & Costello, 2005). Interpretations need to be as informed as possible and thus require teachers to keep notes on their observations of students and to collect samples of students' performance across varied situations. They require an observer who is sensitive to the students' actions and reactions to the situations and demands of the tasks (Clay, 1993a).

Above all, assessments should approximate real reading conditions—thus reading words in context or narratives, expository, or online texts,

for example, situates the assessments. And the assessments we describe help teachers go beyond
whole-class assessments and provide specific data
on students' daily performance, misconceptions
during instruction, and needs that require further
instruction.

> Conditions for assessment should be authentic, mirroring as much as possible reading situations that are *typical* for students.

## PLANFUL AND USEFUL ASSESSMENTS

We think of assessment as an inquiry journey collecting data over time and
constructing understandings of students' performance. Teachers begin the
journey when thinking about students such as Shakeela, Aslam, or Jenny.
Initially teachers may have general information, such as what is provided
in the cases above. More specific information is required, however, to plan
appropriate and responsive instruction. We recommend the following assessments as a starting place to learn about each student who is experiencing difficulty.

### Assessment Situated in the Students' Perspective

The goal for these assessments is to bring to the forefront, quite explicitly, students' rich knowledge sources and experiential history and the
social cultural influences on their learning to read. Multiple researchers
have documented how issues such as differences in everyday experiences and interactions with peers and family members (Johnston & Costello,
2005); different expectations of teachers, students, and parents for school
learning and participation (Au, 2000); and histories of language learning
and linguistic differences (Artiles, 2003) can affect students' reading performance in schools. Despite this body of knowledge, however, students
generally are all treated the same (Gormley & McDermott, 2011). Few if
any adjustments to testing conditions or instruments are provided, and
the knowledge sources of students or information about what interests
them in reading and writing are discarded or thought to be irrelevant
to teaching decisions. Students are often misdiagnosed (McDermott,
2004) or placed in special education when differences are thought to be
difficulties.

Assessments that are situated in the students' perspective are designed to reveal students' language, cultural, and experiential resources so
that these resources can be leveraged within the assessment process and

instruction. One form of these assessments invites continuous conversations with students and their families. Conversations should be two-way, open, and foster a sharing of visions and expectations. Some teachers develop family history projects where students and families work together to develop stories about their families; often these are placed on classroom blogs or in class publications. Katie Devlin, a first-grade teacher in Winnipeg, Canada, develops Personal Museums, where students and families share information about their histories and special events about the student, such as birth date and events on that day, origin of the student's name, and so on (Risko, 2011).

Landis, Kalieva, Abitova, Izmukhanbetova, and Musaeva (2006) conducted interviews with community members to learn about the history of the community and community events. Students analyzed these interviews drawing comparisons and contrasts in events and perceptions, generating questions for further interviews. From this data collection, students wrote informational pieces that could be shared at community or school events. Similarly, involvement in community projects, such as the study of toxic waste in New York City (Torres-Guzman, 1992), revealed students' abilities to address complex problems, higher order thinking, high interest, and extended engagement in reading and writing, all attributed to the authenticity of the activity (Newman, Marks, & Gamoran, 1995).

Other researchers draw from students' "youth culture" to engage discussions and/or to observe how students participate in reading and writing activities. For example, what are students' preferences for music or videos and why? What understandings do they have of the lyrics of country or rap music? How much time do they spend on the Internet and how is the time spent? Do they track information around particular topics, such as reality shows versus discovery- and science-oriented information? Compton-Lilly (2009) describes how a teacher uses downloaded images from a student's favorite video game with teacher-added captions to create texts that become increasingly more complicated to support his growing repertoire of skills and his interests. Pickering and Painter (2005) organized discussions about expectations for classroom community drawing on students' knowledge of the animated characters Shrek and Bart Simpson.

Dworin (2006) describes how a family story project that was developed in a bilingual fourth-grade classroom was helpful for providing family information and helped the teacher learn about students' bilingualism and biliteracy skills. Similarly, providing opportunities for students to discuss vocabulary and texts translated to their first language can not only enhance comprehension (Orellana, Reynolds, & Martinez, 2011) but also provide valuable information about students' vocabulary knowledge, text inferences, and bilingual capabilities (Iddings et al., 2009), as we illustrated in Chapter 2, with our discussion of Seth's and Erin's instruction.

## Assessment Situated in Authentic Reading Activities

There are multiple methods for assessing oral reading and comprehension. The purpose for listening to students' oral reading is to capture what students say and do while reading. As teachers listen to students' oral reading, they record actual behaviors (e.g., rereading, mispronunciations), and these behaviors are later coded and analyzed to determine language cues and reading skills and strategies students may be applying to their textual reading. The data provide some clues about students' reading strengths and instructional needs; teachers' inferences can be developed further with subsequent oral readings across various texts, by asking students to talk about the texts they read orally and silently and by interviewing students about their reading. Assessing students in different ways (e.g., oral reading, silent reading) and with different texts provides additional information, as skills used while reading high-interest texts may be different from those used during reading of less interesting texts. Similarly, easy-reading texts may require fewer strategies, such as word identification strategies, than instructional-level texts. Thus oral reading samples require teacher observation and interpretation, and the closer the text is to students' authentic experiences, the more likely that data will be a fair estimation of students' reading skills and strategies.

On the one hand, oral reading, as we describe below, is an authentic act—students are reading real texts and talking about their understandings. Yet for most students, particularly struggling readers and older readers, reading aloud is not authentic, and few students expect to have their behaviors recorded while they read. Thus there are aspects of oral reading for assessment purposes that are artificial. Johnston (1997), Y. Goodman (1996), and others recommend sharing the purpose of oral reading and the data and asking students to comment on their performance. This process makes oral reading assessments more accessible to students and signals a value for students' self-analysis. These interviews also provide additional information for teachers.

Comprehension is assessed when students tell what they remember and how they interpret text ideas. Students can be asked to retell what they remember, summarize the text, answer teacher questions, and pause frequently during the text reading to explain what they are thinking (often called a think aloud procedure). With these assessments, comprehension is assessed when students are reading orally or silently.

The following sections describe the forms of oral reading and comprehension assessments that we recommend.

***Assessing oral reading with miscue analysis.*** Begin by having the student read orally a full-length text or big chunks of text that hold meaning (such as a chapter of a narrative or a topical section of an informational text). (See Goodman, Watson, & Burke, 1987.) Often we use chapter books and choose a chapter other than the first one. Students, who have read the first chapter, then are somewhat familiar with the text's purpose, organization, style of writing, and vocabulary prior to reading aloud for assessment purposes. While the student is reading, the teacher records observed actions (e.g., noticing the humor expressed by the author and commenting on it, rereading for self-correction of mispronounced words) and oral reading miscues (students' changes to the printed text). Possible student miscues are listed in Figure 3.2.

The teacher then analyzes the oral reading actions interpreting language cues and strategies students may be using to aid pronunciation of unknown words and make sense of the text. Language cues include those that represent semantic (meaning), syntactic (grammatical), and/or graphophonic (letter sounds) information (for an illustration of this, see Figure 6.1 in Chapter 6). When determining language cues students are using, the analysis reveals *what* forms of language information a student may be using. For example, a student may rely on graphophonic cues producing words that have some or most sounds of the words in the text. (We will discuss language cue systems further when we describe running records in this chapter.)

The analysis of miscues also reveals students' strategies—*how* they approach their reading task, as displayed in Figure 3.3. The analysis of strategies reveals if students are overrelying on particular cues, such as specific sound segments (e.g., beginning sounds) in words to aid pronunciation and/or if students are rereading to self-correct and monitor their own reading.

Kenneth Goodman (1973, 1996) explains that students can miscue based on their understandings of the text or the cueing systems in play. He argues that students are constantly interpreting cues, but at times their representations are different from what an author intended.

The analysis of miscues, then, are *telling informers* for teachers, as they provide clues about students' use of language information and strategies for identifying words and ideas and making sense of texts they are reading.

*Figure 3.2. Examples of Student Miscues During Oral Reading*

| Oral Reading Action | Change in Text/Markings | Description of Action |
|---|---|---|
| Substitution | *turnets* <br> and turrets | Can include real word(s) substituted for another word or words; or can be a mispronunciation of word(s) |
| Insertion | And then she *also* <br> appeared ∧ | Word, words, or phrases are inserted |
| Omissions | its (cornices) | Word, words, sentences may be omitted |
| Repetitions | The huge manor | Word, words, or sentences may be repeated |
| (Rereading for) Self Corrections | *hug (sc)* <br> The huge manor | Changed text is corrected with a rereading |
| Rereading for fluency | *Pause* <br> The huge manor, <br> *fluency* | Rereading to correct phrasing, voice of characters, flow of text |
| Rereading with repetition of miscue | *hug, hug* <br> The huge manor | Rereading but not self-correcting |
| Abandoning correct reading | *huge, hug* <br> The huge manor | Rereading and changing text from initial accurate reading |

It provides information about those that may need further development through instruction.

*Miscue analysis coupled with retrospective miscue analysis.* Y. Goodman (1996) states that interviewing students about their oral reading miscues, through a retrospective miscue analysis procedure, adds additional information to support teachers' interpretations. Asking students questions such as "How did you figure out the character's name?" or "Why did you go back and reread this section?" helps students develop personal awareness of strategies and skills in use (Bransford et al., 1999). The assessment process, then, becomes a tool for empowering and nurturing students' interpretations and constructed meanings and their reasoning about decisions (Tierney, 1998).

*Oral reading assessment with running records.* Clay's (2000) data collection and analysis procedures are useful for analyzing students' oral

*Figure 3.3. Oral Reading Strategies*

| Strategy | Description |
|---|---|
| Reliance on graphophonic cues | Reads first letter or some letter combination (e.g., beginning and ending sound of word) to predict pronunciation of unknown words; can also segment words into sound units to aid pronunciation |
| Reliance on syntactic cues | Makes text sound "right" by substituting words that fit the grammatical structure of the text (e.g., verb for verb), not necessarily meaningful |
| Reliance on semantic cues | Uses context clues to select a word that makes sense in the sentence or larger text |
| Cross-checking | Monitors and rereads to use all three language cues to self-correct and predict unknown words |
| Self-monitoring | Rereading to fix up strategies, often includes cross-checking |
| Reads up to and around words and circles back to pronounce words | Reading and checking reading as an aid to predict and confirm meaning of words |
| Inserts, omits, changes words | Often used to make sense of text when confronted with unknown words; can also produce words that are not meaningful or associated with the three language cues |

reading. As a student reads aloud, the teacher records a check mark for each word read correctly, changes to the text that are made during oral reading (e.g., word substitutions, repetitions), and students' behaviors (e.g., expressions of excitement, pauses). Markings like these are illustrated for Aslam's oral reading later in this chapter (in Figure 3.10). Students read small segments of text (on average, about 100 running words), and several samples across different texts (e.g., two to three oral reading samples a week) to substantiate interpretations of students' use of language cues and reading strategies.

Like the miscue analysis, teachers analyze performance for use of semantic, syntactic, and graphophonic cues. Miscues (called "errors" by Clay) are judged, for example, to determine if changes to the intended text make sense for the story. As with the miscue analysis procedures described above, miscues are judged to determine students' use of strategies (e.g., do the text changes make sense? ) and language cues (e.g., semantic cues). Questions guiding this analysis are provided in Figure 3.4.

*Figure 3.4. Questions Guiding the Analysis of Running Records: Use of Language Cues and Strategies During Oral Reading*

| Use of Cues and Strategies | Questions for Analysis |
|---|---|
| Use of Semantic Cues— Meaning Cues | Do the changes/errors make sense? <br><br> Do they make sense to the overall story? <br><br> Do they make sense for the text part read up to the error? <br><br> Do the changes/errors make sense due to student's prior knowledge and experiences? other similar texts that student read? <br><br> Is the student relying on illustrations to influence changes/errors that make sense? <br><br> If errors/changes do not make sense, why is this the case? See above examples as possible reasons for errors. For example, the illustrations don't support the text ideas but influenced the error. |
| Use of Syntactic Cues— Language/ Grammatical/ Structure Cues | The structure/grammar of the sentence up to the error should be a plausible English representation of the text. <br><br> Did the student's construction sound like his/her knowledge of English and English grammar? <br><br> If the student's construction does not represent a plausible representation of English, what other cues may have influenced the errors/changes (e.g., another first language, mimicking the language of a familiar author)? |
| Use of Visual Cues— Graphophonic Cues | Does the error/change look like the word(s) in the text? part of the word(s) and which parts? <br><br> Does the error/change represent a plausible construction of the word sounds? sounds for part of the word(s) and which parts (e.g., initial blend sounds, suffixes, medial long vowel sounds)? |
| Use of Strategies | Is student reading fluently and with prosody? <br><br> Is student using appropriate phrasing and punctuation? <br><br> Are self-corrections based primarily on one or two of the language cues (e.g., graphophonic cues, meaning/context clues)? <br><br> What may have contributed to the student's self-corrections? <br><br> Does the student reread to adjust fluency or to attempt to decode or attempt to make sense of the text? <br><br> Does the student reread and abandon correct reading? <br><br> Do insertions and omissions affect the meaning and how? |

*Oral reading and fluency.* Reading fluency is defined as reading with accuracy (reading words in text correctly), automaticity (reading words without effort), and prosody (reading with appropriate expression drawing on semantic and syntactic information) (Rasinski, 2004). More specifically, *automaticity* encompasses accurate reading with a quick recognition of words while reading. *Prosody*, or reading with expression, refers to the reader's ability to represent and signal the meaning of the text—with appropriate rhythm, pitch, intonation, and phrasing (Samuels & Farstrup, 2006). In contrast, students may read word by word, in a monotone voice and/or with awkward phrasing and pauses. This is referred to as a *lack of fluency* or dysfluent reading. Patterns of fluency are derived from the markings made during a miscue analysis or when coding for running records. For example, a high number of check marks indicates high accuracy at the word level was attained. The absence of excessive pausing or repetitions provides information about automaticity. Additionally, teachers add comments, such as "reads with expression," "reads with appropriate intonation and phrasing," to refer to students' prosody. Analysis of the patterns are determined when teachers ask questions such as, Did the student's reading sound like natural speech? Did the student read with expression and to convey meaning with appropriate emphasis? Timothy Rasinski (2004) provides rubrics for recording fluency data at http:// www.prel.org/products/re_/assessing-fluency.htm

*Comprehension assessments.* For a retelling assessment, students tell what they remember from the passage. Retellings can be scored in different ways. Dena McAllister, while a graduate student at Vanderbilt University, developed the form shown in Figure 3.5 (McAllister, 1996). On this form, the teacher can record story information recalled (page 1) and judge the quality of information and engagement (page 2).

Retellings can also be judged more holistically, with rubrics, such as the rubric provided on the Developmental Reading Assessment, 2nd Edition (DRA2+) (Celebration Press/Pearson Learning Group, 2005). For example, using a scale from 1 to 4 (with categories of *very little comprehension, some comprehension, adequate comprehension*, and *very good comprehension*) teachers can judge the students' retellings on areas such as key facts, important details, and accuracy of information.

If students are asked to retell the text as a summary, a rubric such as the one in Figure 3.6 can be used to evaluate the kinds of information included in the summary.

*Figure 3.5. Retelling Assessment Form*

Name _____          Date _____

Examiner _____          Story _____

Mark those that apply: Immediate/Delayed, Written/Oral, Reading Comprehension/Listening

| *Quantitative section (Recall of important facts)* | *Unaided* | *Aided* | *Notes* |
|---|---|---|---|
| Setting | | | |
| Time | _____ | _____ | _____ |
| Place | _____ | _____ | _____ |
| Character names: Main | _____ | _____ | _____ |
| Character names: Supporting | _____ | _____ | _____ |
| Plot | | | |
| Opening statement-introduces story (May include above information) | _____ | _____ | _____ |
| Initialing event-beginning of problem | _____ | _____ | _____ |
| Goal - objective in solving the problem | _____ | _____ | _____ |
| Other events - succeeding attempts to solve problem | _____ | _____ | _____ |
| Summary | | | |
| Resolution of problem | _____ | _____ | _____ |
| Ending statement | _____ | _____ | _____ |
| Story events in sequential order | _____ | _____ | _____ |
| Story theme - lesson or main idea | _____ | _____ | _____ |

**Total quantitative (12):**

_____ _____

_____

## *Figure 3.5. Retelling Assessment Form* (continued)

| Qualitative section (Shows more comprehensive understanding) | Unaided | Aided | Notes |
|---|---|---|---|
| **Beyond the main points** | | | |
| Evidence of inferences/connections | _____ | _____ | _____ |
| Includes description/explanation of character | _____ | _____ | _____ |
| Mentions feelings of characters | _____ | _____ | _____ |
| Alternative story idea - another solution, etc. | _____ | _____ | _____ |
| Includes supporting detail, storytelling style | _____ | _____ | _____ |
| **Self-Awareness** | | | |
| Relates story to personal experience | _____ | _____ | _____ |
| Mentions enjoyable section | _____ | _____ | _____ |
| Self-monitoring: aware of difficult areas | _____ | _____ | _____ |
| Self-concept: attitude was confident, willing | _____ | _____ | _____ |
| **Accuracy of retelling** | | | |
| Includes pertinent story vocabulary | _____ | | _____ |
| Sentences are clear, and not run together | _____ | | _____ |
| Pauses are not extensive | _____ | | _____ |
| No incorrect information given | _____ | | _____ |

**Total qualitative (13):**

_____   _____

**Total retelling (25):**_____(N/A_____)

**Scoring**

1. Administer and mark retelling according to the normal procedure - allowing the student to tell all remembered information (unaided) before asking any questions about the story (aided).

2. Give one point for each answer, partial credit of 1/2 can be given.

3. Put N/A (not applicable) for items not included in story text or do not apply for other reasons, and note this next to the total score.

4. During the aided retelling, items which could not be asked should be left blank. Items which were asked and received no answer should be marked with a "0."

*Source:* Form developed by Dena McAllister, graduate assistant of V. J. Risko at Vanderbilt University, 1996

*Figure 3.6. Rubric to Evaluate Student Written or Oral Summaries*

0 = No evidence of construction of meaning.

1 = Some evidence of construction of meaning, building some understanding of the text. Presence of defensible, and possibly some indefensible, information.

2 = A superficial understanding of the text, with evidence of meaning construction. One or two relevant but unsupported inferences.

3 = A developed understanding of the text with evidence of connections, extensions, and examinations of meaning. Connections among the reader's ideas and the text itself are implied. Extensions and examinations are related to the text but explicit references to the text in support of inferences are not present. When more than one stance is possible, the response may remain limited to one stance.

4 = A developed understanding of the text with evidence of connections, extensions, and examinations of meaning. Connections among the reader's ideas and the text itself are explicit. Extensions and examinations are accompanied by explicit references to the text in support of inferences. When possible, the response indicates more than one stance or perspective on the text; however, only one stance is substantially supported by references to the text.

5 = A developed understanding of the text with evidence of connections, extensions, examinations of meaning, and defense of interpretations. Connections among the reader's ideas and the text itself are explicit. Extensions and examinations are accompanied by explicit references to the text in support of inferences. When possible, the response indicates more than two stances, all substantially supported by references to the text.

6 = A complex, developed understanding of the text with evidence of connections, extensions, examinations of meaning, and defense of interpretations. Connections among the reader's ideas and the text itself are explicit. Extensions and examinations are accompanied by explicit references to the text in support of inferences. Responses indicate as many stances as possible based on the activity, all substantially supported by references to the text. These responses reflect careful thought and thoroughness.

**Codes:** A: Blank. There is no response.

B: The writer's response is off task or off topic. It does not address the question that was asked.

C: Unscorable. The writer's response cannot be read (e.g., it is illegible, incomprehensible).

D: Copied from test text.

*Note:* From "The Maryland school performance assessment program: A new view of assessment," by B. A. Kapinus, G. V. Collier, and H. Kruglanski, 1994, in S. W., Valencia, E. H. Hiebert, & P. P. Afflerbach (Eds.), *Authentic reading assessment: Practices and possibilities* (pp. 255–276). Newark, DE: International Reading Association. Reprinted with permission.

It is important to choose texts carefully and prepare students for the above oral reading and comprehension assessments. Students may be unfamiliar with these forms of assessment; thus practice sessions that may involve teacher modeling and guided practice (e.g., how to retell a text) may be needed so that students understand what is expected from them and how data will be collected.

Teachers choose texts that are authentic to instruction and include those that students may be reading independently at home or school; those that relate most directly to their life experiences and world view (Tatum, 2008). Included are texts that may be easy reading for the students to be assessed and those that are more difficult. Clay (1993b) describes levels of texts as "easy or independent reading" (95% word accuracy), "instructional" (90 to 94% word accuracy), and "frustrational" (below 90% word accuracy).

Teachers often choose a few texts representing what students may be required to read and those that students select (two to four texts). Often assessments are conducted on more than one text over time. Next teachers select a text or fully developed passage from the set assembled to address particular goals they may have. For example, Ms. Isaac knows that Shakeela is most comfortable reading texts with repetitive phrases, but she may want to assess her performance on a different kind of text, perhaps a narrative written for second graders. Ms. Callan may choose to have Aslam read part of a text that he is reading in his literature class to determine what may be posing problems for him. And Mr. Marlin may want to hear Jenny read from a class text to provide specific information about the skills and strategies she is using and those that require instruction.

***Case students' reading and comprehension.*** Both Shakeela and Jenny read a full-length text. Shakeela read "The Frog Prince" that appeared in her second-grade literature anthology. This version of "The Frog Prince" closely matches the version written and illustrated by Galdone (1975). Her teacher noted that she read with expression and that she made very few miscues. Figure 3.7 shows a few examples of her miscues, representing patterns of her oral reading.

On line 193 (see Figure 3.7), Shakeela read and reread trying to make sense of the sentence. She had several trials with the word *witch*, correctly pronouncing the initial consonant sounds each time. She seemed to know that her mispronunciations did not make sense, but she was unable to fix it. In the second example, on line 88, Shakeela repeated and self-corrected her

*Figure 3.7. Shakeela's Oral Reading*

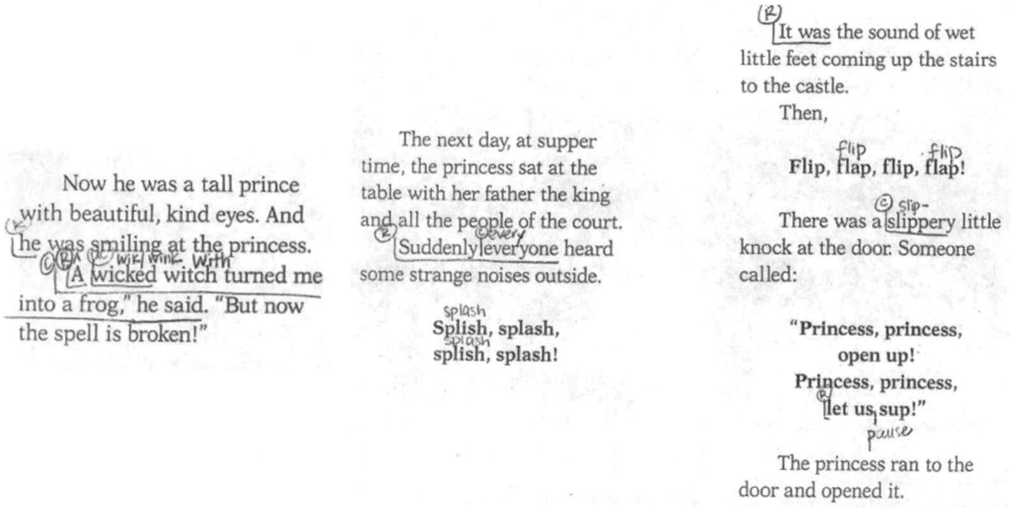

Now he was a tall prince with beautiful, kind eyes. And he was smiling at the princess. "A wicked witch turned me into a frog," he said. "But now the spell is broken!"

The next day, at supper time, the princess sat at the table with her father the king and all the people of the court. Suddenly everyone heard some strange noises outside.

Splish, splash, splish, splash!

It was the sound of wet little feet coming up the stairs to the castle. Then,

Flip, flap, flip, flap!

There was a slippery little knock at the door. Someone called:

"Princess, princess, open up! Princess, princess, let us sup!"

The princess ran to the door and opened it.

reading of *every* to *everyone*, and on line 97 she self-corrected *slip* to *slippery*. In both instances, she worked through the sounds in the total word to pronounce it correctly. On these two pages, she substituted *splash* for *splish* two times and *flip* for *flap* two times. No attempts to self-correct were apparent, but her teacher interpreted this to mean two things: (1) Her substitutions still made sense; and (2) Shakeela seemed to follow the pattern of the word groups—*ash* in *splash*, and *ip* in *flip*.

Her retelling after the reading was strong. She recalled all the details of the story, told them in sequential order, and explained correctly that the moral of the story is "if you make a promise, you should keep it."

These data are useful for planning Shakeela's instruction. This reading provides evidence that Shakeela is reading her grade-level text with comprehension and with a balanced use of semantic, syntactic, and language cues and meaning-oriented strategies. Keeping this trajectory moving in a positive direction requires a continuation of a balanced approach to reading, maintaining her cues and strategies and reading for meaning but now applied to learning new vocabulary, reading more complicated and varied texts, and supporting methods to deepen her comprehension while reading more complicated texts.

Jenny, a second grader who is described by her teacher as a "beginning" or emergent reader, had two assessments. She listened to the story "The Little Red Hen" and retold it almost word for word, line by line. She said that she had heard the story before but that this one was a "little different."

She began her retelling with the phrase "once up a time" and continued to tell the story, expressing fears (that the fox will get her) or exclaiming joy (when Red Hen tricked the fox). She frequently repeated phrases from the book, such as "I won't" when characters indicated that they would not help Red Hen do the housework. And she judged the characters' actions, indicating that "they were lazy" or "they shouldn't get cake if they don't help Red Hen."

Her oral reading of *Moo Moo, Brown Cow* (Wood, 1991) provided information about her cueing systems. The text is organized in a series of couplets that end with rhymes. There is a pattern to the presentation of information. A parent animal is introduced and described (e.g., brown cow and black sheep) followed by a description of baby animals (e.g., spotted calf and wooly lambs). Yet this text has potential for being difficult unless students have experience with the rhyming couplet style, and the vocabulary requires a high level of specific knowledge about animal names. For example, gosling is the child animal paired with the goose, kids are paired with goats, piglets with pigs, and froglets with frogs.

Jenny read the entire text. A portion of the recordings is provided in Figure 3.8. On first inspecting the oral reading data, Mr. Marlin noticed that Jenny did not understand the pattern of the text (i.e., parent-child animal relationship). Furthermore, she was unable to read words that were difficult for her (e.g., calf, ducklings) and she often skipped over the number and color words. After reading the text, she explained that the text was "about different animals, the cow, the sheep, the goat, the kitten."

With further analysis, Mr. Marlin noticed that Jenny was working hard to make sense of a text that was difficult for her. For example, she used graphophonic cues, often reading through the sounds of a word and either pronouncing it correctly, such as *k-i-d-s* then pronounced as *kids*, or approximating the word to read part of it correctly, such as *duck* in *ducklings*. She used semantic clues to describe *lambs* as *wonderful*, to read *kitten* for *kitty*, or when reading *children* for *kids*.

This analysis provides information for planning Jenny's instruction. First, Mr. Marlin will choose narratives, perhaps a narrative format similar to "The Little Red Hen" on her emergent reading level. Previewing the book with a picture walk could help Jenny understand the text format and build expectations for meaning, while signaling words that will appear in the story. Mr. Marlin plans to teach word identification skills building on the ones Jenny is using already (e.g., use of semantic cues, use of at least beginning parts of words) to include reading through entire words (e.g., *duck* to *duck* + *ling* to *duckling*).

*Figure 3.8. Jenny's Oral Reading*

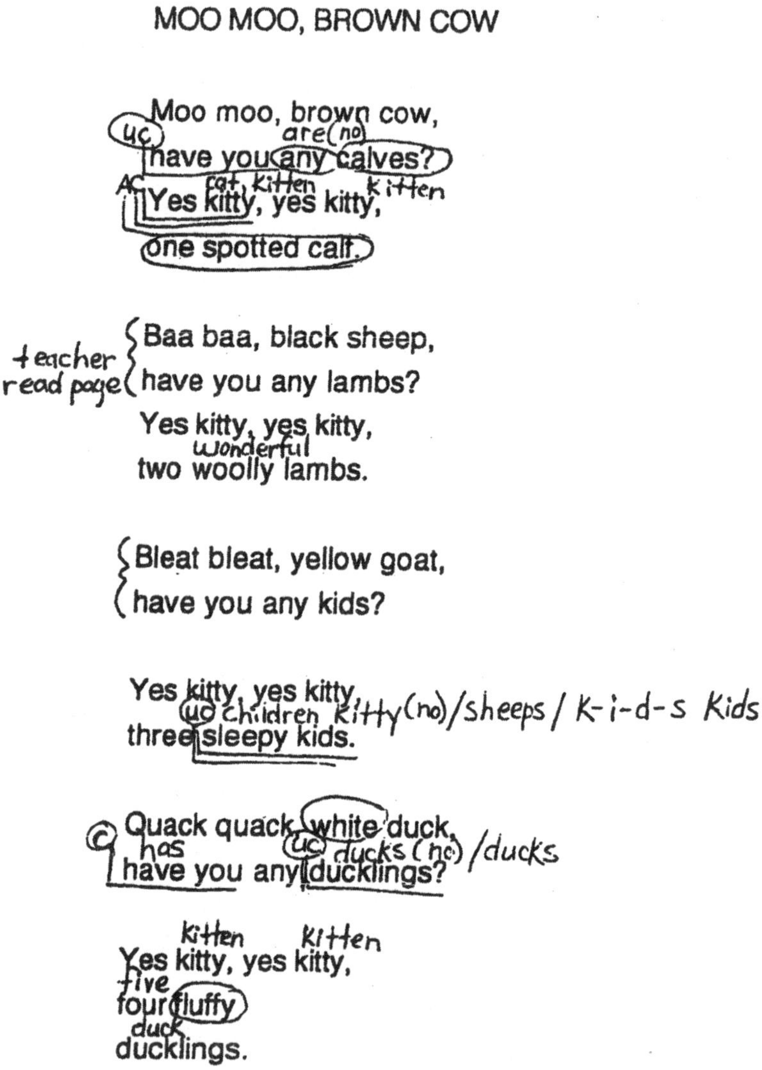

## MOO MOO, BROWN COW

Moo moo, brown cow,
*uc*                    *are (no)*
have you any calves?
*A*          *cat kitten      kitten*
Yes kitty, yes kitty,
one spotted calf.

*teacher*  { Baa baa, black sheep,
*read page* { have you any lambs?

Yes kitty, yes kitty,
*wonderful*
two woolly lambs.

{ Bleat bleat, yellow goat,
{ have you any kids?

Yes kitty, yes kitty,
*uc children kitty (no) /sheeps / K-i-d-s kids*
three sleepy kids.

*C* Quack quack, white duck,
*has          uc ducks (no) /ducks*
have you any ducklings?

*kitten      kitten*
Yes kitty, yes kitty,
*five*
four fluffy
*duck*
ducklings.

Aslam's teacher, Ms. Callan, asked him to read aloud portions of the first chapter of the book *The Wolves of Willoughby Chase* by Joan Aiken. Additionally, she asked him to read silently other parts of the chapter and to stop in selected places to explain his thinking, using a think aloud procedure. Both the oral reading markings and a transcription of Aslam's thinking during the think aloud activity are recorded on the text page provided in Figure 3.9. Ms. Callan analyzed his oral reading using Clay's (2000) procedure for analyzing running records; this analysis appears in Figure 3.10.

Ms. Callan noticed that Aslam read many words correctly and self-corrected three of the eight words that initially had miscues. When miscueing, Aslam relied primarily on graphophonic (classified as visual) cues. With substitutions, Aslam worked his way through total words, missing medial sounds. The words he misread seemed to be words that were not in his vocabulary, such as *chaise*, *postern*, and *portmanteau*.

The think aloud procedure revealed Aslam's careful reading of the text and his ability to make conjectures and inferences and use problem-solving strategies about intended meanings of ideas that were not clear to him immediately.

There is much that Ms. Callan learned that has direct implications for instruction. First, she planned to focus on vocabulary development, plus take time for conferencing with Aslam and provide opportunities for small-group guided reading sessions. During the conferences and small-group meetings, Ms. Callan would model her thinking while reading and encourage Aslam and the other students to share their thoughts and reactions to the texts they were reading. Thinking aloud seemed to be a supportive comprehension strategy for Aslam as taking time to reflect on and analyze the story parts contributed positively to his comprehension. Peer think alouds with teacher modeling would extend this strategy to emphasize the importance of careful reading and developing analysis and inferences while reading. Even though this text on Victorian England does not seem to be a good match with Aslam's prior knowledge, he is making good sense of material that may be out of his interest and knowledge base. If this content is viewed as important, making connections to other texts may be appropriate. For example, connections can be made with Sherlock Holmes texts, since Aslam likes to read mysteries, or with his interest in the history of monarchs in England.

## Assessing More Than Single Skills

We recommend that assessments should involve students in authentic reading activities. That means we ask students to read and talk about what they are reading. And as we demonstrate above, there are several tools that can be used, including oral reading, oral reading interviews, think alouds, and comprehension measures. Each of these tools holds potential for making inferences about a wide array of students' reading skills and strategies, including students' comprehension processes.

*Figure 3.9. Aslam's Oral Reading and Think Aloud Statements*

---

*The Wolves of Willoughby Chase* by Joan

Aiken

corners/sc

1 The huge manor house stood alone, its cornices    ✓ ✓ ✓ ✓ ✓ ✓   <u>Cornices</u>

2 and turrets sharp against the dark winter sky.    ✓ <u>turrets</u> ✓ ✓ ✓ ✓ ✓ ✓   <u>turrets</u>

3 The gameskeeper, musket in hand, stood by the

4 postern gate, keeping the howling wolves at    ✓ ✓ <u>mus /sc</u> ✓ ✓ ✓ ✓ ✓   musket

5 bay. Inside two young girls clung together on    <u>posted/postern</u> ✓ ✓ ✓ ✓ ✓   postern

6 the ottoman listening for the wheels of the    p ✓ ✓ ✓ ✓ ✓ ✓ ✓

7 chaise. And then she appeared, Miss Slighcarp,    ✓ ✓ ✓ ✓ ✓ ✓ ✓ ✓ sc

8 the new governess with full valise and bulging    <u>cha se</u> ✓ ✓ ✓ ✓ <u>Slighca</u>   chaise    Sligh carp

9 portmanteau. Even the wolves who roamed the

10 surrounding forest were less dangerous as    ✓ ✓ ✓ ✓ ✓ <u>Va lis</u> ✓ ✓   Valise

11 Bonnie and Sylvia were to discover/And as    <u>port man too</u> ✓ ✓ ✓ ✓ ✓ ✓   Portman teau .

difficult as life at the manor became, it was even    ✓ ✓ ✓ ✓ ✓ ✓

worse when the orphans were sent off to Miss    ✓ ✓ ✓ ✓ ✓

Slighcarp's sister, Mrs. Brisket. With only a

young boy to help them the captives face many    [What were you thinking?]

chilling moments in this dark tale of murder and    I'm thinking this is

greed.    a dark, gloomy, and scary

   place – wolves around

   2 young girls "clinging" to

   each other, forests are less

   dangerous then what will

It was dusk – winter dusk. Snow lay white and shining    happen –

over the pleated hiss, and icicles hung from the forest    [How did you decide on

   name of new governess?]

   Sligh (sounds out) –

   and then I throw the word

   carp. What an odd name!

### Figure 3.9. Aslam's Oral Reading and Think Aloud Statements *(continued)*

trees. Snow lay piled on the dark road across
Willoughby Wold, but from dawn men had been
clearing it with brooms and shovels. There were
Hundreds of them at work, wrapped in sackling because
of the bitter cold, and keeping together in groups for fear
of the wolves, grown savage and reckless from hunger.

Snow lay thick, too, upon the roof of Willoughby Chase,
the great house that stood on an open eminence in the
heart of the wold. But for all that, the Chase looked
an inviting home-a warm and welcoming stronghold.
Its rosy herringbone brick was bright and well-cared-
for, its numerous turrets and battlements stood up
sharp against the sky, and the crenelated balconies,
corniced with snow, each held a golden square of
window. The house was all alight within, and the
joyous hubbub of its activity contrasted with the
somber sighing of the wind and the hideous howling
of the wolves without.

In the nursery a little girl was impatiently dancing up
and down before the great window, fourteen feet
high, which faced out over the park and commanded

Tell me what you were thinking as you read these words —

Willoughby Chase is the house, Willoughby Wold is a place. Maybe the house is on a hill in the forest —
like the place Trent-on-a-Wold that we read about.....

The house is odd -- warm and welcoming, but battlements - does not sound warm - then joyous activity

oh - turrets - on the building as we saw with the Victorian pictures of building

*Figure 3.10. Aslam's Running Record Analysis*

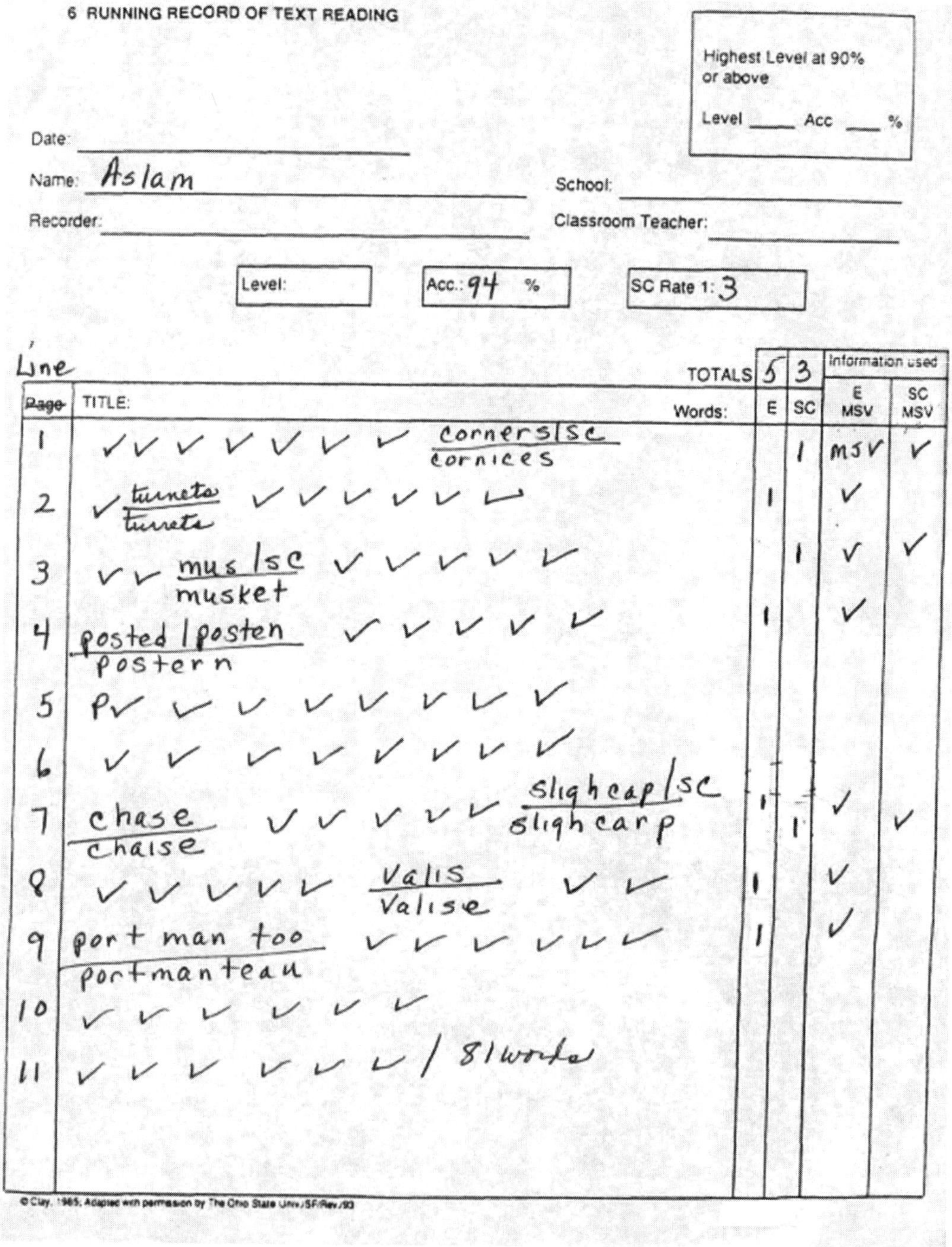

6 RUNNING RECORD OF TEXT READING

Highest Level at 90% or above

Level ____ Acc ____ %

Date:

Name: Aslam

School:

Recorder:

Classroom Teacher:

Level: | Acc.: 94 % | SC Rate 1: 3

| Line (~~Page~~) | TITLE: TOTALS / Words: | E (5) | SC (3) | Information used: E MSV | Information used: SC MSV |
|---|---|---|---|---|---|
| 1 | ✓ ✓ ✓ ✓ ✓ ✓ ✓ corners \| sc / cornices | | 1 | MSV | ✓ |
| 2 | ✓ turnets / turrets ✓ ✓ ✓ ✓ ✓ ✓ | 1 | | ✓ | |
| 3 | ✓ ✓ mus \| sc / musket ✓ ✓ ✓ ✓ ✓ ✓ | | 1 | ✓ | ✓ |
| 4 | posted \| posten / postern ✓ ✓ ✓ ✓ ✓ ✓ | 1 | | ✓ | |
| 5 | ✓ ✓ ✓ ✓ ✓ ✓ ✓ ✓ ✓ | | | | |
| 6 | ✓ ✓ ✓ ✓ ✓ ✓ ✓ ✓ ✓ | | | | |
| 7 | chase / chaise ✓ ✓ ✓ ✓ ✓ slighcap \| sc / slighcarp | 1 | 1 | ✓ | ✓ |
| 8 | ✓ ✓ ✓ ✓ ✓ ✓ Valis / Valise ✓ ✓ | 1 | | ✓ | |
| 9 | port man too / portmanteau ✓ ✓ ✓ ✓ ✓ ✓ ✓ | 1 | | ✓ | |
| 10 | ✓ ✓ ✓ ✓ ✓ ✓ ✓ | | | | |
| 11 | ✓ ✓ ✓ ✓ ✓ ✓ ✓ / 81 words | | | | |

> Assessing only part of the reading process or reading actions underrepresents what students know and can do.

Often, published assessments that are closely aligned with the state tests or a district's curricular goals are less than optimal (NRC, 2001) since they focus mostly on literal comprehension more than higher levels of comprehension (Applegate, Applegate, McGeehan, Pinto, & Kong, 2009). Thus listening to how students strategize about unknown words in text or the connections and interpretations they generate while reading is extremely important for understanding how students are making sense of the text. They provide rich sources of information to guide instruction and they go beyond narrow approaches to assessments.

The reauthorization of the Individuals with Disabilities Education Improvement Act (IDEIA) of 2004 in the United States requires data-based instruction that is situated in the use of repeated assessments, administered on reasonable intervals, to measure students' learning in instruction. The goal for the IDEIA is early identification of students experiencing academic difficulties, such as in reading, and implementing a multitier assessment and instructional plan to prevent the development of more serious difficulties. Multiple assessments that provide information about multiple skills and strategies are optimal for understanding students' strengths and specific instructional needs, and their responses to instruction (McIntosh, Graves, & Gersten, 2007).

No specific assessments are required by the IDEIA legislation, but many states are identifying different levels of assessment (Wixson & Valencia, 2011) for different purposes. These include screening instruments (designed for data collection before instruction, such as referring to scores on standardized tests administered by the district); diagnostic tests (individual assessments to determine specific strengths and needs, such as a miscue analysis or comprehension measures); formative progress monitoring measures (gathering data during instruction at specified time periods and could include work samples, running records, observational records); and summative outcome assessments (providing data at the end of the year to examine progress and learning, and may include administering some of the above assessments as a final measure for the year or a readministering the screening instrument used at the beginning of the year).

## Assessment Providing Both Formative and Summative Information

Teachers administer a variety of assessment tools, and many of these are required by school districts and/or federal policies. Yet teachers report that many assessments do not provide useful information or they are ill-prepared for using data to form instructional decisions (Peverini, 2009). Popham (2008) analyzed various forms of assessment and asserted that commercially made tests providing continuous checks on performance, including formative assessments and benchmarks, are limited in their application to instructional decisions with no research supporting their educational benefits for students.

Typically, these assessments are aligned with more global standards and goals and not matched well to situated applications of a curriculum or day-to-day instruction. Cech (2008) described commercially made formative assessments as "illusionary," a promise not fulfilled and not addressing essential elements.

> Formative assessments assess learning and performance in action.

Formative assessments, in general, are those that are embedded in instruction providing careful and continuous assessment of student performance. To be credible, they should determine the following things: what will be measured (e.g., use of language cueing systems); the conditions for assessment (e.g., running records on instructional texts); the frequency of data collection (e.g., 2 minutes of oral reading three times a week per student); and how data will be used to adjust instruction (e.g., small groups of students practicing prediction and confirmation strategies to aid comprehension while reading) (Popham, 2008). As Hurley and Blake (2000) proposed, each assessment has an objective-linked purpose.

Popham recommends formative assessments developed by teachers or at the school or district level to assess performance in the local context to insure they are assessing what is being taught. Such assessments are effective and associated with large student gains. In their analysis of 250 research studies in which teachers gathered data on what students were learning during instruction, Black and William (1998) concluded that students made gains that were considered large and meaningful.

Numerous researchers (Y. Goodman, 1996; Johnston, 1997; Popham, 2008) report on the importance of involving students in formative assessments. Students share their reasoning for choice of answers or constructed meanings, providing insights into their meaning-making processes and their connections to the text readings. Collaboration with students can lead to timely feedback and enrich a district's assessment process (Fiene & McMahon, 2007). One way to collaborate with students, as noted by Fiene and McMahon, is for both teachers and students to keep notes about their thinking during the instructional process. Students can record their initial thoughts and reactions to material read and continue to elaborate on these notes as reading continues. Teachers can record notes on their observations and their assessment of students' understanding. Teachers examining both sets of notes can design appropriate and timely instruction such as extending students' thinking by modeling questioning and inferencing skills, such as text organization through the use of graphic organizers.

Summative assessments provide a broader view of student performance. Summative tests include a range of assessments, such as high-stakes tests that are commercially developed and end-of-unit tests that are teacher made. Use of these assessments can provide information about progress across a year or years of instruction, or with unit tests, information about content that may need to be revisited within subsequent units. The assessments we describe in this chapter, such as miscue analysis, running records, or text retellings can be used as both formative and summative assessments. They can be used to monitor progress on regular intervals, providing daily and/or weekly data that inform instruction, or as end-of-term or end-of-year measures to record progress over time.

## Assessments Situated in Multimodal Representations

Classroom assessments should represent the multiple forms of texts that students read, including digital and video texts, graphic novels, and other forms of multimodal presentations of ideas. And they should represent the multiple ways that students are interacting with texts, such as accessing multiple layers of information simultaneously with online texts, tracing several story lines within graphic novels, following directions to engage in video games, using nonlinear tools for composing texts, and examining original documents available through online museum resources (Meadows, 2003; Silva, 2008; Stornaiuolo, Hull, & Nelson, 2009).

Assessments should provide information about how students engage in these multimodal texts, the strategies they use to engage in the activity and for learning, and what they are learning. Otherwise, assessments are not capturing the wide range of skills and strategies students have acquired.

For example, observing how students compose digital stories can provide valuable information about their critical thinking, media literacy skills, and report writing (Ohler, 2006), and content knowledge in specific disciplines (Sadik, 2008). Sadik provides a 12-point rubric to assess students' composing

> Multimodal assessments are embedded in the multiple and digital real-time activities of reading and writing.

skills (e.g., content, point of view, organization, pacing) while developing digital stories.

Lenski, Ehlers-Zavala, Daniel, and Sun-Irminger (2006) and Carrier (2006) recommend multimodal assessments for supporting students who are learning English as an additional language. They describe multimodal examples (e.g., pictures and drawings, gestures) that would serve as scaffolds for communicating the information on assessments. Further, they suggest that students demonstrate their knowledge and understandings through multiple modes. To ensure fair and equitable testing conditions, they advocate for alternative ways that students may participate in assessments. For example, students might translate for each other within discussion groups or in collaboration with peers, with teachers observing participation and individual student generation of information. Additionally, students can present what they know with drawings, use of graphic organizers, gestures, and/or use of computer software to identify main points and ideas.

### Assessments Situated in Doable Activity

The assessments we recommend in this chapter require practice and preparation (e.g., choosing texts for miscue analysis, preparing students for retellings). With practice, the assessments can be implemented during conferences with students and while listening to students as they summarize their texts to their peers in small groups. With practice, these assessments become an integral part of teachers' instruction. Peverini (2009), a fourth-grade teacher, advocates for multidimensional, formative, and authentic assessments meeting the assessment goals that we describe in this chapter. And Peverini recommends that teachers move gradually into the use of these assessments—taking time to understand their purpose, developing assessments that are multidimensional and multimodal that are specific to classroom instruction, and choosing a few new forms to begin the process.

### SUMMARY

What kinds of assessment are optimal for providing information that matters for students and instruction? The assessments we describe in this chapter address what we believe is important for guiding instruction because they attempt to represent what students do and know, and they are situated within both students' perspective and goals set for developing readers. Assessments should reveal what interests students, how students engage in reading, and the skills and strategies they employ while reading. They should look like the texts and activities that engage students while reading. Most of all, assessments should provide sufficient information to lead instruction with provisions for continuous assessments so that adjustments in instruction are timely and responsive to students' learning. They should help teachers tailor instruction to promote their students' higher level thinking and problem-solving abilities that are needed to meet the educational challenges confronting them and to participate in the multimodal world in which they live.

Assessment data gathered on the measures we described provide multiple opportunities to identify students' knowledge, strategies, and skills. For example, oral reading and comprehension assessments and interviews reveal knowledge of concepts and vocabulary and knowledge of language structures. Once these knowledges are revealed they can be used to guide culturally responsive instruction, as we described in the previous chapter. These data provide similar specific connections to the instruction we recommend throughout the subsequent chapters for early literacy learners and for acquiring reading strategies and skills.

Repeated use of these measures provides credible data to support interpretations of patterns derived from the data analysis and to support instructional planning in areas we discuss in the next chapters. Across the chapters that follow, we demonstrate how assessment informs instruction and is embedded in daily reading and writing activities. Teachers' keen observations and data collection lay the foundation for providing appropriate and responsive instruction.

REFLECTION QUESTIONS

1. Tape record the oral reading of three students and analyze their performance. Are there differences in their use of language cues and strategies for making sense of the texts?
2. Think about your students' multimodal ways of reading and learning. What assessments would you construct to capture their reading habits and interests, and what they are learning?

# CHAPTER 4

# Using Anchors for Leveraging Problem Solving and Cross-Curricular Connections

Imagine that you viewed the full-length film *A Wrinkle in Time* (Harrison, 2003) in your fourth-grade language arts class. Or in social studies you viewed a student-produced digital text, downloaded from YouTube (Chocolate and Child Labor PSA, 2007) that calls attention to child labor in the Ivory Coast. These video texts are rich with information that aligns with the school curriculum and affords connections to several disciplines. For example, both provide plots with settings, motives of characters, and problems to be solved—explicit representations of story elements that students are learning to use for analyzing plot development. Students watching these videos take on the role of a problem solver as they look for clues to explain why the children's father has disappeared in *A Wrinkle in Time* or for ways to counter child slavery in the child labor video. With *Wrinkle*, connections can be made to science, space travel, planets in the solar system and life outside the solar system, and government structures and rights of citizens in nondemocratic countries. And for the child labor video, connections can be made to economic concepts of supply and demand, living conditions in high-poverty areas in the world, and treatment of workers on farms and in factories.

Both texts are examples of *anchors*—informational-rich contexts, often displayed in videos, that afford the study of real-life problems and afford cross-disciplinary learning. *Anchored instruction* is a form of integrated instruction that is held together by its anchors. And these anchors provide multiple stepping-off points for reading and writing, student inquiry, comprehending novel information, and building knowledge across and within disciplines. As we describe in this chapter, anchored instruction provides:

- Authentic learning
- Access to multiple texts
- Connections to real-world problems
- Connections across the curriculum
- Connections to big ideas and central themes
- Learning how to use knowledge as tools for problem solving

- Production and expertise
- Opportunities for applications to real-world contexts, often in the form of action research taken back to the community

## CASE ANALYSIS: LENIA

Lenia, who is White, is a fourth-grade student who performs well on tests that require short-term recall of facts or spellings (e.g., tests of vocabulary definitions, social studies factual recall tests, spelling tests), but she has difficulty recalling this information over time and frequently is unable to use the facts she has learned to solve more complicated problems or analyze issues. Lenia is quiet in class. Her teachers report that Lenia likes to read when books are less complicated than the fourth-grade books used in the classroom. Her favorite books include mysteries, such as *Who Stole the Wizard of Oz* (Avi, 1981) and *Nate the Great* (Sharmat, 2002), and books written by Judy Blume.

Mr. Nelson is Lenia's fourth-grade teacher. He teaches all subjects in his self-contained class and he is required to teach reading and writing for 90 minutes per day. He tries to make connections between reading and writing assignments (e.g., writing assignments tied to class readings) and with other content areas. Mr. Nelson commented that Lenia needs support reading and comprehending more complicated texts and instruction should focus on word learning, vocabulary development, comprehension, and "lots of practice" reading increasingly higher level texts. He judged her easy-reading level as second grade and her instructional level as third grade. And while he wants to address her specific skills, he observed that many students in his class seemed to have learned to memorize facts to perform well on tests requiring recall. He worries that she and her peers are not realizing the importance of the content areas they are exploring or the reading and writing activities.

### Case Questions

1. How can anchored instruction be implemented to engage Lenia's and her peers' deeper learning of content and use of reading/ writing strategies to acquire new knowledge?
2. How does anchored instruction invite generative learning that involves students in setting purposes for their learning—purposes that are student directed for authentic inquiries and problem solving?

## ANCHORED INSTRUCTION

For several decades I (Vicki) and a group of researchers and literacy educators at Vanderbilt University collaborated with K–12 classroom teachers to develop and implement a form of cross-curricular instruction called anchored instruction. We learned that it benefits all students, but in particular students who are experiencing reading problems (Cognition and Technology Group [CTG], 1990, 1992a, 1992b, 2003). As with Lenia, some students make good progress in early reading development, learning the basics such as word identification and lower order reading comprehension skills. They read texts that interest them, and some are avid readers. Yet some readers seem to hit a plateau, becoming very good "third-grade" readers and experiencing difficulty transitioning to more complicated texts and higher order skills required for knowledge building and knowing how to seek or use new knowledge for life.

Students in fourth grade and through high school make many transitions in reading development, meeting new and increasingly complicated texts and content. Often students have difficulty negotiating these transitions (Camburn & Wong, 2011; Roderick & Camburn, 1999). The instruction we describe is appropriate for supporting these transitions for older students (several of our projects were situated within middle school classrooms), but also effective for younger readers.

Anchored instruction also enhances the learning of young students, as we learned from our teaching with anchored instruction in preschools, kindergarten, and the early primary grades. Its emphasis is on *authentic learning*—learning information and skills for the purpose of using them for real-world applications. In projects directed by Diana Sharp and others at Vanderbilt, we witnessed the advantages of engaging young children in problem solving and higher order thinking while also teaching basic word learning and word identification skills (Sharp et al., 1995). In their review of instructional research, Camburn and Wong (2011) documented positive student outcomes associated with authentic instruction, where students across the grades engaged in problem solving, self-directed inquiry, and higher level reasoning.

Authenticity is a central concept of anchored instruction. There are multiple ways to address authenticity, such as inquiry-based learning projects where teachers and students generate questions that interest them around real-world problems (e.g., climate change due to natural evolution vs. global warming, pollution) and draw on the content of multiple texts, including their textbooks and the Internet, and out-of-school learning resources (e.g., community leaders, parents) to answer those questions. Projects that draw on cross-curricular connections often support forms of authentic learning and productions. For example, students might examine historical artifacts, scientific evidence, and economic trends to trace the history of the Great Depression and draw connections to contemporary periods of recession that affect the economy worldwide and in their own neighborhoods. Similar to our anchored instruction, Jewett, Wilson, and Vanderburg (2011) discussed how reading a common text (*Seedfolks* by Paul Fleischman, 2004) schoolwide led to authentic learning events. Their project, for example, involved middle school students and their families discussing segregation and respect for diversity within their school and neighborhood community.

An additional example of anchored instruction is a project in which the arts are integrated within reading and writing activities entitled Arts for Learning Lessons. It is part of the Young Audiences Arts for Learning program, founded in 1952, the nation's first and largest arts-in-education network (http://www.youngaudiences.org). Now funded in part by a federal i3 (Investing in Innovation Fund) grant, the Young Audiences Arts for Learning Lessons project is designed to significantly increase student literacy by developing arts-based instructional strategies for use by elementary school teachers, Grades K–8. Working with learning scientist John Bransford (The Learning Sciences Group at the University of Washington), the lessons are designed for implementation by classroom teachers and are augmented by extended residencies led by performing and visual artists. This form of anchored instruction can be seen in a YouTube video entitled Arts for Learning: Young Audiences of Oregon and Southwest Washington (2010) (http://www.youtube.com/watch?v=AQu0oPaQgbs). In this video, students demonstrate their collaborative work while producing their interpretive works and explain what they are learning in the process.

Anchored instruction has specific characteristics (Love, 2004/2005; McLarty et al., 1990). In addition to authenticity, the characteristics described below have elements in common with inquiry and project-based instruction, cross-curricular instruction, and instruction that is responsive to the cultural and linguistic histories of the students. Anchored instruction fosters collaborative and shared thinking about real-world and social issues that affect students and their communities and that students can affect. We believe anchored instruction is highly appropriate for Lenia and her classmates for deepening learning and understanding the importance of the new knowledge they are acquiring.

Unfortunately, these forms of instruction occur more frequently in high-SES schools than low-SES schools (Camburn & Wong, 2011). And these rich contextualized forms of instruction are more often provided for higher achieving readers than for students with reading problems even though studies indicate that more of a focus on isolated skills and foundational skills is less effective for low-achieving students (Camburn & Wong, 2011). Willingham (2009) makes a similar argument against instruction that overly stresses basic skills and minimizes comprehension and deeper learning of content, indicating that students requiring the most contextual and content-learning supports are those receiving it the least.

## CONCEPTUALIZING INSTRUCTION

As with all instruction, careful assessment of students' strengths and needs are identified and instructional goals are set. In the case of Lenia, assessments revealed a need to emphasize comprehension. Consequently, Mr. Nelson set goals to build Lenia's understandings of the big ideas or central concepts of texts and to support her ability to draw connections between concepts and text details. He wanted Lenia to develop comprehension strategies, such as question asking, predicting, and self-monitoring of understandings. He explained that these goals were consistent with his goals and the goals of his school district and that they were applied to his teaching for all his students. With instructional goals set, Mr. Nelson then began to question how he could align these goals with anchored instruction principles and where he would start to build that alignment.

### Teaching with Anchors

Instruction begins with the study of the chosen anchor. Anchors can be events in students' lives, a historical happening, a scientific breakthrough, a text, several compatible texts, or a film, as examples.

#### Comprehending the Anchor

For an anchor to be effective, it needs to provide a sufficiently rich context so that students can revisit it for additional clues or information. Anchors should afford multiple connections to content across the curriculum, connections to real-world problems, and relevance to students' experiences and what interests them. For our work with anchored instruction, we typically use videos as the anchor. These videos can be commercially made (e.g., *A Wrinkle in Time*, *To Kill a Mockingbird*, *The Chronicles of Narnia*, *Harry Potter*, *Lyddie*) or developed by a team of teachers and students and posted as YouTube videos (e.g., Chocolate and Child Labor PSA). Coherence of content within the anchor is important for helping students make connections across what might seem to be disparate facts presented in written or video texts. Often the teacher needs to guide students in forming linkages across texts to reconstruct the plot development of narratives or messages within informational pieces.

We believe there are distinct advantages to using videos as an instructional resource. A particular reading level is not required to access the content of videos; thus videos provide accessible content for most students. Yet guided viewing for all students is often helpful for deepening comprehension and aiding students' noticing of multiple levels of information.

Videos are dynamic, visual, and spatial—there is much to notice and with each re-viewing, additional information is identified and can lead to deepening knowledge and recognition of multiple aspects of the texts represented within the texts (e.g., characters' motives and problems, settings that provide a historical and social context, emotions of both central and less central characters, and so on) represented in the videos. Video representations of stories, historical events, scientific experiments, and others often invite students' curiosity, question generation, problem identification, and problem solving (Bransford, Vye, Kinzer, & Risko, 1990).

For Mr. Nelson's fourth-grade class, instruction could begin with the introduction of the video *A Wrinkle in Time* (directed by Kent Harrison). This video is a rendition of the book of the same title written by Madeleine L'Engle that is often popular with upper elementary and middle grade students. This story is about a sister and brother, Meg and Charles Wallace Murry, who rescue their father from captivity on the planet of Camazotz. In the process, the universe is saved from the clutches of the evil power, IT. They are helped in their struggles by their friend Calvin O'Keefe and three odd women, Mrs. Who, Mrs. Whatsit, and Mrs. Which.

There are several concepts that develop across the many, overlapping episodes. These include a battle between good and evil; the difference between battles that are universal and those that are individual; that being different is okay; that one should be true to oneself; that determination and loyalty are important character traits; that self-sacrifice may be needed to solve problems; and that individuals can face challenges and succeed.

In the opening scene of the video, Meg Murry is watching a shooting star in the sky and thinking back to a conversation she had with her dad before he disappeared. After her father asked her to make a wish on the star, she talked about how difficult it is to be her (approximately 10 years old) and that she didn't "live within her skin," that she felt "stupid" and that "no one likes me." Her father explained that she did things her own way, at her own pace, and this made her special. The scene then returns to the present and Meg, as the narrator, tells us that her dad left her family, disappeared without a word, and has been gone for over a year. She tells us that her parents are brilliant scientists and her dad was working on a secret project before he left. And she explains that her mother is "weirdly" confident that her father will be back. When Meg goes into the house we meet her three brothers—two are twins and a third is called Charles Wallace, not just Charles. Charles Wallace talks to no one outside of the family, he seems to be brilliant, and his mother describes him as "new." This is an engaging opener to the film—bringing elementary students into the life of Meg and her family.

## Generating Questions

Several questions can be generated after viewing this 10-second scene. These questions might include the following: What could have happened to Meg's dad and why isn't Meg's mother worried about his disappearance? Could it be that his mysterious science project is the cause for his disappearance? Did he make himself disappear? Is he working for the government and have government officials taken him to a secret place until he finishes his project? Where is this story taking place? What is the time period of this story? Do they live in the United States? In Washington, D.C.? What do you expect to learn about Charles Wallace? From these questions and others that will follow, students watch the film to answer their questions and those of others, developing shared knowledge among the teacher and students.

## Building Mental Models

They have opportunities to develop rich knowledge, often referred to as *mental models* of situations and problems (Johnson-Laird, 1983) that are embedded in the film. These rich mental models help students build pattern recognition (e.g., patterns of Meg's behaviors leading to her feelings that no one likes her; patterns of Charles Wallace's behaviors that make him different from others; patterns of how scientists do their work; patterns in the clues that might explain why and how Meg's father disappeared). Pattern recognition and mental models are built within a rich story context and developed over time through discussions and study of the film. Facts are noticed during the watching of the film (or during reading of a text) rather than introduced randomly, and the process is different from an introduction to the film that lists all the characters and their attributes.

Anchored instruction addresses the inert knowledge problem that Lenia is experiencing (CTG, 1990). Many students have similar difficulties: They remember facts but are unsure of their usefulness, and when asked to apply these facts to solve problems or respond to real-world issues, they do not know which facts they should access or how they are helpful for problem solving. And sometimes students can recall information when prompted but fail to recall this information spontaneously when involved in solving problems that are relevant to the information they have "learned." Often these students are labeled as poor problem solvers or as having difficulty applying knowledge when in reality they have not been taught other aspects of knowledge development, namely *procedural knowledge*—how to use novel information—or *conditional knowledge*—when it is appropriate and relevant to the task at hand.

## Exploring Cross-Curricular Connections

To overcome the inert knowledge problem, instruction provides sustained exploration of curricular and content information, while drawing on students' knowledge and experiences, and also ways to use this information to solve content-embedded problems (e.g., use of math or science formulas to calculate the distance explorers might travel across a mountain vs. traveling around it, while drawing on decisions of mountain climbers or cross-country hikers confronted with similar questions).

Facts are contextualized within the rich texts where they are introduced. Dewey (1933), Vygotsky (1978), and others have demonstrated that learners, often guided by others, become experts and knowledgeable individuals with immersion in principles, concepts, and ideas that are interesting to them and that they see as useful. Immersion to develop expertise is in contrast to a quick mentioning of information or shallow introductions of new facts, skills, or strategies without opportunities to experience the repeated effects of using these facts, skills, or strategies as tools for deepening knowledge or problem solving. Without the understanding of usefulness of information, students often believe that memorization alone is the end goal for the learning activity.

## Learning with Understanding

Learning with understanding should occur throughout anchored instruction. One example relates to the goal of teaching students to recognize elements of story grammar. Often we teach students to label setting, character traits, and plot development, including initiating events, actions and reactions, outcomes, and story conclusions or solved problems. Students learn to label these elements in stories, especially within stories that are fairly simple with few episodes or uncomplicated character development. However, students seldom use this information to advance analytical thinking that may be needed to distinguish important ideas, such as character traits (characteristics that are predictable across most events) vs. character states (conditions under which actions may not be typical for characters).

## Thinking Analytically

During anchored instruction, the goal is to use the knowledge of these elements to complete a careful read of the text, to study motives of characters and how these affect actions and how they change depending on story events and conflicts. After viewing the film at least one time to develop the overall context of the story line, we asked our students to go back through small segments of the film to analyze story information, analyzing traits of characters or how events in one episode foreshadowed events in subsequent episodes (CTG, 1990).

As applied to Mr. Nelson's teaching, analysis of the first scene can lead to students' writing or constructing a map representing Meg Murry's character traits. See Figure 4.1 for an example of what the map may look like.

## Building Expertise

Deepening knowledge for building expertise continues by revisiting the text and the written or map work.

This general map (see Figure 4.1) is the starting point for adding more information related to reasons Meg was frightened and how she reacted to being afraid, why she felt she didn't belong, and so on. Rewatching the initial segment of the film provides additional clues about each of these elements, and these clues are typically inferred by studying Meg's conversation, her facial expressions, or her actions. Students can elaborate on their map elements as they confirm their choices of character traits. Or they may choose one element from the first map and add more details, such as the element of being brave (see Figure 4.2).

These maps provide a method for keeping a record of students' interpretations and reactions to events or character development, display students' reasoning about content and the connections they are generating, and serve as an organizer for writing about Meg.

### Knowledge as a Tool

Another activity that might engage students in this content is the reading of the book that inspired the movie and comparing the two. Thus a careful analysis of each chapter would help students use story grammar

*Figure 4.1. Meg Murry's Character Traits*

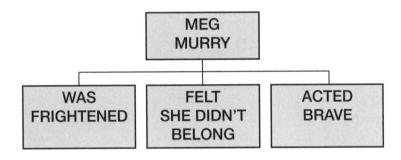

*Figure 4.2. Additional Clues About Meg's Character Traits*

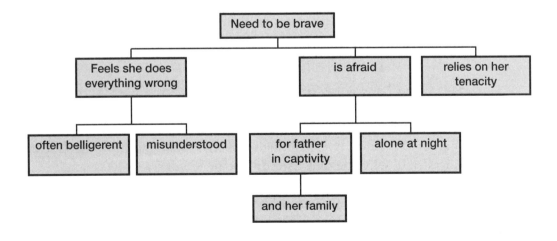

elements to analyze the content, as with the first chapter. Knowledge of the story grammar elements then becomes a tool for developing new knowledge and analyzing the text for comparison.

For example, Chapter 1 may be described as follows:

*Initiating event 1*: Storm
*Reaction*: Meg is frightened and recalls wrong events of the day
*Actions*: Goes to the kitchen for food and finds family, then Mrs. Whatsit
*Reaction*: Meg is worried, Mother is calm, Charles Wallace is trusting
*Outcomes*: Father is missing, Mrs. Whatsit provides a clue—The TESSERACT!

And as students discuss the development of story ideas, story-specific vocabulary words are used as tools for explanation and description. For example, the word *Tesseract* helps students explain the time warp element of *Wrinkle*. Meg may be characterized as *frenzied*. And the strange environment of storms and hurricanes may be described as *wraithlike, vicious, savagely moving, frivoling, or ephemeral*.

## Providing Effective Learning Environments

As we illustrated above, concepts, content information, skills, and strategies are taught to support understanding instead of memorization. In their report *How People Learn* (1999), Bransford, Brown, and Cocking provided research supporting both the goals of deepening students' knowledge and developing well-organized knowledge and also instruction that invites multiple demonstrations of how knowledge can be used to solve problems. Students learn to apply knowledge for problem solving, such as resolving the issue of Meg's fear and learning how she draws on her courage to find her father.

It is exciting to visit classrooms where meaningful learning is occurring, and students are not easily classified as *abled* or *disabled, interested* or *disinterested*. Students are actively engaged in independent reading and inquiry; they are asking and answering their own questions and those of others; they are reading and writing every day; and there are few boundaries that compartmentalize the curriculum (i.e., teaching science, social studies, language arts, and other disciplines as separate subjects). And while there are many ways to organize classrooms for meaningful learning, we find that many of these involve some forms of integrating the curriculum.

Integrating the curriculum to forge authentic connections across the disciplines might occur in classrooms where teachers support inquiry learning that engages students in research projects that address content themes and issues (e.g., what is meant by "time travel"?) and that takes students to reading about social conditions and individual rights in countries (or other planets, as in *Wrinkle*) that are not organized around democratic governance. Or students might pursue the study of other possible forms of life within and outside the solar system. Dramatic arts projects could lead to a study of political and social conditions contributing to characters' motives and actions, or a study of climatic changes that also affect characters' actions. And in the process students are strengthening their *procedural knowledge*—principles and steps for applying what they are learning—and *conditional knowledge*—recognizing when information they know can be useful.

## Problem Solving

As students explore the film, they might focus on character traits and motives, as described above. And while this skill is often developed in instruction to meet curricular guidelines, the study of character traits and motives has multiple levels of information that can deepen students' comprehension about the characters and why actions occurred, and also provides links to information about the historical period or the economic times or the character's education that could explain actions and events.

For example, Meg's father is a scientist and students may read to identify clues about his secret experiment and the possibility that his secret work has something to do with his disappearance. They may ask questions like these: Were there clues about his disappearance in the very first scene, with the shooting star and Meg examining the sky? What did it mean that a vast world might exist beyond the earth? The author sets up the problem of the father's disappearance, and students are drawn into the discussion to generate possible reasons for the disappearance and possible places where he may be.

## Connecting Concepts Across the Curriculum

And students will generate additional problems and questions, such as why does Meg feel so different from her peers and what did she mean that she can no longer "live within her skin"? Connections to students' own feelings of insecurity and worries about not being popular may be discussed with connections made to other texts and how these issues are resolved. Such discussions encourage students to examine the content from different perspectives: their own, the perspectives of the text characters (e.g., mother's perspective, Meg's perspective), and/or the perspective drawn from other resources (e.g., how insecurity was addressed by national leaders).

### Taking Different Perspectives

Students may also explore Charles Wallace's silence. Some students may hypothesize that Charles Wallace has "no speech at all" and yet learn he talks with his family. Part of problem finding also involves analyzing the text for accuracy, and the study of the setting or time period helps to situate and explain the science experiment that involves Mr. Murry.

As students generate questions and identify problems embedded in the video context or printed text, multiple connections can be made to fourth-grade curriculum; for example, the father's disappearance can be associated with explorers in early U.S. history or with outer space travel and how this has evolved over the decades. Or characteristics of the planet of Camazotz can be compared with characteristics of planets in the earth's solar system. Living in a country that requires complete conformity to survive can be compared to similar historical events in other countries. This is illustrated in Figure 4.3.

*Figure 4.3. Wrinkle and Cross-Curricular Connections*

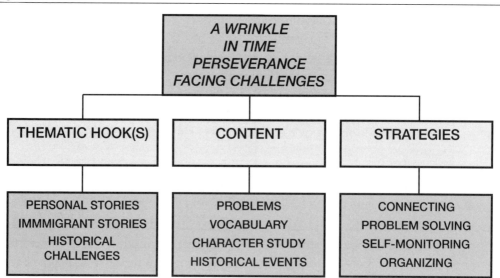

Another example is the curricular connections developed by Mr. Nelson as found in Figure 4.4.

## Organizing Multiple Grouping Arrangements for Reading and Writing Instruction

As we describe above, the video of *A Wrinkle in Time* serves as the core text for the entire class. All students have access to the content and the class discussions developing shared knowledge about the embedded concepts and plot development.

Once the anchor has been viewed and reviewed to address instructional goals, the teacher can now begin to differentiate instruction to extend student learning. Some students may be brought together in a group to read the book version of *A Wrinkle in Time* and write an opinion column that compares and contrasts the book with the movie. Other students may read another adventure book that is written at a lower or higher level than *A Wrinkle in Time*, matching interests and reading levels.

### Access to Multiple Texts of Different Complexities

Other students may be invited to or choose to read mysteries; this could be Lenia's choice, for example. Or students may read graphic novels, such as science fiction novels or a novel from the Narnia series that depicts

*Figure 4.4. Perseverance and Cross-Curricular Connections*

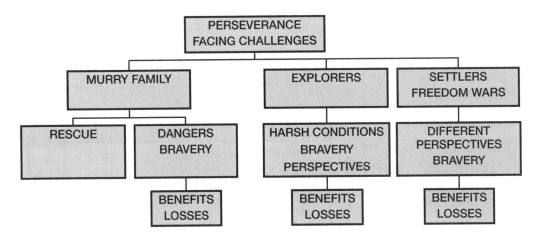

adventures in strange places. Multiple level books are made available so that students transition to books that are easy-reading books and that build on the central concepts of *A Wrinkle in Time*, and books that are at the instructional level and can be used for guided reading instructional groups. With the reading of additional materials, students are matched with particular projects, such as writing the weekly news about explorers in history, or developing digital stories of mysteries that are read, and so on.

## Productions and Deepening Expertise

The additional readings and guided instruction and peer sharing in small groups lay a foundation for encouraging students to pursue inquiry projects, guided by their own questions. Students can work in small groups or independently as they pursue their interests. These projects may include a dramatization of *A Wrinkle in Time* from Meg's perspective, a project that Mr. Nelson believed would be interesting to Lenia. Or students may explore further the scientific information in the film to verify plausibility and create digital stories that provide alternative explanations of Mr. Murry's disappearance. Some students who are interested in graphic novels may develop their own, using their illustrations or images they download from the Internet. As we write this chapter, there are no graphic novels of *A Wrinkle in Time*, although several are in the development stage by different publishers. It could be that the students in Mr. Nelson's class will lead the way in producing a graphic novel that interests them and that can be shared online with a larger audience. The goal for these projects is to deepen knowledge and to demonstrate to students how to apply what they are learning to real-world issues. And as students generate their work, then reading, writing, dramatizing, and producing become tools for sharing what they are learning.

## SUMMARY

Anchored instruction is an example of the conceptual instruction we described in Chapter 1. Its goals are to integrate skills, strategies, and content within a balanced and comprehensive whole. Knowledge builds on what students know already and on connections they generate and questions they ask. Anchored instruction revolves around an opener that sets the scene for multiple connections to content that will be pursued in subsequent units of instruction. Often this opener is a video, a story, or informational piece that is viewed in its entirety and that provides multiple stepping-off points for inquiry and learning.

Anchored instruction is grounded in multimodal learning as students explore, learn, and produce information that is represented in multiple texts. Embedded in the exploration are opportunities for building expertise, analyzing content from different perspectives, engaging in problem-finding and problem-solving experiences, and generating personal connections and applications. As we have learned from teachers and students, this form of instruction is particularly appropriate for struggling readers, such as Lenia, for developing new knowledge, skills, and strategies.

Anchored instruction provides access to content (through videos and different levels of texts) and text complexity is addressed. Gaining knowledge enables reading of more complicated texts and students have opportunities to read and search for information across texts, including online searches. We continue the discussion of guided and dynamic learning events in the chapters to follow, explicitly in Chapters 6 (word learning), 7 (vocabulary), and 8 (guided comprehension instruction). Student directed learning, active engagement, taking on of different perspectives, tackling complicated texts, and generating productions to develop expertise will be developed further in Chapter 8.

REFLECTION QUESTIONS

1. How would you develop a unit of instruction that addresses the characteristics of anchored instruction? What content themes would be emphasized? What anchor would you choose and why? How do you envision cross-curricular connections?

2. The anchored instruction example in this chapter applies to Lenia and her fourth-grade classroom. How could you develop anchored instruction for younger children? For older middle school students?

# CHAPTER 5

# Changing Strategies to Meet
# New Demands for Student Success

Changing the reading trajectory of struggling readers must begin early in their school experiences. Early identification of students who struggle, based on formative assessments of students' reading development and linguistic and cultural capital, can be used to develop a profile of students' strengths and needs, as well as a plan of instruction. In our case studies of Colin and Lenia, we note that both students' reading struggles were evident at the fourth- and fifth-grade levels. As teachers, we need to know when students' reading difficulties begin and how their early perception of themselves as readers affects their responses to reading instruction. With this information teachers can begin to gain greater perspective about the robust instruction needed to accelerate the reading progress of students like Colin and Lenia.

We begin this chapter by examining a portrait of a child embarking on her journey to become a reader. As reflective educators, we must think about students' individual and collective journeys to make changes in our teaching and in student learning. It is with this intent that we reflect upon Maria's literacy journey and on the principles that we believe should undergird early literacy instruction:

- Success in early literacy promotes future success in reading.
- Children need multiple opportunities to hear, use, and experiment with language to develop their skills in literacy.
- Children need many opportunities to be exposed to and involved with a variety of literacy materials at home and in school.

## CASE ANALYSIS: MARIA

Maria's parents are native Spanish speakers who recently relocated to the Upper Midwest. Maria was 3 years old when the family arrived and settled

in a predominantly Latino neighborhood within a largely urban community. She spent her first 2 years at home with her mother and baby brother.
The next year Maria and her brother were sent to a home day care center
located near her home. This allowed her mother to work part-time to supplement the family's income. The next year Maria's parents enrolled her
in a half-day kindergarten program that operated in a charter school for
Latino children. It was there that Maria developed an interest in reading
picture books written in Spanish. At the end of kindergarten, Maria told
her teacher that she was a good reader and said she wanted to read the
books that "my mama and papa read." In first grade her skills and interest
in reading continued to develop.

At the end of first grade, Maria's family moved to another part of the
city that was closer to her father's job. This meant that Maria had to change
schools and live in a more racially diverse urban community that had
few Spanish-speaking or bilingual families. In school Maria was placed
in a second-grade English-speaking classroom with one other Spanish-
speaking student. At that time she was administered the QRI, an individually administered informal reading inventory (Leslie & Caldwell, 2006),
as one of the formative assessments used for placement. Her instructional
level in word recognition was at the first-grade level and her comprehension was at the preprimer level. She demonstrated problems in responding
to both explicit or literal questions and implicit questions about narrative
and informational text. Maria was identified as a struggling reader and
left the room each day, along with the other Spanish-speaking student, for
small-group instruction with the EL teacher.

Because Maria leaves the classroom for EL instruction during Reading
Workshop and returns during the last half of the workshop, she has few opportunities to develop friendships based upon shared literacy experiences.
She seems more comfortable exploring books independently or with Isabella, her EL classmate, when she returns. While her conversational skills
in English are relatively good, she seems more comfortable using Spanish
to talk to Isabella about the books she is reading.

Although Mrs. Galton, Maria's teacher, sits next to her for a few minutes and either points out words that she feels are difficult or asks Maria questions about the book, the limited time remaining in the workshop
prevents any direct instruction in reading. Mrs. Galton believes that the
EL teacher is responsible for Maria's reading instruction, which she feels
is different from what she provides in the classroom. Mrs. Galton feels
Maria would probably benefit from another year in second grade. Mrs.
Galton observes that Maria listens as children share their reading during

Reading Workshop, but never participates by asking questions or making comments. This confirms her plan to recommend that Maria be retained in second grade.

The EL teacher provides one-to-one instruction, which focuses on Maria's vocabulary and comprehension skills. She uses pictures and actions to teach English vocabulary and explicit teaching to increase her word recognition skills. As a bilingual educator with skills in Spanish, the reading specialist encourages Maria to respond to questions about text in Spanish when she cannot express her thoughts in English. This helps Maria demonstrate her comprehension of text written in English while she is increasing her knowledge of English vocabulary. Echo reading and repeated reading are also used to develop fluency in reading, and the texts read were used as models for writing. Maria is making progress in her reading. An example of Maria's growth can be seen in the narrative that she wrote with the help of her classroom teacher:

> My grandfather is coming to visit soon. We call him Papa Grande. We will wake him up by singing Zippity Do Dah in the loudest voice ever. We will wake papa and mama and say, "Bring Alex down." Alex is my baby brother. Papa Grande gives us surprises in his suitcase. Sometimes he reaches for them in his suitcases and sometimes he gives them to us in our hands.

Although Maria is making progress, she still struggles with reading and does not see herself as a reader. For teachers, there are questions that this case study generates.

## CASE QUESTIONS

1. What significant changes can we make in the trajectory of literacy development for struggling readers in the early stages of learning to read?
2. What should we do to meet the reading needs of English learners, in our mainstreamed classroom, who have varying degrees of proficiency in English?
3. How can we increase the self-efficacy and promote the cultural identities of beginning readers who struggle in reading?

## EARLY LITERACY EXPERIENCES

Most children begin school wanting and expecting to learn a variety of things. Some leave the familiar surroundings of home and family nourished by a supportive family who have provided them with a steady diet of rich language, family experiences involving reading and writing, expectations for success, and knowledge and experiences that will support their school-based learning. Other children have lesser degrees of this diet. Home experiences with literacy are expanded by early literacy experiences. The quality of and mere exposure of children to early childhood instruction that fosters emergent literacy are influenced by economic and cultural factors. For example, many Latino and other immigrants from low socioeconomic levels do not enroll their children in early childhood programs (Karolyn & Gonzalez, 2011; Takanishi, 2006), which puts their children at a greater disadvantage in beginning literacy experiences. Regardless of the circumstances of their lives, however, children's expectations for learning to read are undoubtedly the same.

Children within language-rich homes and supportive family environments as compared to those in less language-rich homes and less supportive family environments will find their path toward becoming readers to be a smooth one because of their intrinsic motivation to read and the motivation attributed to home and/or school factors. These children understand that reading must make sense because they have the necessary decoding, vocabulary, and fluency skills to engage in the reading process, and they see themselves as "real readers." However, the children in less language-rich home and unsupportive family environments struggle with one or more aspects of reading, do not see themselves as readers, and lack the home and school scaffolding necessary for beginning reading. This is becoming an increasing concern to educators and researchers alike.

The struggling reader label is socially constructed from students' relationship with their teachers and fellow students and their performance in meeting the standards of achievement of the schools' reading curriculum. Triplett (2007) believes that literacy educators must challenge the labeling of children as struggling readers and recognize the ability of teachers to create classroom and school learning environments, choose and incorporate curriculum and instructional practices, and foster relationships where all students are successful.

> The struggling reader label is a constructed concept that must be challenged.

Students who struggle with reading are considered to be on a slippery slope, either cascading down a mountain toward special education placement and eventual school dropout or being saved by timely reading interventions that will place them on a solid ground of self and school identities as readers. The Response to Intervention (RTI) legislation (IDEIA, 2004) creates a means for teachers and schools to identify and scaffold struggling readers in the early stages of reading development through intensive and targeted instruction and thereby reduce the overidentification of students for special education or subsequent underachievement in reading (Bursuck & Blanks, 2010). The multitiered design of RTI models recognizes the complex nature of reading difficulties and allows time to assess and opportunities to provide classroom and supplementary instruction before referrals are made for special education placement. The first tier of most RTI models specifies that children should receive exemplary research-based reading instruction provided by classroom teachers. Because this first-tier intervention involves classroom instruction and screening measures to identify the approximately 80–85% of elementary school students who are achieving below grade level, this is the level where the most support is needed. High-quality instruction and knowledgeable teachers go hand in hand. They are critical since children who are at the greatest risk for failure in reading due to poverty, linguistic, socioeconomic, and cultural factors often receive the least effective instruction in reading, placing them at risk for greater difficulties in reading (Stichter, Stormont, & Lewis, 2009).

Instruction based upon multiple and ongoing assessment is a necessary aspect of teaching and is essential for early identification and prevention of reading problems. Selecting tools for determining areas of need and monitoring children's response to instruction are essential aspects of early intervention (Griffiths, VanDerHeyden, Skokut, & Lilles, 2009).

> Early intervention is important for preventing more serious reading problems from developing.

## Perspectives About Early Readers Who Struggle

Early identification is central to preventing reading failure. Screening kindergarten children to determine their knowledge of letters is believed to be one way to identify young children who are at risk for reading difficulties (Allington, 2011a). Determining when to begin supplemental instruction for kindergartners considered at risk for reading failure is the next issue schools face. Cooke, Kretlow, and Helf (2010) found that kindergarten children who received one year of small-group, supplemental reading instruction outperformed children who only received a half year of reading intervention. They recommend using supplemental programs that address the academic needs of individual children (i.e., language and communication) and provide academic support (modeling, gradual and explicit skill progression, and simple and direct language use).

> Highly effective instruction is specific to students' needs, is provided by highly qualified teachers, and is sustained over time.

Consequently, the trajectory of early reading failure could be potentially broken if children receive high-quality reading instruction delivered by knowledgeable kindergarten teachers. It is important to note that the number of students who fail in reading due to a diagnosis of learning disabilities and other disabilities is relatively small, at approximately 2–9% (Chard et al., 2008). The remaining students who struggle can be helped with high-quality classroom instruction. According to Chard and Kame'enui (2000), the majority of instruction that struggling readers get might be out of alignment with contemporary research on preventing reading difficulties. Their particular concerns focused on the misalignment between research and the type of reading experiences and materials used; the type and frequency of oral reading; and the early word reading growth demonstrated by struggling readers on major assessments of oral reading.

## CONCEPTUALIZING INSTRUCTION

High-quality classroom instruction in reading that is differentiated according to students' needs, coupled with early intervention instruction, has been found to be associated with higher levels of reading performance for young readers who struggle with reading (Mathes et al., 2005). Systematic and explicit instruction in phonemic awareness, phonics, vocabulary, comprehension, and fluency (National Institute of Child Health and Human Development [NICHD] 2000) based upon empirically tested practices are essential components of the type of instruction recommended in multitiered models of intervention. In a three-tiered intervention model, Tier 1 involves research-based instruction in the classroom. Tier 2 adds small-group differentiated instruction and supplementary programs to research-based classroom instruction (Tier 1). Tier 3 builds upon Tier 1 and Tier 2 instruction and provides greater differentiation, such as one-to-one instruction (Rinaldi & Samson, 2008). The supplementary programs used in reading interventions vary, with no one method considered the best method for working with struggling readers. This is evidenced in research by Mathes et al. (2005) in which two methods (Proactive Reading and Responsive Reading) were examined. Proactive Reading, aligned with behavioral theory, was derived from Direct Instruction, while Responsive Reading was derived from a cognitive-apprenticeship model. In other research, Scanlon, Vellutino, Small, Fanuele, and Sweeney (2005) found that both small-group and one-to-one intervention are equally effective in reducing the number of early readers who struggle with reading. They also found a reduction in the number of kindergartners identified as struggling readers after being exposed to classroom reading instruction supplemented by 30-minute tutorial sessions over a period of 25 weeks (Scanlon, Vellutino, et al., 2005). In another study of reading intervention approaches Professional Development Only (PDO) for classroom teachers; supplemental, small-group Intervention Only (IO) for students; and both professional development and supplemental, small-group intervention (PD+1) found that all three approaches were effective in reducing the number of kindergarten children with early reading difficulties (Scanlon, Gelzheiser, Vellutino, Schatschneider, & Sweeney, 2010).

However, the risk of failure in reading for lower socioeconomic level students is greater than that for children from more affluent families due to the quality of the reading instruction that they receive in first grade. As Stuhlman and Pianta (2009) found, first-grade children at the lowest socioeconomic levels are served by a higher percentage of low-quality first-grade classrooms while middle-income students are placed in a significantly higher proportion of high-quality classrooms. In spite of the fact that researchers have identified several classroom instructional approaches that can be used in reading instruction, educators are still concerned about the reading progress made by struggling readers in classrooms where best practices (research-based) are used (Chard & Kame'enui, 2000). Block, Whiteley, Parris, Reed, and Cleveland (2009) conducted research to determine if adding 20 minutes of additional instructional time to the most often used instructional approaches in literacy would affect the reading comprehension of second- to sixth-grade students from mostly (62%) low to low-middle socioeconomic level schools. There were grade-level differences in the type of learning that enhanced students' comprehension. The highest comprehension scores for second, third, and fourth graders were found for silent reading followed by discussion (transactional learning). Independent reading with teacher monitoring (individualized schema-based learning) was found to be effective for third graders. Student choice of reading two expository readings on the same topic in sequence (conceptual learning) was found to be effective for sixth graders. These researchers also found that providing additional time, over and above the traditional basal instruction, did not result in increased comprehension for all readers in Grades 2–6. The important outcome for struggling readers was that when they were given 15–20 minutes of time to read class books coupled with 70 minutes of time for basal instruction, they performed better or comparable to more successful readers on the following standardized measures of comprehension achievement: summarizing and retaining information, identifying main ideas, and recalling details from stories (Block et al., 2009).

## BENEFICIAL FACTORS FOR EARLY READING

### Matching Books to Readers

Young readers need to be exposed to a variety of narrative and informational text to foster their comprehension of text and to engage them in reading (Duke, 2000; Smith & Read, 2009). Matching text to the developmental needs of readers is a very important consideration in working with both beginning and struggling readers (Mesmer & Cumming, 2009). Reading Recovery, an early intervention program developed by Marie Clay (1985) for at-risk readers, used repetition and language patterns to create text that matches the spoken language patterns and reading levels of students with texts. Because Reading Recovery students at the beginning levels are exposed to text that uses fewer words, which are more frequently repeated, and familiar language patterns before moving to more complex text, they experience success in reading. The daily 30-minute lessons provide several opportunities for students to build on their experiences with matched text by reading familiar stories, working with letters, creating written messages, and reading new books, while their progress is monitored by running records.

There are several key findings in the research on matching texts to readers. Hiebert and Martin (2009) reviewed the literature on repetition and pacing of the presentation of unknown words in reading and concluded that repetition of words in texts is overlooked in selecting texts for these readers. While a paucity of research exists in these areas, there are two important findings that have implications for teaching: First, beginning readers' abilities to recognize words accurately and quickly are affected by their familiarity with orthographic and phonological patterns (letter-sound and rimes) in words. Second, beginning readers' rate of learning high-frequency words is greater than their rate in learning low-frequency words. Thus beginning readers will be more fluent in reading as they apply their knowledge of high-frequency words, along with orthographic and phonological patterns when reading connected text. Their increasing fluency and word identification skills will allow the teacher to focus more on vocabulary and comprehension instruction as described in Chapters 7 and 8.

## Time Spent Reading

The time that children spend reading connected text, text focusing on a common theme or related to a specific topic, is important in early literacy development.

The more time teachers provide for students to read in school, the greater the volume of reading by students. Schools must establish more time for reading as an objective and as a necessary part of their literacy framework if it is to be recognized and practiced in classrooms. As Richard Allington (2006) states in his book entitled *What Really Matters for Struggling Readers: Designing Research-Based Programs:*

> Successful early interventions provide access to a variety of texts, multiple opportunities to read connected texts, and increased volume of reading.

> Kids need to read a lot if they are to become good readers. To ensure that all students read a lot, schools need to develop standards for expected volume of reading (and writing). The cornerstone of an effective school organizational plan is allocating sufficient time for lots of reading and writing. Some of the time needed can be reclaimed from non-instructional activities. But it is important that such a plan has the support of teachers. (pp. 55–56)

McIntyre, Rightmyer, Powell, Powers, and Petrosko (2006) found that 66 first-grade struggling readers in classrooms where less connected text was read had greater achievement in phonics compared to children in classrooms where there was much more reading of connected text. The researchers concluded that the children in the first classrooms were developmentally ready for phonics instruction and attributed this to their improved achievement in this area. They also concluded that the developmental phase of reading dictates that some children have daily phonics instruction, and that explicit, systematic phonics instruction be provided for students based upon their stage of phonological development. They, however, recommend independent reading time for students and believe that teachers working with beginning readers should establish mediated reading time, time in which they monitor the engagement of students with text through repeated reading, paired reading, assisted oral reading, and choral reading to make sure that students are really reading.

> ### *The benefits of exposure to print increase from infancy to adulthood*
> In a meta-analysis of 99 studies on the topic, Mol and Bus (2011) found that increased exposure to print is associated with increased academic achievement, reading comprehension, technical reading, and spelling. For young children, exposure to print in books is associated with children's oral language development and understanding of reading. Like McIntyre, Rightmyer, et al. (2006), the findings by Mol and Bus (2011) indicate that independent reading for pleasure benefits struggling readers, as well as readers at all stages of development.

## Reading Aloud

Reading aloud benefits all children, especially struggling readers in the early grades. Repeated interactive read-alouds are effective for young children in generating more oral responses to text from low-ability preschool children (Morrow, 1988). The type of text shared in read-alouds should include a variety of genres. The need for and effectiveness of sharing informational text with young readers through read-alouds is widely supported by research (Duke, 2000; Pappas, Varelas, Barry, & Rife, 2003; Smolkin & Donovan, 2003; Yopp & Yopp, 2000).

## EARLY READING INSTRUCTION FOR LANGUAGE MINORITY STUDENTS

Language minority students whose first language is not English, who are from low socioeconomic backgrounds, and struggle with reading need effective reading intervention programs (August & Shanahan, 2006). In their research on teaching reading to native Spanish-speaking children, Mathes, Pollard-Durodola, Cárdenas-Hagan, Linan-Thompson, and Vaughn (2007) found that these students benefit from explicit and systematic instruction just like native English-speaking children who struggle in reading. They note that language skills in one's native language may or may not transfer easily to a new language. As a result, struggling readers who are also native Spanish speakers have more difficulty transferring and maintaining their language skills over a period of time. This finding is supported by the Early Childhood Study of Language and Literacy Development of Spanish-Speaking Children (ECS) (Tabors, Paez, & Lopez, 2003), which examined the longitudinal growth and trajectory of progress of Spanish-speaking children. Tabors, Paez, and Lopez (2003) found that the oral language skills of Spanish-English bilingual children in preschool and kindergarten were limited in English and Spanish. The limitations in language were found specifically in vocabulary knowledge (Paez, Tabors, & Lopez, 2007; Paez, Bock, & Pizzo, 2011).

However, instruction that capitalizes on students' home languages is effective and can facilitate language and literacy development and academic achievement (August & Shanahan, 2006). For example, instruction that invites students' translation of English text to students' home language facilitates reading comprehension (Orellana, Reynolds, Dorner, & Meza, 2003; Orellana, Reynolds, & Martinez, 2011).

Thus focused instruction designed to improve vocabulary is necessary. Mathes, Pollard-Durodola, et al. (2007) designed a reading intervention program called Proactive Reading and adapted it for Spanish-speaking students.

> Instruction is multifocal, emphasizing vocabulary development, text reading and comprehension, and embedded skills instruction.

The adapted intervention added an oral language component to daily lessons in phonemic awareness, alphabetic knowledge, vocabulary, comprehension, and fluency. Storybook routines and practices considered effective with ELs were also used to develop students' oral language skills. Among the practices were student-teacher dialogue and interaction, repetitive language and routines, and the use of concrete gestures. They found that beginning readers benefited from instruction in a core reading program and instruction in a Spanish version of an instructional intervention.

In addition to using students' first language to aid their second language learning, other classroom-based instructional practices have been found to benefit English learners. Interactive read-alouds provide an opportunity for ELs to hear language and develop their language skills in English (Uribe & Nathenson-Mejia, 2008). Interactive read-alouds also provide opportunities for teachers to assist them in comprehending literature and build upon and extend their background knowledge. Other recommended practices for developing the language comprehension of ELs are shared reading and guided reading. Uribe and Nathenson-Mejia (2008) recommend that shared reading for K–2 ELs should involve teaching different aspects of language (e.g., high-frequency words, spelling patterns, and prepositions) and providing opportunities to hear and practice the correct pronunciation of words. On the other hand, guided reading provides ELs with small-group support in decoding and comprehending instructional-level text. After grouping students in terms of their facility in reading their native language, level of language development in English, or age, teachers can focus on aspects of reading (phonemic awareness, phonics, vocabulary, comprehension, and fluency) and the students' use of the grapho-phonological (sound-symbol), semantic (meaning), syntax (structure), and pragmatic (purpose and use) cues in language.

Guided reading is small-group, differentiated instruction for students with similar needs and performance in reading. It is considered as an effective approach for early childhood teachers to use in working with early readers (Iaquinta, 2006).

Structured guided reading instruction can enhance the oral and written language development of beginning ELs (Bauer & Arazi, 2011). In a version of guided reading known as Modified Guided Reading, teachers guide students in discussions of culturally relevant text. They engage students in making connections between content and language structure and students' lives using strategies like predicting and picture walks. Teachers model reading for fluency, guide students in using strategies for word recognition, and actively use words from the culturally relevant texts to teach word-study skills (i.e., phonemic awareness, structural analysis, and phonics). Modified Guided Reading can provide struggling readers with the scaffolding and explicit instruction to learn English language structures and vocabulary, as well as the culturally relevant materials needed to connect to their lives (Avalos, Plasencia, Chavez, & Rascon, 2007).

> Guided text readings with minilessons is effective, especially when teaching with culturally relevant texts.

## SUMMARY

Classroom teachers are responsible for providing primary reading instruction for ELs, and for coordinating the instruction provided by EL teachers and resource teachers (Smith & Read, 2009). This was not the case for Maria, described in our opening vignette. Her teacher did not have the professional development that she needed to understand how to work with Maria. Teachers must be provided with the professional development needed to assess, monitor progress, and teach EL struggling readers in the context of their classroom. Maria's case reflects a mismatch between her word knowledge and her skills in comprehension. Mancilla-Martinez and Lesaux (2010) believe that language minority students, like Maria, must also receive explicit and continuous vocabulary instruction in order to promote their skills in text comprehension. Maria's story about her grandpa provides a window into her cultural and linguistic background knowledge and family experiences that could be tapped to maintain her initial interest in reading and perception of herself as a reader. It is clear that Maria's interest in reading developed at home where her parents engaged in reading, which created Maria's desire to "read the books that her mama and papa read." The picture books written in Spanish that her kindergarten teacher used further motivated and supported Maria's initial journey as a reader, but did not remove all obstacles to her reading development. Chapters 6–9 will provide information and strategies that will help teachers consider the type of instruction that students like Maria need and will provide them with the insights necessary to build upon the cultural capital that students like Maria bring to reading.

In Chapter 1, we learned that several factors contribute to students' reading difficulties. Among the risk factors for reading difficulties are linguistic and cultural differences, negative perceptions of students' potential and performance, and a disconnect between school and home. Children living in poverty frequently enter school lacking essential skills and concepts (i.e., letter identification, book knowledge) needed for reading, and therefore are considered to be at risk for failure in reading and negative social interactions at school (Espinosa, 2005; Espinosa & Laffey, 2003). These factors influence their motivation to read and progress in reading development. Time and opportunity to read a variety of texts matched to the interests and abilities of early readers, coupled with explicit instruction in reading skills; teacher scaffolding of students' efforts through positive expectations, explanations, and directions; and capitalizing on the cultural and linguistic funds of knowledge they bring, can sustain the motivation that early readers bring to the process of learning to read. Clearly, high-quality reading classroom instruction and early interventions can change the trajectory of reading failure that lies ahead for the youngest and one of the most vulnerable groups of students in today's schools.

## REFLECTION QUESTIONS

1. How can teachers determine when early reading difficulties are developmental or indicators of potential failure in reading?
2. How can classroom teachers differentiate instruction for ELs in the primary grades in ways that affirm them as readers?
3. What are effective ways to inform and engage parents who do not speak English to help their children who struggle in reading?

# CHAPTER 6

# Contextualizing Word Learning and Word Identification

There are different perspectives about how to prepare students for learning new words and the use of word identification skills and strategies. Our position is that word learning and word identification instruction should help students draw on multiple sources of information, including language cues (graphophonic, structure, and meaning), simultaneously as they attempt to identify unknown words. In this chapter we revisit the language cues and word identification strategies defined with assessment procedures in Chapter 3, and provide recommendations for teaching strategies and skills for learning new words. The instruction we describe is contextualized and embedded in authentic reading activities. Students learn reasons for attempting to identify unknown words in print, such as trying to make sense of the text they are reading. Or as one student told us, "I am going to conquer those nasty words"—words that continually pose problems during reading, interfering with fluency or comprehension.

Robust word identification instruction includes the following features:

- Starting with what students know
- Skills blended with meaning
- Whole-part-whole procedures
- Teacher coaching, modeling, and explicit guidance

## CASE ANALYSES: ADAM AND JEREMY

Adam and Jeremy are fourth-grade students who receive reading and language arts instruction from a reading specialist in a pull-out program. Adam goes to the support room for reading instruction for 45 minutes daily and Jeremy receives 90 minutes daily of reading, writing, and spelling instruction. Both students are White and attend an elementary school in a large metropolitan, urban school district.

**Adam**

Ms. Zen, the reading specialist, indicated that Adam is reading grade-level texts but has difficulty identifying unknown words and deriving meanings of these words in context, and often misses the central or main ideas of passages. She is teaching Adam how to identify unknown words and use graphic organizers to take notes as he reads his textbooks. From interviews with Adam and his parents, Ms. Zen has learned that Adam likes to read graphic novels and sports magazines at home and plays video games, but infrequently. She also learned that Adam frequently applied his knowledge of letter and word sounds when texting (on his phone) with friends. For example, he wrote "bi" for *bye* (using the long /i/ vowel sound correctly), and wrote "txt u l8ter" (demonstrating knowledge of the long /a/ sound in *later* by replacing it with the numeral *8*).

Ms. Zen provided information from a recent conference with Adam where she asked him to reread parts of a story from his basal reader. She shared a sample of Adam's oral reading of a story about a man who learns that he likes to sew when he stitches a hole in a porch awning.

> One morning when his wife, Sarah, was out of town, Sam Johnson found that the awning over the front porch was torn. . . . It was morning before he leaned back to look at his night's work. . . . "I had so much fun doing it that I decided to join the quilting club."

Ms. Zen indicated that Adam was "very serious" as he read the passage, often mumbling as he read and reread parts of the passage. He had difficulty reading the words *awning* (saying "aning," then "awing"), *leaned* (saying "lened") and *join* (saying "joan").

Ms. Zen administered the Names Test (Cunningham, 1990), a test of phonics knowledge adopted by the school district. The purpose of this test is to assess students' ability to read real words but ones that are probably not in the students' reading vocabulary, thus requiring application of graphophonic cues to pronounce words that could be in students' oral and/or listening vocabularies. Students are asked to read a list of names containing various letter combinations (single consonants, consonant blends and digraphs, and vowel combinations) that appear in different parts of words.

On this test, Adam worked through the words from left to right, trying different sounds until he concluded that the word he pronounced made sense to him. For example, he read "Chuck Hulk" for *Chuck Hoke*, "Fred Sharewood" for *Fred Sherwood*, "Flo Thurton" for *Flo Thorton*, and "Dee

Skindmore" for *Dee Skidmore*. Ms. Zen interviewed Adam about his performance, and Adam shared that some names were familiar to him, such as Hulk, Chuck, Fred, and Dee. He thought the test was "hard" and concluded that it is difficult to read names for "people I don't know." For the other words, he said he tried to look at the parts of the words and then pronounce the full word. Ms. Zen concluded that Adam had most difficulty with vowels and vowel combinations in multisyllabic words. Some word parts were read correctly, such as initial consonant blends and digraphs, and ending parts, such as *–wood, -ton, -more*.

## Jeremy

Ms. Zen indicated that Jeremy is reading first-grade texts and that she is required to teach language arts with the school basal and school spelling program for the 90 minutes he is in her room. She said that Jeremy seems to be embarrassed about coming to the reading support room and often comes in angry, taking a few minutes to "get acclimated" before participating in the small-group work. Further, she said that the simple basal stories seemed to be uninteresting to him. She knew that he was interested in assembling and painting model cars and trucks, a hobby that he shared with his father. His mother read to him occasionally but indicated that Jeremy prefers making cars after school and before going to bed.

Ms. Zen shared an oral reading sample from a previous day's basal reading lesson.

> People will take trips on the bus
> They will take trips,
> So they can see the city.
> They will take trips,
> So they can see the country.
> People will be very happy to take
> my trips.

When reading this passage, Jeremy often read word by word with little expression, and had difficulty reading the word *trips*, calling it "tri," "types," "tips," and "tr." Ms. Zen observed that this passage lacked an authentic connection to Jeremy's interests.

Later Ms. Zen asked Jeremy to read the words on the Names Test. This test was extremely difficult for Jeremy, and Ms. Zen stopped the testing after the first ten words. He read "Tim Cornell" for Tom Thompson, "Yates

Kirk" for Yolanda Clark, and "Haily Panasonic" for Homer Preston. For these substitutions, Jeremy relied on first letter consonants and sometimes looked at objects in the room for clues (such as the Panasonic TV for Preston). When interviewed, Jeremy indicated that the test did not make sense but that he tried to think of people or things with the same names. He explained that for Tom Thompson, he chose "Tim" (instead of Tom) because "Tim is a friend," and for Thompson, he chose "Cornell" because Tim Cornell "is an uncle."

## CASE QUESTIONS

1. What forms of instruction would build on Adam's strengths and extend his word identification strategies?
2. Jeremy is reading first-grade reading texts with difficulty and disinterest. What forms of instruction would build knowledge of word identification strategies while moving Jeremy to reading varied genre and interesting texts?

## CONCEPTUALIZING INSTRUCTION

We advocate for a balanced approach to teaching word-learning skills. We believe this balance is especially necessary to provide meaningful contexts for learning skills that can be abstract for students and not viewed as applicable to "real" reading. For example, drills on pronouncing vowels appearing in words on word lists and out of context seldom lead to accurate reading of vowels in unknown words that appear in contexts. Yet we have observed that students struggling with reading in second grade and above receive an overemphasis on isolated skill drill. Instead, students need to be taught how to apply what they are learning about words while they are reading and writing texts. And, as discussed in Chapter 1, texts should be those that students *can* (perhaps with instructional supports) and *want* to read.

Marie Clay (1985, 1993b) demonstrated that word study when combined with text reading was highly effective for beginning readers, as shown with multiple studies of Reading Recovery instruction. Morris (1992) and Santa and Hoien (1999) modified Reading Recovery instruction to include a systematic word study with embedded phonic instruction and, like Clay, reported highly significant effects on high-risk first-grade children. Word study was taught along with story reading, comprehension, and writing.

> Highly effective instruction combines code-based and meaning-based methods.

More recently, Morris (2011) analyzed various approaches to teaching sounds of language (phonemic awareness) and concluded that the more powerful approach to this instruction is phonemic awareness taught with other skills rather than as prerequisite skills. And researchers indicate that even very young children are aware of story meaning and successfully adjust their telling of stories through a combination of referencing illustrations and word features to obtain meaning (L. E. Martin & Kragler, 2011). Examples of students demonstrating their use of graphophonic, syntactic, and semantic cues in combination and strategically can be viewed on the Internet at http://www.learner.org/workshops/teachreading3-5/ (Teaching Reading 3–5 Workshop, Annenberg Foundation, 2011). In particular, view workshop 2 where students discuss their choice of word identification cues and strategies.

Vellutino and colleagues (Vellutino et al., 1996; Vellutino & Scanlon, 2002) also demonstrated the advantages of combining code-based (i.e., use of graphophonic cues) with text-based (i.e., text meanings, semantic and syntactic cues) methods for word learning. While structured to provide more attention to code-based learning than Reading Recovery, their instruction was balanced with lessons including the following features: (a) reading and rereading of several texts on students' instructional level (often literature pieces and high interest); (b) learning letters and corresponding sounds and how to use this knowledge to pronounce words; (c) reading new texts with attention to "unknown words" and use of graphophonic cues and discussions of text meanings; (d) practicing high-frequency sight words after readings (often with word cards); and (e) engaging in writing or dictating texts, with attention to representing sounds in words as they are written. Within the lesson components, students are taught to use both graphophonic strategies for pronouncing words and context clues (semantic and syntactic clues) to predict or confirm word choices. Thus all three language cues are used in combination. And consistent with Paris's (2005) research, constrained skills, such as letter names, letter sounds, and word segmentation for sound analysis, are taught explicitly and ended relatively early during the first years of instruction. Comprehension and meaning-oriented skills and strategies are taught simultaneously, and once graphophonic skills are achieved, instruction deepens students' vocabulary and comprehension development (unconstrained skills that continue to grow throughout adulthood).

Several researchers continue the argument in favor of balanced word identification instruction (i.e., combining use of three language cues, embedding word identification skill learning within text reading discussions). Cummins (2007) contended that anything less than a balanced approach results in instruction that limits students' growth. He argued that students with reading difficulties are denied access to a rich repertoire of language and meaning sources of information that can aid word learning. Cummins concluded that this outcome was particularly the case in high-poverty schools where scripted phonics programs received primary emphasis over more balanced approaches to literacy instruction. He advocated for an explicit emphasis on language information, such as the use of context clues or word parts, taught in combination with text comprehension strategy instruction (e.g., "does that make sense?" or "predict what might happen next") and opportunities to read and write extensively. Similarly, Pease-Alvarez (2006) reported that very different forms of instruction occurred in the affluent and low-income schools she investigated, with the low-income schools receiving more scripted (and impoverished) instruction and affluent schools characterized by less scripted instruction and curricula designed to address interests and needs of the students.

McCarty and Romero-Little (2005) documented changes in teaching and test performance of low-income schools on a Navajo reservation and concluded that the newly implemented intensive phonics program had negative outcomes. Prior to the implementation of a scripted teaching of isolated sounds out of words, students' test scores showed a consistent upward trajectory (when compared with a comparison group) when taught with a bilingual, bicultural literature program. The former program provided a balanced approach to teaching word learning, vocabulary, and comprehension skills in combination (similar to Cummins's view, as described above). With the infusion of the scripted phonics program, test scores declined, with higher scores reported in 1999 than in 2003, 4 years after the new program was introduced, and for some students, scores dropped as much as 50%.

We apply the above research findings to identify specific skills that students can use to access semantic, syntactic, and graphophonic (language) information in Figure 6.1. The list below outlines each cueing system and its corresponding skills. For example, students search picture and/or illustrations to find clues to meaning, such as the illustration of the awning on a front porch might be a (language) cue to help Adam understand the meaning of that word. As depicted in Figure 6.1, the cueing systems overlap as meaning might be activated once a word is pronounced or vice versa. At the center of the overlapping cue systems is language information (meaning, structure, and sounds for letters).

*Figure 6.1. Language Cues*

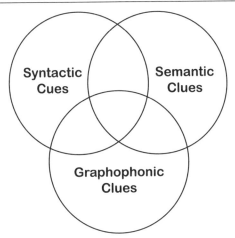

Meaning/Semantic information

- Search pictures, images, and/or illustrations for clues to word meanings
- Refer to context information, including topic/theme, paragraphs, sentence meaning or syntax
- Refer to dictionary
- Ask a peer or friendly soul

Sounds for letters/Graphophonic information

- Use structural or morphemic information, including syllables or other chunks of words, onsets (the initial consonant sound of a word, such as "w" in *wall* or "sw" in *swim*) and rimes (vowel and rest of syllable in a one-syllable word, such as "all" in *wall* or "im" in *swim*), prefixes and suffixes to help pronunciation of word parts and words
- Use sounds of words/phonic information

Structure/Syntax

- Analyze author's style and structure of language, such as repeated phrases and use of multiple adjectives to create affect, to provide clues to words
- Analyze grammatical organization of words in texts

## INSTRUCTIONAL RECOMMENDATIONS

We return to the cases of Adam and Jeremy to demonstrate methods of robust instruction (starting with what students know, skills blended with meaning, whole-part-whole procedures, and teacher coaching).

> The goal of word identification instruction is students' flexible and strategic use of language information. Too often, struggling readers overrely on a limited set of cues or strategies.

### Adam's Instruction

We learned that Adam is reading grade-level texts indicating that his word identification skills have progressed well. We also learned that he likes to read, and Ms. Zen noted his problem-solving approach with unknown words, trying alternative versions of sounds in an attempt to identify words that made sense to him. Yet Adam needs to continue to make progress in this area, in particular identifying words that are more difficult for him to decode and having strategies for accessing words that are not part of his knowledge base. We learned that Adam when confronted with unknown words was not consistent in using semantic clues (e.g., picture clue for awning on the front porch) and that he had difficulty using graphophonic information to pronounce vowel combinations in words (e.g., /oi/ in *join*, /awn/ in *awning*).

A multidimensional approach that teaches more than one way to identify unknown words enables students flexible use of skills and strategies (e.g., what are the sounds in the word? what does this word mean? does the word "sound like language"?) (Gaskins, 2011; Gaskins & Labbo, 2007). For example, Ms. Zen can guide Adam to identify the word *join* by revisiting the sentence "I had so much fun doing it that I decided to join the quilting club." She might point to the word *join* and ask Adam its meaning and if there are meaning clues in the sentence, demonstrating that by reading on in the sentence, the word *club* might be a clue (e.g., do you belong to a club? what did you do to become a member? is there a word that you know that starts with a /j/ sound that describes what you did to become a member?). She could go further to make analogies with words Adam knows. For example, she could ask him to identify the beginning letter in *jump* and the last letters in *coin* to help him recognize the word chunks: "j—oin" (stretched out explicitly to highlight word parts). Saying the sounds together with Ms. Zen, the word is pronounced. This is followed by Ms. Zen asking the semantic and syntactic questions, "Does *join* make sense in that sentence? Does it sound like language?"

Teaching from a multidimensional approach provides balanced attention to the language cues and activates students' use of explicit strategies and self-monitoring (e.g., does that make sense?) in the process (Gaskins, 2005). It also addresses the four components of robust instruction that we identified earlier in this chapter: starting with what the students know; blending skills with meaning; progressing from whole to parts to whole; and involving teacher coaching, modeling, and explicit guidance.

***Context plus phonics.*** Numerous researchers have demonstrated the power of teaching several word identification skills simultaneously, such as the use of context (semantic and syntactic) clues and phonics (Beed, Hawkins, & Roller, 1991; Gustafson, Faith, Svensson, Tius, & Heimann, 2011) to accelerate and improve word identification skills for readers across elementary and middle school grades. This teaching is embedded in carefully guided instruction in the strategic use of skills (Cole, 2006). To guide strategic use of word identification skills, teachers may say:

- Can you predict what that word is, based on what you have read so far? Does that make sense?
- Can you predict what the word may be by looking at the pictures? Does that make sense?
- Reread the first part of the sentence; what word would come next? Does that make sense?
- Read around the unknown word and predict what word may fit. Does that make sense?
- Read around the unknown word and predict what word may fit by looking at the beginning letter, the middle letter(s), and the ending letter. Does that make sense?

***Keywords for analogies.*** Keywords are used to aid word identification (Ehri, Satlow, & Gaskins, 2009; Gaskins, 2011). Thus in the above example of instruction on the word *join*, Ms. Zen used keywords *jump* and *coin* as analogies for pronouncing the word. For another example, Adam may determine that the word *awning* refers to the cover over the porch, as viewed in the illustration. Yet he may not be able to pronounce the word. The teacher would then draw on a keyword analogy. She would ask Adam to stretch out the word, looking for small chunks. She may need to demonstrate the chunking and write the word in two parts: "awn- + -ing." Then she would ask Adam to think of words that might have the same parts. He might generate *walking* for the "–ing" chunk but be unable to think of a word for the "awn-." Ms. Zen would present keywords that Adam can read, such as *fawn* or *pawn shop*. She would help him stretch these words into parts: "f—awn," "p—awn"; then she would draw comparisons between the keywords and "awn- + -ing" to help him pronounce the new word (Ehri et al., 2009). In the process of making comparisons, Ms. Zen would ask Adam to draw analogies between words that are known, as modeled by Ms. Zen saying, "If I know 'awn' in *fawn*, then I know 'awn-ing.'"

*Robust instruction.* In the above demonstration, Ms. Zen builds on what Adam knows in several ways. She provides keywords that are part of Adam's reading and speaking vocabulary to draw analogies between known and unknown words. The skill of looking at word chunks for pronouncing the word *awning* is related back to the text cues to confirm the meaning of the word, thus blending the skills of sounding out the word parts with meaning confirmation. The activity demonstrates whole-part-whole teaching by starting with the text, focusing on words with guided practice, and applying this learning back to reading the words in the text to establish meaning. Throughout the process, Ms. Zen guided Adam's use of language cues and made explicit the structural and phonic elements of the unknown word and the process of using keywords to aid word pronunciation. Systematic practice of these elements during word study that accompanies his text readings will continue to support Adam's use of multiple word analysis skills. Instruction will continue until Adam develops independent applications of these combined word analysis skills. Keeping a notebook of newly learned words and keywords that are offered by Ms. Zen is useful for his work with analogies (Gaskins, 2011) and for reasoning about the sounds of words and for building automaticity, a quick recognition of predictable sound patterns. Ms. Zen will continue to take running records with new texts to monitor Adam's progress with these skills.

### Jeremy's Instruction

Jeremy is developing a basic reading vocabulary as evidenced by his accuracy of reading most words in early-first-grade texts. Ms. Zen has observed that Jeremy has difficulty using graphophonic skills needed to pronounce blends (e.g., /tr/ as in *trip*, /pl/, /fr/) and that he is not using context clues. She indicated, though, that the texts he read were not very meaningful to him and this may be a reason that he didn't search for meaning to help him identify unknown words. From her analysis, Ms.

Zen concludes that Jeremy has not mastered the constrained skills of using graphophonic information. And because the texts he is reading have limited meaning, the use of meaning clues are not as helpful as they could be.

*Emphasis on graphophonic cues.* Jeremy also needs a multidimensional approach, applied to texts that are carefully chosen (e.g., instructional level) and well written (i.e., sufficiently rich content) with particular emphasis on graphophonic cues. Ms. Zen decided to emphasize a systematic approach to teaching sound-letter associations, teaching common spelling patterns, such as onsets and rimes (e.g., /tr/ + /ip/ = *trip*) and sounding through the parts of words (Juel & Minden-Cupp, 2000), with writing to reinforce the use of sounds in words. As reported by Juel and Minden-Cupp, a systematic and intensive emphasis on graphophonic cues is effective for teaching these skills, for teaching multiple skills simultaneously (e.g., sound and letter matches for high-frequency sounds, word segmentations), and accelerating learning of these constrained skills. This instruction when coupled with the keyword approach described for Adam, helps students decode words by drawing analogies between words already known and similar sounds in unknown words (Gaskins, 2011). Linking these skills to students' writing and using context cues to identify unknown words while reading continues the process of referencing graphophonic information in combination with text-meaning information. Additional practice with sounds can be accomplished with word sorts and examining word parts (Clay, 1985; Ganske, 2006; Richgels, 2001). For example, Jeremy could choose words from his vocabulary notebook or the classroom word wall that match on beginning sounds; for the /tr/ sound, he could list words such as *track, train,* and *trampoline.* Or he could sort words according to ending sounds, such as matching words to the /ip/ sound as in *sip, slip, flip, lip.* An example of student sorting words by sounds can be viewed on the Internet in the YouTube video entitled *Word Study: Partner Work with a Sort* (http://www.youtube.com/watch?v=YNWMaxFK9EY&feature=related).

Rasinski (2005, 2011) uses word ladders to draw students' attention to word parts. He provides multiple examples of his word ladders on his website under "Presentation Materials" (http://www.timrasinski.com/presentations/word_ladders_1-3.pdf). For example, students could start with the word *team,* and rearrange letters to form a word, *meat,* that is a food that comes from animals. Or another word, *tame,* that means not wild. For these activities, students are using meaning and graphophonic cues in combination.

***Writing and strategic learning.*** Engaging Jeremy in writing to produce texts that interest him is another strategy that may be effective for extending Jeremy's word study (Williams & Lundstrom, 2007). Students examine a word bank or their own word notebook to find words that would be useful for learning new words. For example, Jeremy's interest in building trucks could lead to writing about trucks (the ones he builds, the different kinds of trucks) with his own illustrations or those that he finds online and downloads for his writing. The word *truck* then becomes a keyword for other /tr/ words that he is learning, what Williams and Lundstrom (2007) call a "Tool of the Trade." And as a keyword, it provides ways to associate known words with new words.

Williams and Lundstrom's instruction then moves to emphasize the strategies they refer to as "Tools of the Mind," and includes strategies such as: say the word or sounds slowly and listen to the sounds, think of how to write letters that represent those sounds, and think of other words you know that have these same sounds (keywords) and write those words. Teachers encourage students to use their words in writing and to keep records of these in their word notebook. Part of the work with the words would include stretching the word into word chunks to draw attention to these sound units to aid pronunciation. Ms. Zen may choose to use larger chunks, such as "tr—ip," or if needed, smaller units, "tr—i—p." This stretching activity makes visible the graphic units and is another strategy that Jeremy can use independently to draw attention to word parts, their sounds, and the blending of these chunks into whole words. Pairing word study and interactive writing activities (guided by Ms. Zen) not only draws attention to specific ways to reason about words and sounds and word parts, but it can capitalize on Jeremy's personal interests and experiences as he generates his own texts, and it demonstrates to Jeremy that the words he knows and his interests are important for reading and writing.

***Fluency and prosody.*** Once Jeremy generates his own written texts and transitions to texts that hold meaning for him, it will be important to build fluency. Fluency activities would include reading and rereading texts for accurate reading and feeling comfortable with the words, as well as for providing opportunities to read with expression and convey meaning with intonations and emphasis on particular phrases or ideas. For example, Jeremy may write about a show where antique cars and trucks are displayed, or he may write about sports car racing. Once written, he could read and reread his texts aloud taking the role of a radio announcer, or Jeremy could develop and narrate a digital story with images that he downloads from the Internet. He could participate in a Readers' Theater activity, where students read from a script or write a script of a text. Multiple scripts are available commercially and free on the Internet on websites such as *Readers' Theater Scripts and Plays* (http://www.teachingheart.net/readerstheater.htm). There is no memorization of lines; students read from the scripts by taking characters' parts and reading the dialogue, or reading the commentaries that explain the dialogue. The focus is on prosody, as described in Chapter 3: reading the text with expression and with gestures. Rasinski (2011) advocates Reader's Theater for helping students feel comfortable reading connected text; the multiple and purposeful rereadings focus less on word pronunciations and more on text meaning.

Young and Rasinksi (2009) offer multiple ways to use Readers' Theater that might be appropriate for Jeremy to build on his own interests and to engage him in enactment of stories that interest him or that he creates. Included in their suggestions are Internet sources for Readers' Theater scripts, such as *Aaron Shepard's RT Page* (http://www.aaronshep.com/rt/) or Timothy Rasinski's website under "Presentation Materials" (http://www.timrasinski.com/?page=presentations).

*Robust instruction.* The activities we describe for Jeremy begin with skills and words that he knows. Added to this is the writing goal for accessing his experiences and knowledge for the context of learning graphophonic cues. An emphasis on graphophonic cues will be systematic and continuous but the practice of these cues will be applied to his writing and reading, blending skills and meaning and whole-part-whole practices. Careful guidance by Ms. Zen will continue. Additional analysis of specific graphophonic cues will be necessary to identify sounds that Jeremy knows and those yet needed. For example, Ms. Zen could use the rubric from *Word Study Lessons* by Pinnell and Fountas (2004) to assess Jeremy's knowledge of phonic sounds when reading and writing. In the study lessons, teachers assess how students use graphophonic cues as they read and follow with specific instruction that might include rereading sections of the texts and/or word sorts. A discussion of the study lessons is provided by Fountas on the Internet in the YouTube video entitled *Phonics and Word Study Lessons from Fountas & Pinnell* (http://www.youtube.com/watch?v=Q0WYcGQFY0k). The careful analysis in the study lessons is similar to the oral reading analyses that we discussed in Chapter 3. Instruction that follows assessment has the goal to accelerate Jeremy's trajectory in building graphophonic knowledge and applications of this knowledge in increasingly more difficult and varied texts.

## SUMMARY

Exemplary word learning and word identification instruction should build on students' knowledge about the purpose and meaning of print and growing knowledge of sound-letter associations. Careful analysis of word parts and writing to apply graphophonic knowledge aims to develop automatic word identification skills and strategies. Good word identification instruction that develops knowledge and use of graphophonic cues is over "relatively quickly" (Stahl, 1992).

Instruction should be explicit and emphasized during early reading development while also addressing use of semantic and syntactic information to predict and confirm word selections in texts. Such instruction should be integrated into a balanced approach to reading instruction and embedded in text reading activities. As demonstrated in Chapter 3, use of language cue systems can be problematic for some students. Instruction that draws attention to the combined use of these cues is highly effective. Word identification skills and strategies are part of the total reading process and, in particular, enable vocabulary learning (meanings of words) and reading comprehension.

### REFLECTION QUESTIONS

1. Writing to practice spellings of words, including invented spellings, can be a powerful strategy for thinking about word sounds and word parts. How can you incorporate writing activities into instruction focusing on word learning?
2. Older students can have difficulty analyzing multisyllabic words. What forms of instruction would you provide to support their skill in reading these words?

# CHAPTER 7

# Developing Concepts and Vocabulary Through Multiple Skills and Strategies

In *How We Think* John Dewey (1910) wrote, "Everyone has experienced how learning an appropriate name for what was dim and vague cleared up and crystallized the whole matter." Vocabulary development is essential for knowledge acquisition and reading comprehension and in empowering students to be independent readers and writers. In this chapter we describe vocabulary instruction as essential to reading comprehension for all learners and important for the success of second-language learners in school. Second-language learners may know the vocabulary equivalents in their first language, and thus instruction focuses on making bilingual connections. For all students, vocabulary instruction must be initiated in the early grades and continued across grade levels (Biemiller, 2001), and it must be comprehensive (Nagy, 2005) and robust (Sobolak, 2011).

Vocabulary instruction is effective when students

- Make connections to their background knowledge
- Have many opportunities for repeated use of words
- Engage in higher level thinking about words
- Use strategies for learning new words independently
- Use words in meaningful learning situations (Allen, 1999; Nagy, 1988; Nagy & Scott, 2000).

## CASE ANALYSIS: CATHERINE

Catherine was one of 29 students in Mrs. Schneider's fourth-grade class in an urban school district. Eighty percent of the students in the class were African American, 15% were White, and the remaining 5% were Latino (all of whom are ELs). While Catherine struggled in reading and her overall progress was below grade level, she maintained a positive attitude about school and reading as reflected in her scores on the Self-Concept and Value of Reading subtests of the Motivation to Read profile (Gambrell, Palmer, Coding, & Mazzoni, 1995), which placed her in the 75th percentile.

Catherine, who is White, seemed to be one of the most academically and emotionally vulnerable students in Mrs. Schneider's class. Catherine's father died in a tragic car accident during the previous school year, thereby leaving her and her four siblings and mother alone. Her grandmother was a stable and nurturing figure in their lives, as evidenced by the stories that she shared in class. Although her third-grade teacher had recommended retention, Catherine's mother decided against it attributing Catherine's low performance to the grief associated with her father's death.

The fourth-grade teachers in the school district used the Gates McGinitie Reading Test, a standardized assessment tool, to assess students' vocabulary and comprehension. The test was administered three times during the school year. At the beginning of the year, Catherine performed well below grade level with her performance equivalent to a student in the second grade at 2.5. Her performance improved steadily to 2.9 in January, and to 3.3 in May.

One day, Mrs. Schneider asked students to write to the following prompt: "What can teachers do to get their students to be better readers?" Catherine responded to the on-demand writing prompt in the following way:

> Dear teacher
>
>     To get your class to be a better Reader is you have to Read all the book you bot [bought] and Read them all twice. And go to the lidrary and get adtoe [about] 4 more books and Read them each 5 times. And I would take the test and if I got an b [B] I would take the test agan intile [until] I get an A+ an it. Then I would go selidrat [celebrate] with my frinds under the giant tree in my back yard.

Catherine's response indicates that she values reading and feels that a reader gets better at reading by reading. She understands that the way to improve reading performance is to read more. She also recognizes the library as a source for securing books, as well as the community (e.g., bookstores or other businesses). These insights are ones that Mrs. Schneider can build upon in her work with Catherine.

Catherine struggled in other areas of the curriculum. On state assessments of reading, social studies, and science, she scored in the 14th, 19th, and 20th percentiles, respectively, for her grade level. Her performance in writing was assessed at the highest level of the average range of performance. Catherine loved to write about a variety of topics, but especially enjoyed writing about her cats and her family; she rarely asked Mrs. Schneider for help with spelling or words to express herself. Catherine's vocabulary and comprehension about cats are reflected in a list poem that she wrote entitled "How to get away from cats."

> How you get away from cats is you need to . . .
> run
> hid
> cheat
> look
> sniff
> be careful
> don't be tricked
> don't be fooled
> and be careful where you are stepping

Catherine's prior knowledge of cats is evident in the information contained in her poem. Her use of the words *tricked* and *fooled* in the advice that she provided about getting away from cats demonstrates that she does not know that the two words are synonyms.

In addition to focusing on writing in her classroom, Mrs. Schneider maintains a direct program of vocabulary development. She uses the state standards in reading for Grade 4 students to help guide her decisions about words to teach. The standards indicate that students must be able to identify the meaning of words using their knowledge of root and base words, and affixes (prefixes and suffixes). They must also identify synonyms and antonyms.

## CASE QUESTIONS

1. What can be learned from Catherine's writing samples that might provide Mrs. Schneider with ideas for ways to increase her vocabulary?
2. How can teachers build upon struggling readers' other language arts skill to promote their vocabulary and reading comprehension?
3. In what way can teachers link culture and vocabulary learning to provide depth and breadth in vocabulary development?

## VOCABULARY INSTRUCTION IN MRS. SCHNEIDER'S CLASSROOM

Mrs. Schneider knows that students learn vocabulary through both direct instruction and incidental reading. She also recognizes that the opportunities to use words in reading, listening, speaking, and writing reinforce words presented in and out of context.

Mrs. Schneider believes that the words presented in her core reading program are the ones that should be taught to her fourth-grade students. She also feels that the routine used to teach these words should be followed in a step-by-step manner. Before students read a selection, she presents words in sentences that are taken from the selection for the day. They are highlighted during reading, and reinforced in independent assignments or projects and in activities in the reading/language arts centers.

She also requires students to maintain a vocabulary notebook in which they record words from other content areas like social studies and science. Students are required to write definitions for the words using the glossary in their textbooks. She evaluates students' understanding of the words through class extension activities and with teacher-constructed worksheets that require students to match the words with their meanings.

In social studies, Mrs. Schneider's class has been exploring the theme of freedom. She began by reading the book entitled *Henry's Freedom Box: A True Story from the Underground Railroad* (Levine, 2007). Mrs. Schneider, Catherine's teacher, frequently incorporated a variety of genres of literature (i.e., poems, informational texts, historical fiction) and writing activities into the theme. Persuasive, descriptive, and informational writing were used to reinforce content teaching and to reinforce writing across the curriculum. One day late in the school year, students were asked to respond to the following proverb:

> "You have freedom but never freedom from consequences." (John Alston)

Catherine's response to this proverb is shown below:

> You do have control of your life but once you do something sooner or later it is going to come back on you and you have to decide wheather it is good or bad. For example, what goes around comes around. So you say you want to take druge. Your conesguess [consequence] is you die or end up in jail or you can take the good result and go to college.

Catherine's response reflects her understanding that freedom has consequences. She has a fairly deep understanding of freedom (e.g., people having control over their thoughts and actions), and she is able to support her understanding of consequences with specific authentic examples.

Mrs. Schneider took several words from *Mississippi Bridge* (M. D. Taylor, 1990), one of the books read as part of the text set used to explore the theme of freedom in social studies. The story takes place in Mississippi in the 1930s and provides a historical context for understanding the Jim Crow laws that denied Black people certain freedoms. In this story, the freedom denied is refusing to allow Black passengers to ride the bus if doing so would fill the bus and prevent some White people from getting on the bus. Some of the words selected from the text and related to the topic were *sharecroppers, tenants,* and *discrimination.* Excerpts from the text provide a rich context for understanding the meaning of *sharecroppers* and *tenants.* Text does not always provide readers with clues to the meaning of words, so it is important to consider this in thinking about how to scaffold for struggling readers.

> Their family (the Logans) owned a whole bunch of acres just west of us and that was something, them being colored. Folks said they'd been owning that land for near to fifty year, but them having land, when we was tenants ourselves living on somebody else's place, ain't never set too well with Pa. Being tenants wasn't bad as being sharecroppers seeing that we owned our own mule, paid for our own seed and such, and paid our rent for the land in cash money 'stead of crops. (pp. 24–25)

The meaning of the third term, *discrimination,* can be inferred from the events in the story described below and reinforced by connecting the events to the background knowledge that many of the students in the class have of discrimination. Combining story events and students' funds of knowledge can lead to greater student engagement with the story. One event involved a Black woman who went into a store at a bus stop while waiting for the bus. She asked the White store owner if she could try on a hat that she liked and he told her she would have to purchase the hat before she could try it on. He laughed at her and used a racial slur after she said that she probably could not afford the hat anyway. In contrast, he encouraged a White customer, who was also waiting for the bus and liked the same hat, to try the hat on as she debated whether or not she could afford to purchase it. Another event involved Blacks who were ordered to get off the bus just before it left town, in order to make room for two late-arriving White passengers. Because of the discrimination suffered by the Black people who were put off the bus to accommodate the White people, they were spared from injury or death as the rain-soaked planks of the bridge leaving town gave way and the bus plunged into the river.

The discussion of the book and the events helped students like Catherine make connections to a previously read book, *Rosa Parks: My Story* (Parks, 1992). Mrs. Schneider then used morphemic analysis to reinforce students' understanding of the suffix (-tion) and Latin root (crim) and embedded prefix (dis) in the word *discrimination*. She then used the poem "I, Too" by Langston Hughes (1990) to help students better understand discrimination and to make connections between it and freedom. Students were asked to record the vocabulary words in their social studies notebooks. They were told that they would be given a quiz over the terms at the end of the unit. However, the term, *discrimination*, might still be a difficult word to read for struggling readers like Christine.

## CONCEPTUALIZING INSTRUCTION

Vocabulary instruction should be envisioned as a process that intensifies over time, across varying text, and according to different learners' needs. The process must be a priority in accelerating the progress of struggling readers, through research-based and differentiated instruction based upon students' linguistic and cultural differences. We will examine the research in these areas and the direction it provides for teachers.

### Making Vocabulary Instruction a Priority

Limited emphasis is placed on vocabulary development in the school curriculum (Beck & McKeown, 2007). However, the National Reading Panel (NRP) report identified vocabulary as a necessary component of early literacy instruction (NICHD, 2000). The findings are embedded in legislation such as Early Reading First (ERF) and Reading First (RF), which were authorized under the Elementary and Secondary Education Act of 1965, but amended by the No Child Left Behind (NCLB) Act of 2001 to focus on using scientifically proven reading instruction to improve the achievement of disadvantaged students who struggle academically. For example, ERF legislation, which was specifically created to address the language and development problems of language minority and economically impoverished preschool children, has resulted in instruction found to promote the vocabulary development of preschoolers who received ERF-preschool enrichment (Gonzalez et al., 2011).

A comprehensive program of vocabulary instruction is critical for struggling readers regardless of their school settings. The four major components of an effective vocabulary program include:

1. Wide reading (i.e., reading from a variety of genres and text types)
2. Teaching individual words
3. Teaching word-learning strategies (i.e., using word parts and context)
4. Fostering word consciousness or a cognitive and affective disposition toward learning words. (Graves, 2000)

An effective vocabulary teacher keeps the following guidelines in mind (Blachowicz & Fisher, 2000):

*Guideline 1*: The effective vocabulary teacher builds a word-rich environment in which students are immersed in words for both incidental and intentional learning, as well as the development of "word awareness."

*Guideline 2:* The effective vocabulary teacher helps students develop as independent word learners.

*Guideline 3:* The effective vocabulary teacher uses instructional strategies that not only teach vocabulary but also model good word-learning behaviors.

*Guideline 4:* The effective vocabulary teacher provides explicit instruction for important content and concept vocabulary, drawing on multiple sources of meaning.

## What We Know About Vocabulary Development

Students' knowledge of vocabulary reflects their understanding of text. Many struggling readers in the upper elementary grades often have smaller sight vocabularies than oral vocabularies and experience difficulty understanding abstract text (Kieffer & Lesaux, 2007). Likewise, students in high-poverty schools struggle to comprehend and read grade-level materials fluently (Greenleaf, Schoenbach, Cziko, & Mueller, 2001) and English learners fail to demonstrate vocabulary gains (Jalongo & Sobolak, 2011; Taboada, 2009).

> Teachers must actively teach vocabulary if they want to increase students' understanding of text and independence as readers and writers.

Sobolak (2011) found that first-grade students from low socioeconomic levels benefitted from more intense (i.e., time) and interactive variation of robust vocabulary instruction in which Tier 2 words (high-utility) taken from *Steck-Vaughn Elements of Reading Vocabulary* were taught. The format for instruction included presenting key vocabulary words in read-aloud storybook selections followed by sharing student focused definitions. Other components included illustrations, examples (i.e., nonexamples, and context situated), graphic aids, home-school materials, and writing activities.

For struggling readers, explicit instruction is recommended to promote vocabulary learning (Biemiller, 2001; D. B. Taylor, Mraz, Nichols, Rickelman, & Wood, 2009). During explicit instruction teachers could begin with think alouds in which teachers model the strategies that they use to determine word meanings using context, spelling patterns, and word parts (i.e., prefixes, suffixes, and roots). As part of the think aloud, teachers can share their personal experiences with words to provide students with a model of making connections to one's background knowledge. Presenting keywords in a sentence context will enable students to draw upon additional clues to word meanings. Teachers should ask students questions such as, "Do you know this word?" "How do you know this word?" "Does it look like, sound like, or mean the same as a word that you have seen or heard outside of school (i.e., in church, on television, at home)?" This type of instruction involves other tools such as knowledge rating scales that can be used collaboratively with students in small-group instruction to determine students' word knowledge or graphic organizers to show the relationship between words. Teachers can also model, support, and extend vocabulary knowledge through the use of strategies (e.g., KWL, Semantic Feature Analysis), metacognitive thinking about words (i.e., Vocabulary Self-Awareness Charts), and independent practice (i.e., vocabulary cards). As a follow-up to explicit instruction, teachers can make students word conscious by featuring Tier 2, useful words (e.g., *fantastic, glimpse*) that are often found in reading materials (Beck, McKeown, & Kucan, 2002), on word walls and have students construct models of the words, write poems or songs, create digital stories, or engage in authentic writing (i.e., newspaper article, want ads) projects.

Children's vocabulary development is influenced by their early experiences with language in their homes. Parents' knowledge of vocabulary development and ability to support their children in this process are significantly related to their economic circumstances. Children of high-income parents from professional backgrounds are exposed to 3.5 times more words per hour compared to young children living in poverty.

Middle-class children also hear at least 2 times more words per hour compared to children living in poverty (Hart & Risley, 2003). While the Hart and Risley (1995) study is often cited to support views of language deficiencies in children and their parents living in poverty, several researchers believe that it pathologizes the language and culture of these children and families. Teachers are reminded that the "language differences are just that—differences" (Dudley-Marling & Lucas, 2009, p. 369), as opposed to deficits. Most importantly, teachers must respect and build on the cultural, linguistic, and intellectual knowledge that children have in instructing them (Dudley-Marling, 2007; Dudley-Marling & Lucas, 2009).

Vocabulary development must be a key component in literacy instruction for all children and at all grade levels (NICHD, 2000). Children's early vocabulary development predicts their later success in reading comprehension in middle school and high school. The vocabulary of English learners is smaller initially than native speakers, with native speakers typically knowing at least 5,000 to 7, 000 English words before kindergarten (AERA, 2004; Senechal & Cornell, 1993). Bilingual students' early reading skills are dependent upon their knowledge of vocabulary (Proctor, August, Carlo, & Snow, 2005). This is important when one considers the research by August, Carlo, Dressler, and Snow (2005) who found that monolingual English learners exceeded Spanish-English bilingual learners in breadth and depth of their knowledge of word meanings. Consequently the comprehension of grade-level text was less for ELs when compared to their English-only counterparts.

## Teaching Practices: Grade-Level Differences

The extent of children's vocabulary knowledge is correlated with teachers' instructional practices in vocabulary. In looking at the case study of Catherine, we can see some additional practices that might be used based upon guidelines for vocabulary instruction and research on vocabulary development. If Mrs. Schneider is to meet the needs of struggling readers like Catherine, she must use a variety of approaches for older readers (Ebbers & Denton, 2008) and diverse readers (Baker, Simmons, & Kame'enui, 1998).

It is important to teach words that support students' reading comprehension.

In all of the approaches used, words should be chosen that are essential to understanding the text but also those that might be problematic for the different reading levels of students in the class. The terms *boycott* and *segregation* are essential to all students' understanding of the story of Rosa Parks, but specific words like *passenger* and *refuse* might be difficult for struggling readers like Catherine. Mrs. Schneider must encourage Catherine's individual interest in words by encouraging her to choose new words and interesting words to learn. We recommend that she begin by having her identify two to three new and interesting words encountered in incidental reading. A format that we have found effective for recording such words is presented in Figure 7.1.

Mrs. Schneider should encourage the use of vocabulary notebooks or word cards as tools for struggling readers to use in reviewing new words and as resources for independent writing. Words that are taught prior to cross-curricular instruction can be collected and reviewed after instruction. Students can also use them in speaking and writing activities.

> Go digital with vocabulary instruction.

Another practice that Mrs. Schneider might implement is frequent sharing of new words or new meanings of words that have been acquired. Modeling the strategies to determine the meaning of the new words will be helpful in promoting higher level thinking about words. Making connections to known words and to life experiences or culture will also reinforce cultural connections that we believe are essential for learning.

Mrs. Schneider might also use technology as a support tool to develop Catherine's vocabulary and that of other struggling readers in her class. Dalton and Grisham (2011) describe ten eVoc strategies that provide explicit instruction and encourage student independence in applying word-learning strategies. Among the strategies described are visual displays, digital vocabulary field trips, online vocabulary games, students' use of media to demonstrate their vocabulary knowledge, and using online word reference tools that are also teaching resources. One strategy that Mrs. Schneider might begin with is to create a visual display that shows relationships between words found within a text. Word maps are

*Figure 7.1. New Word Entry*

Word: _____

Sentence where word is found: _____

Definition: _____

Visual image created by the word: _____

My experience(s) connected with the word: _____

one type of visual display that can be created using Wordle and WordSift, free word cloud tools available on the Internet. In Wordle (www.wordle. net), text can be pasted into the applet and a visual display is created based upon the frequency of words in the text. WordSift (www.wordsift. com) provides the reader with additional supports: word map, sentences, and related images. The tool also sorts words by difficulty and identifies the words that are academic words, which can be a useful tool for ELs.

Figures 7.2 and 7.3 provide two examples of a word cloud to highlight keywords based on an excerpt from Martin Luther King's "I have a dream" speech found in *I Have a Dream: The Story of Martin Luther King* (Davidson, 1986). The keywords can be introduced in prereading activities designed to determine students' background knowledge of word meanings and focus their attention on concepts related to the "Freedom" theme being taught.

## Examining Teaching Practice

In a study of the vocabulary practices of teachers in prekindergarten and kindergarten, Silverman and Crandell (2010) examined five instructional practices considered to be effective in vocabulary development to determine if they correlated with higher vocabulary performance: (1) acting out and illustrating words during read-alouds; (2) analyzing words semantically; (3) applying words in new contexts; (4) defining words explicitly in the rich context of storybook discussions; and (5) word study focused on attending to letters and sounds. Silverman and Crandell found that children with different levels of vocabulary knowledge performed differently to instructional practices. The practices that were found to be effective for children with limited initial word knowledge were: acting out and illustrating words during read-alouds, applying words in new contexts, defining words in the context of storybook reading, and word study. Explicitly teaching vocabulary during shared reading might be modeled by teachers in the following ways: stopping at words believed to be difficult for students, looking for familiar word parts, breaking the words into these parts to help pronounce them, and rereading the word in the sentences from the text. The final step involves modeling how to use context to help students determine the meaning of the words (McGee & Richgels, 2004).

Similarly, whole-class reading aloud followed by small-group instruction (two to five students) can potentially increase vocabulary and comprehension of students in the early stages of reading. Fien et al. (2011) found increased vocabulary and retelling of expository text for first graders with

*Figure 7.2. Wordle*

dream
rooted
created
equal
American
live
truths
men
day
true
creed
one
nation
rise
meaning
self-evident
deeply
hold

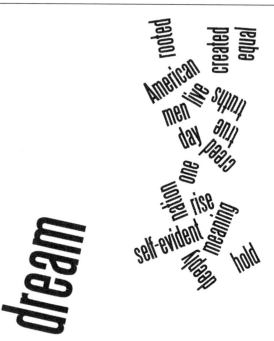

*Figure 7.3. Wordle*

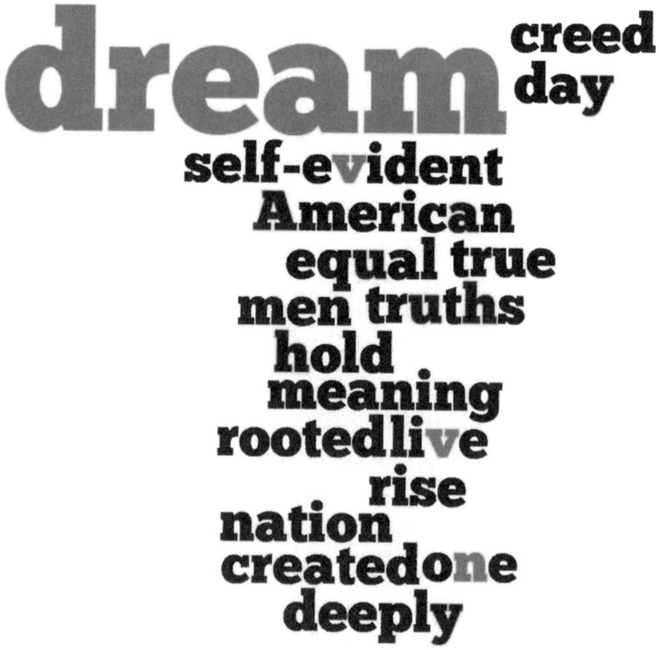

dream
creed
day
self-evident
American
equal true
men truths
hold
meaning
rootedlive
rise
nation
createdone
deeply

low vocabulary and comprehension skills in the intervention group. All students were exposed to a Read Aloud Curriculum consisting of three expository and four narrative lessons with science content grouped according to animal themes. Explicit vocabulary and comprehension instruction was provided during 28 thirty-minute lessons. The intervention group received an additional 20 minutes of small-group instruction twice weekly. This group of students was exposed multiple times to words, provided with definitional and instructional information about words, and participated in activities designed to encourage deep thinking about words (discussing examples and nonexamples, extended conversations, sentence context).

Extended vocabulary instruction during storybook reading compared to incidental exposure to words is an effective intervention for struggling readers (Coyne, McCoach, & Kapp, 2007). Based on their research, Coyne et al. (2007) recommend teachers use a trilevel approach to vocabulary instruction and intervention in kindergarten:

1. Read storybooks to children that contain a variety and range of difficulty vocabulary.
2. Select words from these books that can be targeted for embedded instruction, instruction in which students are provided with simple definitions for words when they are encountered in text. The sentence with the target word is reread using the replaced definition in the sentence. The words selected should be unknown to students but are important to understanding words in an academic context. They are needed to understand words in other texts.
3. Select a similar set of words from the story that is essential for understanding important story ideas and concepts.

Teachers can also use children's books with labeled drawings (Barone, Mallette, & Xu, 2005). Among the books that can be used are *Q Is for Duck: An Alphabet Guessing Game* (Elting & Folsom, 2005), *Talk to Me About the Alphabet* (Raschka, 2003), and *Bembo's Zoo* (de Vicq de Cumptich, 2000).

Teaching practices with older students should actively engage students in learning and making connections with words and content in various subjects. One strategy that can be used is the interactive word wall strategy in which students associate the features and meaning of words with ideas, experiences, and concepts that are familiar to them; this strategy builds on students' choice in identifying words to learn; and provides experiences with words that allow for meaningful repetition and experiences with words (Harmon, Wood, & Kiser, 2009). The instruction sequence begins with (1) teachers selecting Tier 2 or conceptually important words; (2) teachers introducing words in a rich context followed by class discussion about each word's meaning; (3) engaging in word wall activities (e.g., with context, symbols, and colors) designed to assist the reader in making connections; (4) teachers modeling how to use meaningful prompts and sentence completions before having students make word associations in small groups; and (5) sharing information learned through class presentations about the words added to the word wall.

## VOCABULARY INSTRUCTION FOR ENGLISH LEARNERS

My (Doris's) experience assessing Latino struggling readers in Grades 1–4 who attend a university-based reading clinic is that they struggle the most in understanding narrative and expository text. These students, whose parents have varying degrees of proficiency in English, can easily pronounce words on graded word lists from an informal reading inventory. Many score two to three grade levels above their school placement in word identification. Language minority learners (immigrants born in the United States into Spanish-speaking homes) face a dual challenge in learning language (Mancilla-Martinez & Lesaux, 2010). They must learn both vocabulary and English language structures. However, many immigrant children in varying stages of English language development serve as linguistic and cultural interpreters for their families. In a study of children in immigrant families, Orellana, Reynolds, Dorner, and Meza (2003) found that fifth- and six-grade children played major roles in paraphrasing or phrasing information from Spanish to English for their parents and families on a daily basis. They worked with their families to jointly construct the meaning of different texts, and as they interpreted the texts, they also translated knowledge about mainstream culture (e.g., medical, legal, and educational systems). The research demonstrates that the students process higher levels of competence in literacy in their home environment than they might display at school. It is clear that, as pointed out by Klingner and Vaughn (2004), every teacher must be prepared to work with English learners to increase their vocabulary and improve their comprehension of text. The culturally familiar home practices of students can be used as a meaningful starting point for planning instruction in vocabulary and comprehension (Au, 2006).

## Research Implications for Instruction of ELs

The challenge for English learners is to close the initial gap in vocabulary and expand their vocabularies, especially their academic vocabulary. In order to achieve this goal, direct/explicit instruction must be used to teach vocabulary and provide students with multiple opportunities to use the words taught in speaking and in writing (Rupley, Blair, & Nichols, 2009; Tinajero, 2004). Direct/explicit instruction in vocabulary utilizes explicit explanations, modeling, and guided practice.

August et al. (2005) identified three principles and practices from related research to assist teachers in providing effective vocabulary instruction for Spanish-speaking ELs. The first principle is *to build on the first language knowledge.* Teachers should teach students to use *cognates,* similar words in two languages that are derived from the same language (Tompkins, 2006). Some English-Spanish cognates are dance–*danza*, bicycle–*bicicleta*, and map–*mapa*. Teachers should discuss cognates with students and encourage them to identify them in their reading. Research by Nagy, Garcia, and Durgunoglu (1993) suggests that teachers might do the following: (1) have students circle the cognates found in text; (2) have students work in pairs to determine if they know the Spanish word for the cognates; (3) have students use the Spanish word in the context of the text to check for its appropriateness; (4) have students repeat the process with other cognates; (5) provide opportunities for guided practice; and (6) offer practice in adjusting the cognate used to promote comprehension. This type of practice will extend children's knowledge of both concepts and labels for words.

> The teacher who is effective in providing explicit instruction interacts with students in a meaningful manner and supports students in their efforts to learn new words.

The second principle is *to ensure that ELs know the meaning of basic words.* This requires teachers to directly teach students these words, called Tier 1 words by Beck, McKeown, and Kucan (2002). These words are high-frequency words with both regular and irregular spellings (e.g., *car, place, house*).

The last principle is *to review and reinforce words.* This can be done when students' words are placed on word walls or used for differentiated instruction in minilessons conducted in Reading Workshop, read-alouds, and other teacher-directed or student-initiated language activities.

## Vocabulary Interventions for ELs

For students who struggle with the acquisition of new words, intervention must be provided (AERA, 2004). Reading extensively in a variety of genres is essential for developing high levels of both vocabulary and reading comprehension (Cummins, 2003). Woods, Harmon, and Hedrick (2004) recommend that teachers make connections between below-grade-level trade books (i.e., fiction and nonfiction) and content area topics presented in their classes, provide opportunities for multiple exposures to key terms, and encourage extension activities beyond the classroom. In robust vocabulary instruction students learn the similarities and differences in meaning between the select word and related concepts, along with the varied uses of the word in different contexts. Robust vocabulary instruction has been found to improve the word learning of African American students from low socioeconomic backgrounds and students with vocabulary skills below grade level (Beck, Perfetti, & McKeown, 1982; McKeown, Beck, Omanson, & Perfetti, 1983; McKeown, Beck, Omanson, & Pople, 1985). Lovelace and Stewart (2009) used robust vocabulary instruction to effectively promote the word learning of African American children. However, the use of multicultural literature with robust vocabulary instruction did not influence students' retention of the words presented.

Instructional strategies that have been found to be effective for developing the vocabulary of native English speakers have also been found to be effective with second language learners (Fitzgerald, 1995; Gersten & Baker, 2000). Some strategies include student journals, students explaining and illustrating examples, students completing vocabulary charts, and teachers providing concrete experiences supplemented by visual aids. Nation (2003) recommends that students make word cards with English words on one side and the translation in the first language on the other side and that students study word parts (prefixes, suffixes, and roots) and use a bilingual dictionary or a monolingual dictionary where the first language meanings of the words are added to the second language meanings after words are first learned in context.

## Vocabulary Implications for Diverse Middle School Students

In order to comprehend academically complex content material successfully, diverse middle school students need direct instruction in vocabulary (Kieffer & Lesaux, 2010). For example, Kieffer and Lesaux recommend actively teaching morphological units (prefixes, suffixes, and roots) directly to middle school ELs using examples related to topics, content, and themes. Palumbo and Sanacore (2009) believe that teachers can help middle school minority students increase their vocabulary by integrating literacy and content area instruction. At the classroom level this involves the following:

1. Reviewing word recognition and word analysis skills (e.g., prefixes, suffixes, and Latin and Greek roots), as well as phonics elements (e.g., rimes and vowel patterns)
2.. Using a variety of research-based strategies (e.g., word maps, wide and varied reading)
3. Providing frequent opportunities for repeated practice with words to develop fluency through repeated reading activities (e.g., Readers' Theater, Curriculum-Based Readers' Theater, radio reading)
4. Providing time for students to read and opportunities to share authentic, cross-curricular texts

Hall, Burns, and Edwards (2011) recommend that teachers teach diverse students in middle school using culturally grounded instruction, which utilizes students' funds of experiential knowledge to help them learn academic vocabulary. The steps involved include the guidelines introduced by Graves (2000) that we gave earlier in this chapter, but add the need to immerse students in language through rich reading and writing activities.

## SUMMARY

Developing the vocabulary skills of struggling readers must be an instructional priority for teachers in all grades. Teachers must also make sure that they provide vocabulary instruction to meet the needs of the diverse students in class who struggle with reading (Hall et al., 2011). In looking back to our case study of Catherine, we can see that struggling readers need direct/explicit teaching with meaningful interaction with their teachers. They also need teachers to support their efforts to learn words independently. Teachers who recognize the influence communities, families, and cultures have on students' vocabulary development and understanding of a variety of text (McIntyre, Hulan, & Layne, 2011) and use this knowledge to develop word consciousness in students will equip them with the skills they need to reach higher levels of achievement.

Robust vocabulary instruction has the needed evidenced-based foundation to guide teachers in working with struggling readers. For young readers, robust vocabulary instruction involves selecting and teaching words from expository texts as opposed to narratives to emphasize content vocabulary and concepts that can be challenging and complex (Beck & McKeown; 2001; Coyne, Simmons, & Kame'enui, 2004). It also involves devoting instructional time to teaching high-utility words, words that students will encounter in writing, comprehending, and responding to text, and using active instructional techniques (i.e., questioning, explaining, and clarifying) to teach these words (Beck & McKeown, 2005). We believe that the methods and intensity of vocabulary instruction are essential components of classroom interventions for struggling readers.

## REFLECTION QUESTIONS

1.  In the case of Catherine, how could Mrs. Schneider use her knowledge of Catherine's family situation with the death of her father to choose texts and vocabulary instruction that make connections to handling grief?
2.  How can teachers work more effectively with school resource personnel (EL, special education, and so on) to plan differentiated vocabulary instruction for struggling readers in classroom-based instruction?
3.  What new resources are available for teachers to use for vocabulary instruction in content areas with struggling readers?
4.  What additional support and knowledge do teachers need in order to provide vocabulary instruction for struggling readers at the primary, intermediate, or middle school level?

# CHAPTER 8

# Enabling Students' Reading Comprehension and Access to Complicated Texts with Guided Instruction

Katherine Paterson, award-winning author of children's and youth literature, advises: "It is not enough to simply teach children to read; we have to give them something worth reading. Something that will stretch their imaginations—something that will help them make sense of their own lives and encourage them to reach out toward people whose lives are quite different from their own" (retrieved October 1, 2011, from http://www. literacyla.org/quotes.htm). We would add that worthwhile reading not only engages our imagination but our thoughts and our goals; it is the bridge to constructing new knowledge and traveling to new worlds. And as we pursue new knowledge in texts that we read, we encounter multiple texts. Some texts are more difficult than others, due to density of concepts, vocabulary, organizational patterns, and many other factors.

The variety of text styles is the beauty of texts, but for struggling readers the varying styles and difficulty levels can be hurdles to successful reading. These hurdles, however, can be overcome with appropriate instruction. This chapter focuses directly on instruction aimed at moving students into increasingly more complicated texts, accelerating their reading levels, and providing access to content and texts that might otherwise remain inaccessible to them. It continues our theme of demonstrating instructional actions that can change the trajectory of students who are struggling in school. The game changer for these students is strong comprehension instruction, instruction that

- builds on what students know and builds new knowledge
- is concept oriented
- provides access to multiple texts
- provides cross-curricular connections
- is led by students' own questions and productions demonstrating their knowledge

## CASE ANALYSIS: COLIN REVISITED

In Chapter 1, we introduced you to Colin and his fifth-grade teacher, Ms. Schull. Recall that Ms. Schull's class was reading an excerpt from the C. S. Lewis Narnia series. This excerpt appeared in the reading literature anthology chosen by the school district for fifth-grade literacy instruction. Ms. Schull's class of 27 students sat in small groups of four to six students around square tables. They were taking turns reading aloud text sections that were assigned to them on the spot. Ms. Schull followed a version of "popcorn reading" in which she pulled popsicle sticks with student names at random from a jar to identify who would be the next reader.

When it was his turn, Colin read with little expression, and when he finished, he put his head down on the desk while other children were reading aloud. He did not contribute to class discussions about the text. As we described in Chapter 1, Colin often paused or misread words when he read orally, and he did not attempt to self-correct these changes, even when meaning was changed. Ms. Schull is concerned about Colin's lack of comprehension and interest in the material they are reading in class.

### CASE QUESTIONS

1. How can comprehension instruction provide access to texts when content is unfamiliar or uninteresting to students?
2. What are ways to engage students in the (oral and silent) reading and discussion of texts?
3. Surviving in harsh conditions is a central concept of the Narnia text read in this classroom. How can Ms. Schull help students draw real-life connections to this concept with the use of alternate texts or supplementary activities?

## CONCEPTUALIZING INSTRUCTION

As we have documented across our chapters, instructional planning begins with the students—determining what they know, what interests them, and understanding how they engage in reading and writing. Decades of research has identified numerous comprehension problems that students experience, yet instruction is often misdirected, focusing on bits of the reading process rather than engaging students in meaningful text reading and writing (Gormley & McDermott, 2011). This is especially the case for students experiencing reading difficulties.

Emphasis is on performance (as in Colin's class where students read aloud and fluency is checked), and it is assumed that one text and whole-class instruction will work for everyone. In this classroom instruction does not provide support for reading more complicated literature and subject area texts, leaving students with reading comprehension problems further and further behind. They are not provided access to the texts and content that engage successful students. Impoverished instruction, as we discussed in the word learning and word identification chapter (Chapter 6), is the coin of the realm (Cummins, 2007), and the instructional trajectory is disabling for too many students who experience difficulties with school instruction.

> Strong comprehension instruction can address and resolve each of these possible reasons for comprehension problems. *That is the good news.* However, instruction may not attend to these difficulties, or in some cases can contribute to them. *That is the bad news.*

## Comprehension Difficulties Students Experience

Students experience reading comprehension difficulties for many reasons.

- Sometimes students with reading comprehension problems focus more on pronouncing words correctly or reading with fluency than they focus on meaning. Often this occurs when they have come to believe that "sounding like a good reader" or "reading fast" is more important than comprehension. The turn taking to read aloud in Colin's classroom is sending the wrong message to students about the purpose for reading.

- Others have experiences and background knowledge that are different from what is needed for understanding the texts they are reading. This occurs when students are asked to read texts that have few or no connections to their lives out of school or their cultural and linguistic histories. The texts or content are not experientially, culturally, or linguistically relevant, making it difficult to bring prior knowledge to the text to aid comprehension.

- Even when students have a general understanding of topics, such as traveling to a mysterious place, an insufficient knowledge about specific concepts or information (e.g., the role of Prince Caspian in the struggle for Narnia) may intrude on comprehension.

- Students who have not learned strategies for accommodating text structures and organizations have difficulty accessing the features and organizational styles of some texts and using these features to support their comprehension (Risko, Walker-Dalhouse, Bridges, & Wilson, 2011). For example, new forms of texts, such as digital texts that have multiple visual and audio images, often presented simultaneously, may hold promise for engaging interest and supporting comprehension, but unless used strategically, they can intrude on students' comprehension (Cope & Kalantzis, 2000).

- Students may have insufficient strategies for aiding (e.g., activating relevant prior knowledge, visualizing content) or monitoring (e.g., question asking, rereading for meaning) their comprehension.

- Students may have difficulty with particular aspects of comprehension. For example, some students can identify facts but have difficulty identifying big ideas or main ideas, or making inferences, or evaluating the worth of the text information. These students have learned to do a "close read" of the text, noting details and facts, but have not learned how to relate these to important central concepts. Often central concepts and main ideas are not stated literally, requiring the reader to make inferences and/or draw analogies to similar events or circumstances. To complicate matters, making inferences and drawing analogies requires sufficient prior knowledge to enable students to read beyond the facts.

- Conversely, students may recognize main ideas but have difficulty supporting their interpretations with facts and details that are credible and substantial. As we describe in Chapter 4 on anchored instruction, often students don't use the knowledge they are acquiring for problem solving (e.g., Now that I know this fact or idea, how can I use it for problem solving? What are the conditions and circumstances where it is useful to apply what I am learning?).

## Comprehension Instruction as a Game Changer

Throughout this text we recommend different forms of comprehension instruction. So far we have discussed comprehension instruction that is culturally responsive (Chapter 2), comprehension instruction that is supported by student inquiry learning, cross-curricular connections, and teaching big ideas through anchored instruction (Chapter 4), and comprehension instruction that focuses on strategies for developing vocabulary and concepts (Chapter 7). In this chapter we discuss comprehension instruction that involves guided text discussions that are sharply different from the instruction in Colin's classroom. We also discuss specifically how instruction can accommodate and support students' reading of complicated texts. The long-term goal for students' reading instruction is to provide access to a variety of texts, including those on or beyond the instructional-level. We agree with standards statements, such as the Common Core State Standards, that students should have access to instructional-level texts. Yet teachers need to assess the texts used for instruction and, as we describe, provide instruction and texts that are appropriate for students' successful reading. Taken together, our four chapters focus on reading comprehension and provide multiple instructional directions for addressing reading comprehension difficulties.

*Teacher and students guiding text discussions.* Instructional text discussions should provide both (a) teacher guidance and explicit instruction and (b) student-directed learning that is guided by their own questions and productions. Ensuring that both elements are present during instruction is important for all students, but especially important for the students who may have limited comprehension of the chosen texts or low engagement. Students with comprehension difficulties benefit from teacher demonstrations of strategies and self-monitoring, and both teachers and students benefit from students' generation of questions that are genuinely important to them. Students' participation and question asking can help teachers understand the students' perspectives, their understandings and misconceptions, and help students direct their own learning.

> The long-term goal for guided text discussions is for teachers to guide less and less and for students to direct their learning and applications of information to real-world events and problem solving.

Teacher-guided text discussions enable opportunities for specific instruction on all aspects of reading—student engagement, making connections with text ideas, word learning, setting purposes for reading, vocabulary and concept development, and comprehension. Such instruction occurs most optimally in small groups. Teachers can demonstrate how they use strategies to enhance and monitor student understanding and learning. Instruction then can occur while previewing the text, during the reading when students pause to think aloud and to discuss text ideas, and after the reading. In the rest of the chapter, we organize our instructional suggestions around times when teachers preview or introduce texts, deepen comprehension during and after reading, and invite production (students' use and application of newly learned information). Throughout these instructional suggestions, we emphasize that comprehension is more than recalling the facts and details; it is constructed by bridging personal connections and new knowledge, and it is mediated through students' sharing of ideas and learning from others (teacher, peers).

***Engaging students in text talk and productions.*** The second part of this instruction is providing multiple and daily opportunities for students to talk about what they are reading and learning, to conjecture and ask questions about new ideas and information that is important to them, to confirm their hunches, and to engage in problem solving. And as students acquire new knowledge, they share their interpretations of events and concepts and teach each other, becoming experts or knowledgeable others. Part of the instruction should engage students in productions and applications of what they are learning. They may produce multiple forms of displays to demonstrate what they are learning, such as plays, written essays or arguments, digital stories, or movie trailers. And in the process of producing these displays, students are reexamining their questions and their understandings, reconstructing information in their own words and influenced by their prior knowledge, seeking additional information in multiple texts, and deepening their knowledge.

## Preparing for Comprehension Instruction

As we review the information shared by Ms. Schull, we consider reasons for Colin's behaviors. It could be that the Narnia passage does not make sense to him. He has limited prior knowledge of the characters or the mysterious trips to Narnia, and he expressed disinterest in fantasy; thus the concepts became inaccessible to him. It is difficult to understand texts that have no connections to prior knowledge, experiences, or interests.

***Assessing students' strengths and difficulties.*** Ms. Schull began to gather additional information about Colin. She noted that Colin is "shy" and "quiet" in class, but that when she observed him working in small groups he had a "good sense of humor" and often seemed to be a contributing member to group discussions or project work. She said that he is one of the students who had not read the Narnia books or seen the movies previously, but that he had read portions of a Harry Potter book; he told her that he didn't "like that kind of book."

On the most recent norm-referenced standardized reading achievement test administered by the school district, Colin performed at the 75th percentile on word analysis, 16th percentile on vocabulary, 15th percentile on comprehension, 45th percentile on social studies, and 44th percentile on science. Ms. Schull collected additional assessment information that included oral reading samples, think alouds, and retellings. She noted his higher score for word analysis as compared to the vocabulary and comprehension scores. She attributed the relative higher scores on social studies and science to his interest in these subjects.

Ms. Schull asked Colin to read aloud the second paragraph of a page from the Narnia text and took a running record (see Figure 8.1). Colin paused at times throughout the text (sometimes rereading as evidenced by his subvocalizations) and these pauses seemed to help his fluency as he read on. Colin had five word substitutions (*play* for *playboxes*, *traction* for *junction*, "jour" for *journey*, "ten- tem-time" for *term-time*, and *board* for *boarding*). Three of these were self-corrected; *traction* for *junction* and "tem-time" for *term-time* were not. Not counting self-corrections or pauses as errors, Colin's word accuracy was 99%. Ms. Schull hypothesized that the two words that remained uncorrected did not hold meaning for Colin and the text provided insufficient information to support hypothesizing about their meanings. She noted that Colin did use phonics and word parts (e.g., "play" of *playboxes*, "-tion" in *junction*) while attempting to pronounce the substituted words, including those words he self-corrected.

Two days later, Colin read two paragraphs that occurred later in the story. Once again, there was high accuracy (100% accuracy). All substituted words were self-corrected and pauses were not counted as errors. Notice in Figure 8.1 that Colin reread sections where substitutions occurred, and it seemed that he was rereading for meaning and self-correcting. When Ms. Schull asked him about his self-correction of *wading* (changing the short /a/ vowel sound to long /a/ vowel sound), Colin explained that the first reading didn't make sense and he thought about being at the beach and *wading* (with long /a/ sound) in the water.

Ms. Schull viewed this information as helpful. It seems that Colin is reading for meaning, when there is sufficient text information or prior knowledge to support his fix-up strategies. He also uses phonics and word parts to help him pronounce unknown words. Story-specific word phrases, such as a *train junction* or *term-time feelings,* require prior knowledge and can be accessed with instruction that demonstrates how to seek additional information about story context.

On subsequent days, Ms. Schull had individual conferences with several students. She asked Colin to reread silently the first seven paragraphs

## Figure 8.1. Running Record of Colin's Oral Reading

Oral reading # 1, second paragraph of Narnia excerpt

That had all happened a year ago, and now all four of them were sitting on a seat
at a railway station with trunks and playboxes piled up around them. They were, in fact,
on their way back to school. They had traveled together as far as this station, which was
a junction; and here, in a few minutes, one train would arrive and take the girls away to
one school, and in about half an hour another train would arrive and the boys would go
off to another school. The first part of their journey, when they were all together, always
seemed to be part of the holidays; but now when they would be saying good-by and going
different ways so soon, everyone felt that the holidays were really over, and everyone felt
his or her term-time feelings beginning again, and they were all rather gloomy and no one
could think of anything to say. Lucy was going to boarding school for the first time.

*P. pausing*

Oral reading #2, Paragraphs 26 and 27

"Not a bit of it," said Peter. "if there are streams, they're bound to come down to
the sea, and if we walk along the beach, we're bound to come to them."
They all now waded back and went first across the smooth, wet sand, then up to
the dry, crumbly sand that sticks to one's toes and began putting on their shoes and
socks. Edmund and Lucy wanted to leave them behind and do their exploring with bare
feet, but Susan said this would be a mad thing to do. "We might never find them again,"
she pointed out, "and we shall want them if we're still here when night comes and it
begins to be cold."

*word x word*

of the story and to pause to explain his thinking after each paragraph (see Figure 8.2). Then she asked Colin to continue reading silently two additional pages and when finished to retell what he had read (see Figure 8.3). Good comprehension instruction is responsive to students' strengths and instructional needs.

On both assessments, Colin shared literal details, almost word for word from the text. He organized the information in the same sequence as appeared in the text and often quoted directly from the text. Taken together, Ms. Schull identified additional strengths and instructional needs.

> Good comprehension instruction is responsive to students' strengths and instructional needs.

First, Colin uses several strategies that are helpful for his reading comprehension. At times, he rereads and self-corrects his miscues to make sense. When he substitutes words, he often reads parts of the words correctly—such as reading the final suffix correctly in *junction*, when he said the word *traction*. Second, we noted that he is quiet and shy in class, and the procedure to take turns reading aloud for everyone in the class may be uncomfortable for him. Unfortunately, forms of turn taking for oral reading of texts are popular in classrooms, despite research that indicates it is not helpful for building fluency or comprehension (Ash, Kuhn, & Walpole, 2009) and may contribute to students' stressful and avoidance reactions to reading (Ivey, 1999; Opitz & Rasinski, 1998). Also, students are typically asked to read a paragraph or two and when they are so concentrated on performative aspects of reading (reading for their peers)

---

*Figure 8.2. Colin's Think Aloud Performance on First Seven Paragraphs of Narnia*

P1:  There are four children.  Peter, Susan, Edmund, and Lucy. There was a book, about a Lion and a Witch. They went to a strange country called Narnia. No one noticed they were away.

P2:  They were going back to school . . . the girls going to one school and the boys to another school. They were sad and didn't say nothing.

P3:  They were the only ones at the train station.

P4:  Lucy was crying.  Then they were yelling at each other . . . stop hitting me.

P5:  They were afraid.  They were being pulled away and they were scared.

P6:  They were being pulled to another place.

P7:  Lucy said is it Narnia again?

---

*Figure 8.3. Colin's Retelling Two Pages of Narnia*

There were four kids on an Island. They were Lucy, Susan, Edmund, and Peter. At the beginning of the story they were going back to school and they were sad. They were waiting for their school bus. Someone yelled . . . stop hitting me. Then they were pulled to another place. Maybe Narnia Lucy said. They went to a cool place and they were glad to be there and not at school. But they they were thirsty and hungry. They found a stream and drank the water. They ate their sandwiches and looked for more food. They did not know where they were. They were kinda scared but they were glad to not be in school.

they can lose the flow of the text and connections to ideas across the text as a whole. Third, we learned that he focuses on literal details and that he seldom discusses main ideas or makes connections between texts he reads in school and his life experiences.

**Assessing the text.** The text Ms. Schull chose is a complicated text. It is a narrative, and students who have a history of being successful when reading narratives typically find narratives easier to read. Their familiarity with narrative characteristics, such as plot development or character development, aids their comprehension. Just the opposite could be the case for some students who prefer other forms of texts, such as informational texts or graphic novels.

*The Island* by C. S. Lewis is a narrative, but it is an excerpt from a larger text and consequently does not provide the "full story" of the Narnia series that would help students understand this excerpt; thus it appears out-of-context of the larger rich narrative, *The Lion, the Witch and the Wardrobe*.

Starting with the first paragraph of *The Island*, the text is loaded with information and this information seems to follow a simple listing arrangement, with one fact following another across the sentences and few elaborations on the details. There are four children, introduced by their names of Peter, Susan, Edmund, and Lucy. We are told they had a remarkable adventure as told in *The Lion, the Witch and the Wardrobe* in which the children had entered a mysterious world by walking through the opened door of a magic wardrobe. And when there, the children became kings and queens and reigned for years and years. Yet when they returned home to England, they learned that no time had passed at all. No one noticed that they had ever been away.

In the second paragraph, we learn that this story occurs one year later and the four children are sitting at a junction waiting for a train to take them back to boarding school. One train will come for the girls and another train will take the boys back to their school. Lucy is going to boarding school for the first time. They are feeling sad that the holidays are over and beginning to regret the "term-time feelings" that are overtaking them. As they are sitting there, they feel jabs at their arms. These jabs feel like stings from insects. And they feel they are being pulled away from this train junction.

Students familiar with the story *The Lion, the Witch and the Wardrobe* could read these two paragraphs and fill in the spaces between the sentences by inferring what is about to happen—the students will be taken to Narnia again. But those unfamiliar with the story, such as Colin, might find it difficult to infer all the connections that are needed to understand that this story is a fantasy, that they may go to a world where children can become kings and queens, that the children lived in a place called England, and that it is possible that no one will miss the children while they are gone. Also, they would need to understand vocabulary, such as *wardrobe*, *boarding school*, and *junction*.

***Assessing the instructional goals and reading activities.*** Ms. Schull provided a quick introduction to the reading. She told her students that they would read a story about the children who had gone to Narnia. She asked the students if they knew about Narnia and if they had read the book, *The Lion, the Witch, and the Wardrobe*. A few students raised their hands. Ms. Schull then went on to say that these four children from the Narnia books were waiting at a train junction for a train to take them back to school and then asked her students to predict what might occur. She wrote these predictions on the board as students generated them. They included the following: the four would fall asleep and miss the train; the students would have a new adventure; the four would go someplace else other than school.

This introduction was not optimal. Ms. Schull's very brief introduction to the new text initiated discussion around the first few paragraphs of the story but not the central ideas of the text. Vocabulary, such as *junction*, were not defined or related to the actions of waiting for a train to take them back to school. Further, it is doubtful that students unfamiliar with Narnia had sufficient information to set their own purposes for reading or to generate questions that they hoped would be answered when reading—the teacher had her purpose established, but students did not.

## MAXIMIZING THE BENEFITS OF GUIDED TEXT INSTRUCTION

Ms. Schull's guided text instruction did little to benefit Colin's engagement or comprehension. This instruction should provide both teacher guidance and explicit instruction (e.g., demonstrations of previewing strategies), and student-directed learning (e.g., generating questions that they want to answer as they read). Optimal text instruction involves several elements, starting with the instructional goals for text previews.

Previewing text is very important for students who have comprehension difficulties (Alvarez & Risko, 2010). They are especially important for students, such as Colin, who recall details more than main ideas and central concepts and for students who fail to make inferences and understand nuanced ideas that often are embedded in complex texts. In the short term, teachers are demonstrating how they approach reading a new text by asking questions about the author's intentions for the text and identifying main ideas that might develop as they read the text. In the long term, students who practice this form of previewing with teachers learn to do this independently as a strategy for improving their reading comprehension. Previews can accomplish several goals simultaneously as they (a) focus on central text concepts; (b) activate students' prior knowledge and/or build new knowledge of these central concepts; and (c) evoke students' curiosity and personal questions to guide their engagement and deeper comprehension of text concepts.

## Teaching Central Concepts

Central concepts represent higher order information often implied by authors. They are often related to enduring issues that engage students in making real-world connections and applying problem-solving strategies. For example, students reading about challenges explorers faced during the westward expansion in U.S. history may relate these challenges to those faced by the students in Narnia who are stranded on an unknown island.

Additionally, these concepts represent the deeper meanings of texts, often representing disciplinary information that is required for enriching knowledge in the domains of science, math, social studies, literature, and visual and performing arts. These academic concepts can be particularly difficult for students, especially language minority students, who struggle with comprehension (Lesaux & Kieffer, 2010; Lesaux, Kieffer, Faller, & Kelley, 2010) if they have not had access previously to this content.

Too often, attention to central concepts is overlooked in comprehension instruction (Alvarez & Risko, 2010; Walmsley, 2006). When students can't access meaning for these concepts, they are forced to focus instead on lower level information, the details and facts that are more easily remembered. As students acquire disciplinary knowledge, such as understanding the science of survivorship, they begin to use this knowledge as a tool for solving the dangers of being stranded without food and water.

> Students with reading comprehension difficulties benefit from engaging in discussion about central text ideas during a preview activity.

This use of knowledge is the ultimate goal for success in academic learning (Gee, 2003; Lemke, 1990).

Usually there is more than one central concept and almost always these concepts are implied rather than stated explicitly. Teachers choose the one that makes sense for instruction—the curricular goals, students' interest, or other connections that allow backward mapping to content taught previously or foreshadowing content that is coming up later in the school year.

For the Narnia series, for example, there are at least two choices for the central concepts, such as surviving without food and water on a desolate and mysterious island or magical powers as characterized in mythology and fantasy texts. Either *survivorship* or *characteristics of mythology* is an overarching concept to which story details can be linked.

Recall how Ms. Schull introduced the Narnia passage to her students. She read aloud the brief introduction of the text and asked students to predict what might happen to the children when they were left alone at the train junction. Students predicted that they might fall asleep and miss the train. Additionally, they said that they would find another place to go instead of school or that they will feel sad about leaving their families. Notice that the discussion did not signal attention to the more important and central concepts of this story. Instead, it provided a detour into lower order information that does not set up a pathway for understanding more important text information.

## Activating and Extending Prior Knowledge, But Selectively

Previews are often used to encourage students to activate prior knowledge. We want students to realize that they know something about the text they will be reading. There are two caveats that we emphasize when thinking about activating students' prior knowledge: (1) help students be selective; and (2) take time to hear students' comments and questions. Helping students be selective when activating prior knowledge is useful for staying focused on the topic; going too far afield to less important details (e.g., living on an island, dangers of traveling on the water to a strange land) may distract from, rather than support, comprehension of central ideas. When students share their knowledge about any one of the experiences related to the central themes, such as surviving in Narnia, they make visible their interests and information that can be used to make connections to the text—these are the cultural funds of knowledge (Moll, Amanti, Neff, & Gonzalez, 1992) that they are learning from their family, in their community, and within out-of-school activities that they bring to the reading of the text.

## Previewing to Promote Curiosity and Inquiry

Previews should pique students' curiosity and interest in the text's central concept(s) and at the same time build knowledge. Thus the preview discussion is not an opportunity for the teacher to simply *tell* students the topic (or even the central concept) and ask what they know—a mistake commonly made. Instead, there should be minimal teacher talk with an emphasis on eliciting students' connections and questions. Teachers might join in the conversations to model question asking, making predictions, and identifying what is not understood. At this stage of the conversation, all student offerings are valued and records are kept (perhaps on the whiteboard or on classroom charts); there is no attempt to reach consensus as all questions go forward.

## Previewing to Sow Seeds of Interest

Resources (e.g., illustrations or photos, videos, YouTube student presentations, historical documents, or artifacts) embedded in the previewing activity are a useful and often authentic means for introducing students to the text's central concept and related material. Typically, one resource is all that is needed. For example, Ms. Schull could show a short clip from one of the Narnia movies—a movie clip in which the children are taken to a strange land. After viewing this, students engage in a discussion about what happened and what problems they might face. Students' generation of questions are as important as (and maybe even more important than) teachers' questions (Bransford, Brown, & Cocking, 1999) for guiding self-directed learning and engagement. And if all questions are accepted as valid contributions to the discussion, struggling readers who otherwise might avoid participating slowly begin to become active members of the class discussion; differences between the participation of good and poor readers begin to disappear (Kelly & Turner, 2009).

Other resources that could be equally powerful might include a few pages from a relevant graphic novel, for example, *The Lion, the Witch and the Wardrobe: A Graphic Novel* by C. S. Lewis, illustrated and edited by Robin Lawrie (1995). This novel could be part of the classroom library and familiar to the students or it could be introduced with selected illustrations to start the conversation of *The Island* text. Graphic novels can be highly engaging as they have multiple illustrations that elaborate on content. Graphic novels are particularly good at being graphic—vivid, realistic, detailed. They offer illustrations, dialogue and commentary, and text and color cues to support comprehension. These multimodal texts are a reality of the contemporary and global textual environment (Cope & Kalantzis, 2000; Risko, Walker-Dalhouse, Bridges, & Wilson, 2011). Multiple forms and features, including digital and multimodality features, of texts affect comprehension and personal connections (Mills, 2010; Turbill, 2001).

Alternatively, Ms. Schull could choose historical resources, since these may appeal to students, such as Colin, who are interested in historical materials. For example, she might choose *A Picture Book of Lewis and Clark* by David Adler (2003), *or Lewis and Clark: Explorers of the American West* by Stephen Kroll (1996). Both have powerful illustrations of the hardships and challenges the explorers faced when traveling to remote parts of the United States. Or Ms. Schull could refer to *The Starving Time: Elizabeth's Jamestown Colony* (Hermes, 2001), choosing the photo that depicts the colonists' problems with lack of food and the quote "it is hard to imagine being so hungry that one eats worms" (p. 105) to open discussion.

Engaging students in the discussion of the selected artifact or resource encourages students' noticing and questioning (Bransford, Brown, & Cocking, 1999) while activating interest. Text content is more accessible when students begin the reading with rich information that is relevant to central concepts and with their own questions. And as such, previewing takes little more time than a teacher *telling* students the purpose for reading, questions to be answered, and the "topic for today's reading." Typically, in this form of instruction, teachers own the information rather than the students.

## READING TO DEEPEN COMPREHENSION

Setting the stage for a good exchange of information during the preview follows naturally into reading the text and discussions that elaborate on the central text concept. Rather than stopping after a few sentences or paragraphs to check for recognition of details or facts, relationship of these ideas to the central concept introduced in the preview is emphasized. Text discussions are often shallow and ineffectual (RAND Reading Study Group, 2002) with a focus mainly (or solely) on the details—they encourage students to memorize facts which could be why the details are what students remember the most (Scott, Jamieson-Noel, & Asselin, 2003).

Students with comprehension problems often read texts linearly. This problem can be exacerbated with instruction that "walks" students through the material in a linear progression. For example, the teacher may guide students' discussion by asking questions like "*What is this about?*

*What happens next? What is next?"*—adding up facts that may or may not connect easily to the central concepts. Such a progression neglects major concepts and underrepresents the depth of meaning offered by the author. It also helps explain how readers can become bound by facts and lower order information.

Instead, text discussions during reading should enable students to mentally (or actually) map details onto the central concepts (Asan, 2007; Gowin & Alvarez, 2005). To capture the multiple episodes and story development of *The Chronicles of Narnia*, for example, it may be useful for students to begin drawing a hierarchical concept map as they read, with the central concept "Conflicts of Power" in the center and higher order circle (see Figure 8.4).

In descending circles, arranged hierarchically, are supporting details, such as the evil deeds of new King Miraz, the rescue of Prince Caspian by dwarfs who honor him as their king, the battles between Narnians and the King's army, and so on. Students may attempt to memorize all the facts associated with the multiple conflicts, but by organizing what may

*Figure 8.4. Concept Map for Conflicts of Power*

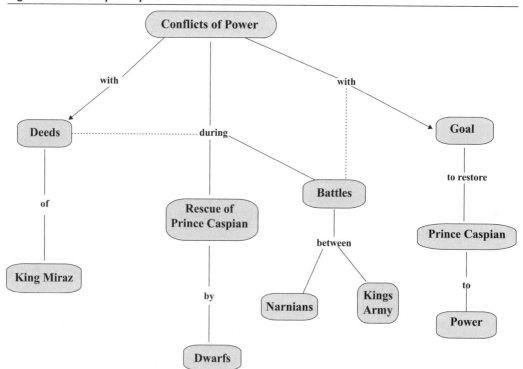

seem to be disparate facts (and conflicts), the concept map helps them draw connections across these and note relationships and how conflicts influence each other and relate to the central goal of overcoming the evil King Miraz and restoring Caspian to power. Guided by teacher modeling of how connections may be made, students are learning strategies for making comparisons and contrasts, linking details to main ideas, and explaining relationships among ideas; all involve strategy learning and the teacher makes these strategies explicit when they are in use for the learning activity.

As students complete the mapping of the ideas, they are rereading to find supporting details to support their hunches, using additional comprehension strategies, as to where to place information on their conceptual map. Other forms of organization can be used, such as story maps that develop the central plot and subplots. These hierarchical organizations help students recall the facts and also trace relationships among major ideas and the facts; knowledge organization is needed to increase the likelihood that students will draw on major concepts when solving problems and when drawing on previously learned information to form relationships with new content (Heller & Reif, 1984).

Embedded in this discussion is attention to vocabulary, both academic vocabulary related to central concepts (e.g., *reign* of king and queen, *confederates* of the army) and supportive vocabulary related to the development of the narrative or expository information (e.g., *term-time feelings, boarding school, jabs like stings*). Teaching words for texts under study increases word learning and text comprehension (Beck, McKeown, & Kucan, 2002, 2008).

Cognitive scientist Daniel Willingham (2010) recently argued that reading comprehension is shallow if we are not teaching the content—of narratives, of history and science texts, of visual arts, and so on. He goes on to assert that we teach reading strategies as though once mastered, students' comprehension will improve. Instead, he argues that the "mainspring of comprehension is prior knowledge" or the new knowledge they are developing that enables them to construct their understandings.

To demonstrate how this might work, please read the following paragraph and answer the five questions. *Do Not Look Ahead to the Paragraph that Appears After the Questions!*

Four kitterings travel through a miscabab. They are in the fettles of Narnia. It is important for the kitterings to be there because they help pugiland Narnia from the florad lerlas. A sigment and symegant mata uglaled them.

1. How many kitterings are traveling? (four)
2. What do the kitterings travel through? (miscabab)
3. Where are the kitterings? (in the fettles of Narnia)
4. Why is it important for the kitterings to be there? (because they help pugiland Narnia from the florad lerlas)
5. What uglaled them? (a sigment and symegant mata)

We have just demonstrated that you could answer these five questions and not understand the passage!

Now go back to the passage above and try to use your comprehension strategies, such as predicting, questioning, interpreting, comparing and contrasting, clarifying misunderstandings, and relating to prior knowledge. Can you predict what might occur next? Or can you interpret what is happening? Can you compare and contrast the kitterings and the mata? Most of these strategies would not help you comprehend this passage without some knowledge of the main concepts and the events. However, when you read the following paragraph, all these strategies can be useful to deepen understandings.

Four children travel through a wardrobe. They find themselves in the land of Narnia. It is important for them to be there because they help to free Narnia from the evil leaders. A mysterious and mystical lion helps them.

Willingham and others are reminding us that knowledge combined with strategy instruction fosters comprehension.

## Deepening Comprehension with Further Analysis

As students complete their reading and discuss information as described above, it is helpful for teachers to (a) ask students to take different perspectives as they analyze what they have just read, and (b) draw students' attention to text features and strategies for accommodating these features to support their comprehension.

***Perspective taking.*** Some students may take the perspective of Lucy, who advises the group to follow Aslan to save time in their travels to save Caspian, deciding on how she came to this conclusion and how she feels when the others don't take her advice. Similarly, students could take the perspective of other characters, tracing their motives and actions and

> Instruction should provide access to multiple levels of text, including complicated texts. Too often students identified with comprehension difficulties are held to lower level texts and denied access to the texts and content that are age and grade appropriate.

deciding how these affect the conflicts and conflict resolutions.

Or at a deeper level, students could take perspectives of fantasy fiction authors, comparing, for example, the writings of C. S. Lewis to those of J. K. Rowling, author of the Harry Potter series. Or they could compare the C. S. Lewis versions of Narnia to the versions of the stories represented in movies, taking the perspectives of the author versus the screenwriters.

Taking different perspectives helps students to deepen their comprehension of the text and build expertise on particular aspects of the text. Students read additional materials for their inquiry project as they develop personal and shared expertise. They explore different perspectives and share their expertise with their peers or in projects they develop. Organizing and presenting what they are learning has multiple benefits for deepening students' own learning, extending their application of academic content and vocabulary (Ogle & Correa-Kovtun, 2010) and advancing abilities to study concepts from different perspectives.

***Accommodating text features.*** Texts' organizational features impact students' comprehension (Meyer & Wijekumar, 2007) and thus are included in instruction focusing on analysis of texts. Many teachers are quite successful in enhancing students' comprehension engagement when they include multiple forms of texts in their instruction (Duke & Bennett-Armistead, 2003), as text sets around central themes can provide a variety of leveled texts to accommodate different reading levels in the classroom. And optimal use of these texts can enrich and deepen students' knowledge and comprehension. Yet with each new text structure come challenges to comprehension for some students. For example, digital texts may have multiple formats occurring simultaneously—images and sounds appearing simultaneously with background music and movements that may be related in tangential ways to the main ideas of the images. Such features are not typical in conventional texts (Cope & Kalantzis, 2000) and students need to be prepared for demands of text that may be unfamiliar to them.

We discussed earlier the possible use of the Narnia graphic novel. As we examine one page (Lewis, 1995, illustrated by Lawrie) (see Figure 8.5), we notice that the organizational patterns of the Narnia text could be problematic for comprehension. This alerts us to the importance of preparing

*Figure 8.5. Text Clues for Reading The Narnia Graphic Novel*

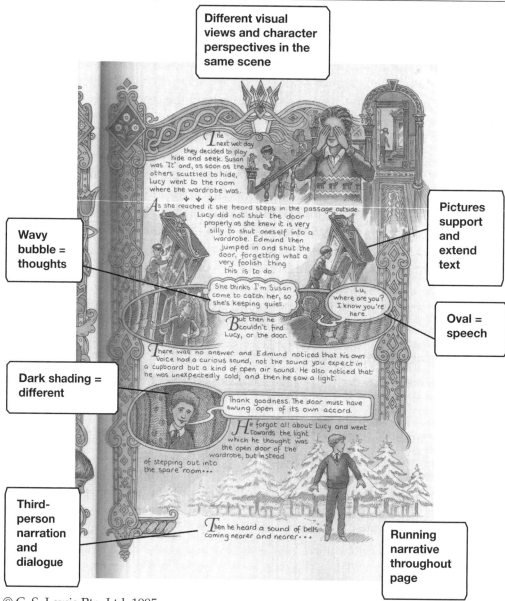

students for the text structure they will encounter. For example, it would be helpful to explain that characters in images are in two different locations but brought together by the illustrator to connect story ideas. The dark shading provided by the illustrator is a clue to the secondary location of a character. The text boxes also take different shapes to alert the reader to different messages, such as narration versus speech of characters. There is much to notice on this page, including how the story line is developed in two different ways—one story line is told through the images and accompanying talk and narration, and the other is told through the running text at the bottom of the page.

Wordless picture books and graphic novels are wonderful resources to support students' comprehension across grade levels (Tiedt, 2000) as the images can really be "worth a thousand words" for some students (Hibbing & Rankin-Erickson, 2003; Maderazo et al., 2010). Yet we noted that students may have difficulty relating the images to the continuing story line, especially when different stories are developed in each. Loss of meaning can occur (Risko, Walker-Dalhouse, Bridges, & Wilson, 2011). Alerting students to text elements and guided discussion of the parts can support students' ability to relate the details to the overall story line that is developing.

Additionally, careful previewing and providing access to central text concepts (as with artifacts such as historical documents or photos or movie clips) is especially useful for preparing students to accommodate more difficult, instructional texts. Knowledge building prior to and during the text reading, instruction on relevant and unique content vocabulary, and guided use of strategies (e.g., How does this new information help me understand text ideas?) can provide the conceptual glue that helps students fill in the gaps of a text that may otherwise be too difficult for them to comprehend (Alvarez & Risko, 2010). And such instruction is directed toward helping students read and understand increasingly difficult texts across genre and content areas.

## Producing/Demonstrating Comprehension

Students reconstruct their own understandings of novel information when they are actively engaged in organizing and reorganizing their ideas for production. Productions include any forms of expression in which students share what they are learning with others, such as writing explanatory papers for an audience, using storyboards to organize their digital stories or informational pieces, writing lyrics to a song representing character feelings, or creating dioramas or dramatic presentations. In the process of producing their understandings to share with others, students monitor and adjust their understandings.

There are many other possibilities for productions, many of which use digital technology. Students could include creating comic strips, perhaps with the support of the Comic Creator on the Read-Write-Think website (http:// www.readwritethink.org/parent-afterschool-resources/games-tools/ comic-creator-a-30237.html) or with The World's Best Way to Make Comics on the Pixton Comics website (http://www.pixton.com). It could include setting up class blogs on protected class-based websites, for students to explain their interpretations of characters' actions or to argue their likes and dislikes about the Narnia series. Providing argumentation may be well suited for blogs that invite dialogue. Conversely, short commentaries could be exchanged through microblogging, where brevity in message is the norm. Edmodo (http://www.edmodo.com) is a secure and free site for mircoblogging (Mills & Chandra, 2011).

With Narnia, in addition to blogging, students might write an argument for the contribution of fantasy fiction for understanding real-world conflicts. Or students might create movie trailers for the Narnia book they are reading. There is an example of a movie trailer with music and video developed by fifth-grade student Emily Morrow on the Internet in the You-Tube video entitled *Narnia Remix Book Trailer* (http://www.youtube.com/ watch?v=-gv4AQqC_fg). Especially helpful beyond students demonstrating what they are learning is taking the productions to real-world applications of knowledge. Movie trailers are examples of real-world materials that might be familiar to students who enjoy movies.

Creating a digital story, such as for a movie trailer, provides opportunities to revisit texts and to confirm understandings. Steps might include developing the content and arranging the sequence of presentation (on a storyboard or outline), writing the script, searching for texts and artifacts to gather and create media to include (images, sounds, video clips), accessing video editing software to produce the materials and add voiceovers/music, editing and citing media, and deciding on methods for sharing (e.g., place on class website with limited access).

Many forms of production, such as movie trailers, blogs, and digital stories involve students working together. Collaborative learning in production of multimedia texts has a positive impact on students' learning (Rojas-Drummond, Albarran, & Littleton, 2008). Multimodal texts have multiple pathways leading to comprehension, and optimally students choose the pathways (Lankshear & Knobel, 2003) guiding their productions.

## SUMMARY

How to provide access to texts when content is unfamiliar or uninteresting to students with comprehension difficulties was a fundamental question for this chapter. This dilemma often confronts teachers and requires careful planning and goals to engage students in question posing and using knowledge to produce demonstrations of what they are learning. Important to optimal instruction is an analysis of the students' strengths and problems, text features, and instructional activities with the goal to determine why students are not succeeding in current instruction. Important to instruction that was optimal for Colin were principles of comprehension instruction that (a) builds on what students know and builds new knowledge, (b) is concept oriented, (c) provides access to multiple texts, (d) provides cross-curricular connections, and (e) is led by students' own questions and productions of their knowledge. And while these principles were situated within the study of fifth-grade instruction, they apply across the grades. Once implemented, these principles can be a game changer for advancing the trajectory of students with comprehension difficulties—they facilitate access to advanced texts and content.

### REFLECTION QUESTIONS

1.  Think of a text that may be used at other grade levels. For example, you may choose the book *Knots on a Counting Rope* (Martin, Archambault, & Rand, 1997), often read to kindergarten students, or a Sherlock Holmes story read in middle school. What are the central concepts you could teach? How would you engage students in ways that show their interest in the content? How could you make connections to students' prior knowledge?
2.  Choose a few graphic novels. Examine them to identify what may appeal to your students and what connections there may be to your students' interests and your instructional goals. Identify text features that may intrude on students' comprehension and explain how you would address those potential problems.

# CHAPTER 9

# Capitalizing on Students' Families and Life Experiences

Parent and family involvement in children's education can have a significant impact on children's achievement in reading (Fan & Chen, 2001), as well as teachers' morale and self-confidence (Henderson & Mapp, 2002). Teachers need the assistance of parents if they are to meet educational demands for increased student performance. We believe that parent involvement should

- Be planned and systematic
- Involve teachers learning about students, families, and communities
- Be a collaborative partnership
- Involve parents and teachers in using community resources (Risko & Walker-Dalhouse, 2009)

## CASE ANALYSIS: WILLIAM

William Thomas is a third grader in a high-poverty school in an urban community in the Upper Midwest. He is the only child in a two-parent family. His mother works the day shift in a local factory, and his father is a long-distance truck driver. William loves to read comic books and material focusing on video games, but quickly becomes disinterested in longer text and expository text. He is interested in things that affect his community and often volunteers to work with the children's group at his church on projects such as cleaning up the neighborhood and serving meals at the local homeless shelter. At the beginning of the year William said that he was a good reader and was a little better than his friends. He admits that he does not try to understand what he reads when it does not interest him and if he does not know what the words mean.

William's parents are both high school graduates. While they read the newspaper and magazines, neither of them reads books for pleasure. They think reading is important and would like William to be a better reader. Mrs. Thomas comes home about 2 hours after William gets home from school. His grandmother comes to the house and stays with William until his mother arrives.

According to Mrs. Thomas, "The books that the teacher sends home for William to read are just too long. When I ask him to tell me what he just read, he simply says, 'I don't know.' I try not to show my anger when he goes on and on about what is happening in one of his comic books and in the magazines about his video games. Yet when William is asked to read a Bible verse in church, he makes me so proud. He reads just like the minister (with a lot of expression). Afterwards, when he gets home, he can tell me everything about what he read. I know that he got the message. If he can understand those things, why can't he understand the books his teacher sends home? I am not happy that William's test scores are low. His teachers keep telling me that I need to help him at home, but I don't know what to do. I think that they feel that I am part of the reason that his reading scores are not so good."

### CASE QUESTIONS

1. Do parents of struggling readers have a greater responsibility than parents of successful readers to work with teachers to improve their children's progress in reading?
2. Are parents of struggling readers *interested* in assuming greater responsibility than parents of successful readers for their children's reading progress?
3. If so, do they possess the knowledge and resources needed to accomplish the task?
4. What expectations for involvement do teachers have for parents of struggling readers?
5. What does this mean in terms of the teacher's responsibilities and relationship with these parents?

## PARENT INVOLVEMENT

As we examine the case study of William, we can see that text selection is a major factor in William's motivation for reading and comprehension of text.

Shields, Gordon, and Dupree (1983) found that the kind of books, not the number of books, was important in examining the differences between

> Book selection for most students is a critical feature in reading motivation.

successful and struggling African American students. Books that could hold children's interests promoted extended interactions between parents and children. Consequently, the books selected and sent home for William to read appear to be teacher-selected texts and not books tailored to William's interests. While Mrs. Thomas needs to see that William completes the required reading, she should be encouraged to help him make important cultural and personal connections that will make the text meaningful to him. Teachers can assist him by including multiethnic literature in text sets that will encourage William to explore themes and topics in the required reading in different genres of text in an effort to increase the relevance of the assigned readings and engage him as a reader.

Closer examination of William's life outside of school indicated that he was concerned about life in his community. This information should be used by teachers to provide him with a purpose for reading a variety of texts (i.e., newspapers, expository and narrative texts, and magazines) that support his social responsibility toward his community. As Wolk (2009) acknowledges, it is imperative for teachers and schools to use literature to promote a sense of social responsibility in their students. This is an opportunity to connect William's in- and out-of-school literacies and promote parent-child discussions about issues that are relevant to their lives. Because William's parents read the newspaper, it could be easily incorporated into a family routine of reading and discussing the issues using shorter, but authentic text.

Mrs. Thomas recognizes that comprehension is an essential component of reading and that questioning is one way to assess understanding. However, it is important to examine the type of questions that Mrs. Thomas might ask and provide her with question stems that can prompt inferential and critical thinking, as opposed to mere recall of explicitly stated information. Letting her know that it is the type of question rather than the number of questions that can promote thinking is also an important point to emphasize.

Clearly, teachers must recognize the different levels of knowledge that parents need to have in order to help their children who struggle with reading. Parent-teacher conferences and home visits conducted prior to or at the beginning of the school year might be structured to include the questions shown in Figure 9.1 that the parents of struggling readers might have but have difficulty expressing.

Once these questions are addressed, there should be ongoing, two-way conversations that inform parents and respond to their efforts to support

*Figure 9.1. Questions Parents Might Have*

1. I was not a good reader when I was in school; how can I help my child to be a better reader?
2. I cannot afford to pay someone to help my child with reading; where can I go in my community to get help for my child?
3. Should I set a specific time and place to work with my child on his/her reading?
4. What routine should I follow to help my child improve his/her reading?
5. Should I insist that my child read when he/she complains that he/she does not want to read?
6. Is it better to let my child choose things that he/she wants to read? Are magazines okay for them to read?
7. Should I only choose for my child books that he/she can read without getting angry or frustrated?
8. Is it better to choose books based upon my child's interests, but that he/she has to struggle to read?
9. How can I tell if my child is making the progress in reading expected of a child his/her age?
10. Why does my child like reading at home, but not at school?

their children. We recommend that home-school journals be sent on a weekly basis as one means of maintaining communication and developing a trusting relationship between the two entities (Kay, Neher, & Lush, 2010). While the structure of these journals might vary, we recommend the format found in Figure 9.2 for journal entries. Teachers must also ask themselves some critical questions as they begin to work with parents of struggling readers (see Figure 9.3).

## CONCEPTUALIZING INVOLVEMENT OF PARENTS, FAMILIES, AND COMMUNITIES

Parents must be part of the network supporting the reading development of struggling readers along with teachers and other school personnel (S. Jenkins, 2009). Parents' knowledge of their children as individuals and of the cultural and home practices that can support or hinder their literacy progress as well as their understanding of specific ways that they can contribute to their children's school success are fundamental to the communication needed to make this network work (Risko & Walker-Dalhouse, 2009).

*Figure 9.2. Structure for Journal Entry*

Date:

Progress Noted in Specific Aspect(s) of Reading

- Information should be anecdotal in nature and supported by references to specific instances of observed behavior and/or scores on formative assessment measures.
- Specific information should be conveyed in clear language that informs parents.

Next Steps

- Limit to one or two strategies that you will use for instruction and/or assessment.
- Include one recommendation for a home practice that might be used to support your efforts.

Questions/Comments

Invite parents to share their questions about the information shared above or make comments on what they have observed at home.

*Figure 9.3. Questions for Teachers*

1. Do I talk to my students' parents about their family's linguistic backgrounds and their educational expectations for their children?
2. Do I use information learned about the backgrounds of students who struggle to make connections between what they know and the content that I teach?
3. How do I attempt to establish a trusting relationship and greater communication with parents so that school and home efforts to improve the reading of struggling readers are aligned?
4. Do I use my students' knowledge, skills, and experiences outside of school to plan reading instruction or help students make connections to what they are learning?

The home environments of children affect their early reading (Snow, Burns, & Griffin, 1998) and continued development as readers, thus distinguishing successful readers from struggling readers. Significant differences have been found between successful readers versus struggling readers in the number of books present in the home, parents' education, and the frequency with which parents taught reading skills (i.e., printed letters, letter sounds, and words) (Kirby & Hogan, 2008).

Family home environments and socioeconomic status jointly and independently discriminate successful readers from struggling readers (Burgess, Hecht, & Lonigan, 2002; Bus, IJzendoorn, & Pellegrini, 1995; Kirby & Hogan, 2008; Snow, 1993). A higher proportion of children in low-income families are at greater risk for low levels of reading achievement when compared to other socioeconomic groups (Ramey & Ramey, 1998; Snow, 1993). The difficulties experienced by these children tend to be consistent in families across generations (Snow, Barnes, et al., 1991) and may seem to be an insurmountable obstacle in changing the reading trajectory of low-income, struggling readers. However, it does point to a greater need to recognize the funds of knowledge that diverse families provide and to build upon them in working collaboratively to meet the needs of the children (Moll, Velez Ibanez, & Greenberg, 1990; Ordonez-Jasis & Ortiz, 2006; B. M. Taylor, Pressley, & Pearson, 2000).

> One way that teachers can challenge their assumptions about the value that families place on reading and their history of literacy practices is through life history interviews.

A. S. Johnson (2010) received valuable information from life history interviews conducted with three generations of an African American family from a rural community in the South. She found that literacy and education were fundamental parts of the culture and traditions of the family. Literacy was used within the home for the following purposes: interactional (i.e., letter writing); instrumental (sharing family recipes and sewing tips); news gathering and sharing about the community (e.g., reading newspapers); financial (e.g., writing checks and money orders; budgeting); spiritual (e.g., Bible reading, reading inspirational materials); recreational (e.g., reading novels; reading aloud); and education. Johnson believes that it is incumbent upon teachers to understand the cultural backgrounds, the histories of literacy practices in students' families that constitute a culture of family literacy that children bring to school, and to use that to engage them in curriculum and instruction that accesses their knowledge.

The task might seem daunting to some, but the necessity and urgency of doing so is evident. It is important to note that teachers are not left to tackle the task alone. Research about the level of involvement of diverse parents in their children's education is mixed. Drummond and Stipek (2004) in a study of the involvement of low-income parents found that most of the African American, White, and Latino parents involved in the study believed that they are responsible for being involved in their children's education. They placed particular importance on working with their children in reading in the early grades, and this was especially true of the parents of struggling readers. Drummond and Stipek (2004) also found that the level of involvement was greater for parents whose children's teachers provided the parents with suggestions about helping their children. This is consistent with the results of an informal survey of first- through sixth-grade teachers in which Ganske et al. (2003) found that the issue of family involvement was one of the concerns in working with struggling readers and writers. Teachers were concerned specifically about how to communicate information about the literacy expectations in their classrooms. Ganske recommended that teachers be proactive in communicating with parents in the early part of the school year. Clarity and simplicity in language will make the information accessible to parents of varying reading abilities. Children who struggle need the assistance of their family when they are working on reading and writing tasks at home.

Not all children receive this support at home and need intervention programs to support them and assist parents. Cooper, Crosnoe, and Pituch (2010) found that the home-learning activities of poor children who were transitioning into elementary school differed from those provided by parents that were more affluent. These differences, however, did not explain the lower achievement levels of the children. The parents involved their children in fewer organized activities, were less involved in their children's schools, and engaged them in fewer cognitively stimulating materials.

As part of their research to determine the effectiveness of a parent involvement intervention program, Manjula, Saraswathi, Prakash, and Ashalatha (2009) began by examining the extent of parent involvement of parents who had children with reading and writing difficulties and those whose children did not have difficulties in these areas. They found that the majority of students (80% with reading difficulties and 67.1% with writing difficulties) received no educational support and worked independently. Thirty-nine percent of children with difficulties in reading received educational support from their parents compared to 60% of children without difficulties in reading. Similar findings were noted in comparing the support for writing for children with difficulties versus children without difficulties (30% vs. 78.9%). Children and their parents participated in an interactive intervention program in which the children were exposed to modules that focused on learning and recognizing vowels, consonants, letters, and words, and acquiring speed in reading and writing. Exposure to an intervention program increased parents' sensitivity to the need to be involved in helping their children and resulted in significantly greater achievement by children with difficulties in reading and writing (Manjula et al., 2009).

## STARTING WITH PRESERVICE TEACHERS

Teaching preservice teachers how to involve parents and families in children's literacy development is a missing but needed dimension of teacher education (Abrego, Rubin, & Sutterby, 2006; Uludag, 2008; Walker-Dalhouse & Dalhouse, 2006). Many educators echo the need for university programs to include family involvement as an essential dimension of teacher preparation in an effort to build and sustain viable partnerships that will extend children's literacy development (Abrego et al., 2006; IRA, 2002). Teacher education programs that include parental involvement instruction and activities produce preservice teachers who view parents in a more favorable light and express greater confidence in working with them (Uludag, 2008). Such programs also help improve their skills in working with parents and in building partnerships to foster children's literacy development (Abrego et al., 2006).

These skills and understandings are useful for working with all parents, but are essential for working with parents of increasingly diverse school and community populations (M. Martin, Fergus, & Noguera, 2010) and struggling readers of all ethnic, racial, linguistic, and cultural groups (Walker-Dalhouse & Dalhouse, 2006). In a survey of the mostly Latino preservice teachers who worked with Latino children ages 3–7 years old in a community, university, and school partnership, Albrego et al. (2006) felt that despite the skills and understandings gained, there were lingering concerns about preservice teachers' attitudes toward Latino parents. Although the preservice teachers indicated that they valued the families and their devotion to their children's academic success, the preservice teachers' attitudes toward them were sometimes condescending. The researchers concluded that preservice teachers might need greater understanding of the funds of knowledge (Moll, Velez Ibanez, & Greenberg, 1990) and strengths of Latino families. Overall, preservice teachers benefit from field experiences in university-school or university-community programs that provide them with opportunities to interact and communicate with parents (Uludag, 2008).

### Providing Courses for Preservice Teachers

Rohr and He (2010) provided additional evidence for the value of providing preservice teachers with opportunities to work with struggling readers and their parents. They found significant changes in the attitudes of preservice teachers toward parent involvement and about their preparedness to work with the parents of these readers after the preservice teachers took a reading methods course in which they were engaged in a one-to-one tutoring experience with struggling readers. In a postassessment of the preservice teachers' attitudes toward parents of struggling readers, they found that 100% of the preservice teachers did not believe that parents were mostly responsible for their children's difficulties in reading compared to 16% who thought so initially. Another significant pre-post change was in the number of preservice teachers who initially thought that parents of children who were struggling readers are unmotivated and disinterested in their children's academic work (60% vs 8%). In another study, while 60% of the preservice teachers felt that they were not prepared to work with parents of a diverse group of students before tutoring, the attitudes changed with 60% expressing confidence in their ability to do so after tutoring (Rohr & He, 2010). Consequently, the preservice teachers were more positive about the extent to which their teacher education program had prepared them to interact with parents of struggling readers.

When intervention programs are designed, they must take into consideration the cultural values, beliefs, and home routines and the material demands that interventions make on individual families. In a study of school-home literacy initiatives involving African American families in urban environments and immigrant ESL families, Dudley-Marling (2009) found that the parents interviewed in his study were committed to their children and their education. However, the school-to-home literacy interventions (shared and independent reading) used in the study sometimes conflicted with their cultural values, beliefs, and family routines, and parents' expectations. Dudley-Marling concluded that for school-to-home literacy initiatives to be effective, school personnel must listen to and be responsive to the needs, values, and expectations of diverse families.

> Interviewing families to develop family stories has multiple instructional benefits.

## Using Family Stories to Spread Understanding

Listening to and getting to know ethnically and culturally diverse families is important in increasing preservice teachers' sociocultural understandings and in enabling them to begin thinking about their teaching in culturally responsive ways.

A useful tool for preservice educators to use in this process might be a collection of family stories as gathered by Kidd, Sanchez, and Thorp (2004). Preservice teachers, who were engaged in an internship, interacted with parents from diverse backgrounds and in the process engaged them in conversations in attempts to become acquainted with the families. They shared with each other the stories that the families had told them. The stories provided them with the opportunity to learn about the families and their cultures. The stories also provided the preservice teachers with the opportunity to examine the influence of their own backgrounds and experiences on their teaching. Such opportunities increase the cultural awareness and responsiveness of preservice teachers (Kidd et al., 2004).

Another option for enabling preservice and experienced teachers to understand ethnically, culturally, and linguistically diverse, as well as low-income families is through constructing counternarratives (López-Robertson, Long, & Turner-Nash, 2010) after participating in home-community visits of diverse children and their families. The process involves identifying prior assumptions about diverse children and/or their families and spending time in varied contexts recommended by families to examine their literacies, community support, values, and language background. The teacher's prior assumptions can then be reexamined in light of these experiences. The process has potential for eliminating teacher biases and heralds efforts to better understand and educate all children (López-Robertson et al., 2010).

## INVOLVING UNIVERSITIES AND SCHOOLS

The general perception that parents of children who struggle are less involved in their children's education (Compton-Lilly, 2000; Nieto, 2000) and the increasing need for parent involvement in children's education embedded in current educational legislation (U.S. Department of Education, 1994) point to a need for changes in teacher preparation. Colleges of education and schools must work independently and collaboratively to prepare preservice and inservice teachers to work with the parents of struggling readers. While courses on working with parents in the general education of their children are valuable, specific courses that focus on reading methods and that provide students with tutoring experiences with diverse parents and children are more beneficial (Rohr & He, 2010).

In a case study of a high-performing elementary school for immigrant children, M. Martin et al. (2010) noted that the language and literacy needs of children could be met by forming a "network of

> Partnerships between universities and schools can also support children who struggle, as well as their parents.

professional practice," with the child and teacher at the core of the network. Working with community services or agencies was essential for providing health and social support and enrichment for the children, in addition to educational programs and social support for parents. Forming a university partnership was key to ongoing teacher professional development to help teachers meet the academic and the social-emotional development needs of immigrant children. Preservice education was also enhanced as university personnel worked cooperatively with the school to provide an on-site setting for teaching literacy methods courses.

Finding low-cost alternatives for universities to work with struggling readers can meet the needs of children in changing economic times. For example, Fingon, Frank, and Kawell (2010) described how a few literacy faculty members, classroom teachers, and graduate students who served as tutors, along with the local reading council, were able to organize, implement, and manage a summer reading camp for struggling readers and their families. Students received either small-group or one-to-one instruction while parents participated in workshops on word identification, writing, and ways to support children's home reading.

## SUMMARY

One-to-one and small-group tutoring can empower struggling readers and provide needed support for their families. Parents want to help their children despite the circumstances of their lives. This can be gleaned from the plea of William's mother described in the opening vignette. In a review of research of the effectiveness of parental involvement on the reading skills of elementary students, Fitton and Gredler (1996) found that parents can be instrumental in improving and maintaining their children's performance in reading. While advocating education for parents of struggling readers in specific reading techniques such as paired reading and direct instruction, they also called for further research examining the reading methods used by parents in home settings.

Parents of young struggling readers want to support school efforts in reading instruction, but may lack knowledge of specific strategies and access to the resources to implement them (Sokolinski, 2010). Literacy in Families Empowers (LIFE), a family literacy program for families of first-grade readers of all socioeconomic levels was created by Sokolinski (2010) to provide parents with the knowledge and skills needed to create tools and use school-based strategies to promote listening comprehension and reading enjoyment of informational text. It is clear that all parents need to be taught to use literacy practices that have been proven to be effective for literacy achievement (Shields et al., 1983).

REFLECTION QUESTIONS

1. What can teachers do to prepare parents of readers who struggle to help their children improve in reading?
2. What differences exist in the way that teachers interact with and/or involve parents of English learners, and those who are economically, culturally, and ethnically different in the instruction of their children who struggle in reading? How might teachers provide more information to help these families?
3. To what extent do teachers and schools listen to parents of struggling readers? Do their recommendations extend or align home literacy practices with school literacy practices?

# CHAPTER 10

# Fostering Independence and Success in Reading

Throughout this book we advocated for instruction that creates new visions of learners who are described as struggling readers. At the heart of this instruction is the goal to leverage students' knowledge, experiences, and passions in ways that set aside narrow views of what it means to be a successful reader and learner. This instruction demonstrates to all students the belief that they can succeed, and largely they can succeed because of their capabilities and differences (and not in spite of them, as is too commonly expressed).

We situated our discussion of instruction within brief case descriptions of students who are experiencing reading difficulties and attempted to interrogate the conditions contributing to students' difficulties in schools. The cases we described are presented in Figure 10.1. For these cases, we offered possibilities for collecting assessment information that acknowledges students' perspective and cultural and linguistic histories, and that can inform supportive and responsive instruction. Our goal is to promote instruction that is just and democratic, that defines *teaching* as more than "best practices" or "aligning curricular goals with national standards." We believe having highly knowledgeable teachers who are grounded in understandings of appropriate practices and expect students to achieve national standards is necessary, but insufficient for meeting the needs of the students who are labeled each year as *deficient*. Teaching is about the students we teach, and this is the standard that teachers hold for themselves, this is the goal that keeps teachers coming back each year transformed by their successes and transforming the students they teach.

For prospective teachers, it is believing that they can make a difference, not in a paternalistic way, but by creating learning partnerships in which students, parents, and families inform and are informed by their efforts.

At the heart of this book is the case study of Colin that opens this book in the first chapter and is revisited in Chapter 8. Through the study of this case and the ones presented in each chapter, we asked that you scrutinize with us the teaching practices that can disable students such as Colin, practices that can distance students from feeling confident in their abilities, and extend your thinking about the practices that can be used in your

*Figure 10.1. Cases Represented in* **Be That Teacher!**

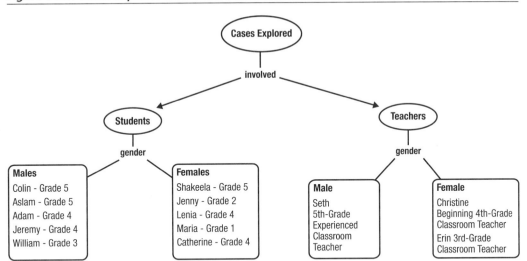

present and future classroom to effectuate positive changes in the trajectory of learning for students who struggle. With each case, we attempted to disrupt "taken for granted" practices (Vander Zanden & Wohlwend, 2011) that are not optimal for inviting students' access to learning new content and entering new texts and visiting new worlds.

Several features characterize the instruction we envision. One feature is the goal that we established in our first chapter, the goal of establishing conceptual instruction. Conceptual instruction is robust and balanced; skills and strategies are taught to provide access to content and most importantly, content that is useful and usable—for answering students' questions, for participating in day-to-day events, and for advancing knowledge and building a foundation for continued learning in students' worlds. Curricular expectations are met within rich learning environments, such as those that we describe in our cultural modeling and anchored instruction chapters. Conceptual instruction makes certain that students have access to new knowledge and multiple genres and levels of texts, as we discuss in each of our chapters. Too many students described as struggling readers remain "beginning readers" throughout their school years because instruction does not accelerate their trajectory, denying access to knowledge, skills, and strategies.

A second feature is that instruction should be productive, responsive, and empowering. From assessment practices to comprehension instruction, transformations are needed. The focus is on students actively engaged in and directing their own learning and producing projects with new literacies that range from digital texts to dramatic or musical productions. Students are reading multimodal texts, such as graphic novels and online texts, more than they are reading conventional print texts, yet assessing and teaching practices are not capturing and responding to students' experiences and capabilities (Gormley & McDermott, 2011). Assessments and instruction too often are not relevant to students' lives. And while we honor and respect differences within our pluralistic society, curricula are devised to teach all students in the same way, resulting in a divide between those students who can overcome such instruction and those who cannot or choose not to do so.

We recognize that while standards and legislative initiatives establish parameters of instruction beyond our individual classrooms, we must not perceive them as burdensome and demanding more and more teacher accountability for learning. The challenges are real in differentiating instruction to meet students' needs, and the energy required is great, but the potential for changing the learning outcomes for students who struggle can be well worth the effort. Every teacher can be THAT teacher who breaks the cycle of failure for struggling readers.

# Teacher Resources

## BOOKS

### Assessment

Afflerbach, P. (Ed.). (2010). *Essential readings on assessment.* Newark, DE: International Reading Association.

Afflerbach, P. (2012). *Understanding and using reading assessment, K–12* (2nd ed.). Newark, DE: International Reading Association.

Barone, D., & Taylor, J. M. (2007). *The practical guide to classroom literacy assessment.* Thousand Oaks, CA: Corwin Press.

Clay, M. (2000). *Running records for classroom teachers.* North Shores, New Zealand: Pearson/Heinemann.

Goodman, Y., Watson, D., & Burke, C. (1987). *Reading miscue analysis: Alternative procedures.* New York: Richard Owens.

Johnston, P. (1997). *Knowing literacy: Constructive literacy assessment.* York, ME: Stenhouse.

Popham, W. J. (2008). *Transformative assessment.* Alexandria, VA: ASCD.

### Culture

Compton-Lilly, C. (2009). *Breaking the silence: Recognizing the social and cultural resources students bring to the classroom.* Newark, DE: International Reading Association.

McIntyre, E., Hulan, N., & Layne, V. (2011). *Reading instruction for diverse classrooms: Research-based, culturally responsive practice.* New York: Guilford Press.

Mueller, P. (2001). *Lifers: Learning from at-risk adolescent readers.* Portsmouth, NH: Heinemann.

Voss, M. M. (1996). *Hidden literacies: Children learning at home and at school.* Portsmouth, NH: Heinemann.

### Comprehension

Albers, P. (2007). *Finding the artist within: Creating and reading visual texts in the English language arts classroom.* Newark, DE: International Reading Association.

Allison, N. (2009). *Middle school readers: Helping them read widely, helping them read well.* Portsmouth, NH: Heinemann.

Harvey, S., & Daniels, H. (2009). *Comprehension and collaboration: Inquiry circles in action.* Portsmouth, NH: Heinemann.

Harvey, S., & Goudvis, A. (2007). *Strategies that work: Teaching comprehension for understanding and engagement.* Portland, ME: Stenhouse.

Jenkins, C. B. (2000). *The allure of authors: Author studies in the elementary classroom.* Portsmouth, NH: Heinemann.

Tovani, C. (2004). *Do I really have to teach reading?: Content comprehension, grades 6–12.* Portland, ME: Stenhouse.

Wilhelm, J. D. (1998). *"You gotta be the book": Teaching engaged and reflective reading with adolescents.* New York: Teachers College Press.

### Early Literacy

Hiebert, E. H. (2009). *Reading more, reading better.* New York: Guilford Press.

Miller, D. (2009). *The book whisperer: Awakening the inner reader in every child.* San Francisco, CA: Jossey-Bass.

### English Language Learners

Reyes, M. de la Luz. (Ed.). (2011). *Words were all we had.* New York: Teachers College Press.

Uribe, M., & Nathenson-Meja, S. (2008). *Literacy essentials for English Language Learners: Successful transitions.* New York: Teachers College Press.

### Technology, Multimodal—for Assessment, Vocabulary, Comprehension

Cummins, J., Brown, K., & Sayers, D. (2007). *Literacy, technology, and diversity: Teaching for success in changing times.* Boston: Pearson/Allyn & Bacon.

### Vocabulary

Beck, I. L., McKeown, M. G., & Kucan, L. (2002). *Bringing words to life: Robust vocabulary instruction.* New York: Guilford Press.

Beck, I. L., McKeown, M. G., & Kucan, L. (2008). *Creating robust vocabulary: Frequently asked questions and extended examples.* New York: Guilford Press.

Blachowicz, C., & Fisher, P. J. (2010). *Teaching vocabulary in all classrooms.* Boston: Allyn & Bacon.

Graves, M. R. (2009). *Teaching individual words: One size does not fit all.* New York: Teachers College Press and Newark, DE: International Reading Association.

Johnson, D. D. (2001). *Vocabulary in the elementary and middle school.* Boston: Allyn & Bacon.

### Word Identification

Gaskins, I. W. (2005). *Success with struggling readers: The Benchmark School approach.* New York: Guilford Press.

Pinnell, G. S., & Fountas, I. C. (2003). *Phonics lessons: Letters, words, and how they work.* Portsmouth, NH: Heinemann.

Strickland, D. S. (2011). *Teaching phonics today: Word study strategies through the grades.* Newark, DE: International Reading Association.

## POSITION STATEMENTS FROM NATIONAL AND INTERNATIONAL PROFESSIONAL ORGANIZATIONS

### Assessment

IRA/NCTE Joint Task Force on Assessment. (2010). *Standards for the assessment of reading and writing* (Rev. ed.). Newark, DE: International Reading Association; Urbana, IL: National Council of Teachers of English.

### Word Identification

International Reading Association. (1998). Phonemic awareness and the teaching of reading: A position statement from the board of directors of the International Reading Association. Newark, DE: International Reading Association. Available at http://www.reading.org/downloads /positions/ps1025_phonemic.pdf

## ONLINE RESOURCES

### Comprehension

Willingham, D. T. (2010). Teaching content is teaching reading [YouTube video]. Available at http://www.youtube.com/watch?v=RiP-ijdxqEc

### Culture

Northwestern University, School of Education and Social Policy. (2009). Guided autobiography. Available at the Foley Center for the Study of Lives website: http://www.sesp.northwestern.edu/foley/instruments/guided

### Graphic Novels—Learning About Graphic Novels and Teaching with Them

"The benefits of comic books in the classroom" [YouTube video]. (CTV News anchor Marni Kuhlmann speaks with Jay Bardyla, owner of Happy Harbour Comics in Edmonton and Stacy Keeler, Teacher at Lamont High School). Available at http://www.youtube.com/watch?v=DTgaqVOIOfQ&feature=related

"Building literacy connections with graphic novels" [YouTube video]. (Courtney Angermeier). Available at http://www.youtube.com/watch?v=RHBQSMve2s8

"Creating comic books: Penciling the story for your comic books" [YouTube video]. (Mark Poulton). Available at http://www.youtube.com/watch?v=vKusp7dBfEs

Plasq [Website]. (Teacher Don Cuggy recommends this site as a resource that provides students with a tool to create panels, a layout, speech bubbles, and more). Available at http://www.plasq.com

"Teachers create educational comic book" [YouTube video]. (Teachers Gary Smith and Steve Prince talk about the graphic novel they created, an African American history story). Available at http://www.youtube.com/watch?v=z2iliW5TFYQ

"Use of the graphic novel in the classroom" [YouTube video]. (Sarah Riddell and Cailey Martin). Available at http://www.youtube.com/watch?v=hGddauVuqPg

### Parents/Families/Teachers

Colorín Colorado. Available at http://www.colorincolorado.org

### Vocabulary

Visual thesaurus. Available at www.visualthesaurus.com
Vocabulary.co.il. Available at www.vocabulary.co.il
Vocabulary.com. Available at www.vocabulary.com

### Books for Children and Youth

International Children's Digital Library. Available at www.childrenslibrary.org
International Reading Association, Children's Choices reading list. Available at www.reading.org/Resources/Booklists/ChildrensChoices.aspx
International Reading Association, Teacher's Choices reading list. Available at www.reading.org/Resources/Booklists/TeachersChoices.aspx
National Geographic Society. Teaching resources by topic available at http://education.nationalgeographic.com/education/collections-topics/?ar_a=1
United States Board on Books for Young People (USBBY), Outstanding International Books List. Available at http://www.usbby.org/list_oibl.html

### Teacher Resources

Annenberg Foundation (2011). *Advancing excellent teaching in American schools.* Washington, DC: Author.
ReadWriteThink. (International Reading Association/National Council of Teachers of English). Available at www.readwritethink.org

# References

Abrego, M. H., Rubin, R., & Sutterby, J. A. (2006). They call me Maestra: Preservice teachers' interactions with parents in a reading tutoring program. *Action in Teacher Education, 28*(1), 3–12.

Afflerbach, P. (2007). *Understanding and using reading assessment, K–12.* Newark, DE: International Reading Association.

Allen, J. (1999). *Words, words, words: Teaching vocabulary in grades 4–12.* Portland, ME: Stenhouse.

Allen, J., & Hermann-Wilmarth, J. (2010). Cultural construction zones. *Journal of Teacher Education, 55*(3), 214–226.

Allington, R. L. (2006). *What really matters for struggling readers: Designing research-based programs* (2nd ed.). Boston: Pearson Education.

Allington, R. L. (2007). Intervention all day long: New hope for struggling readers. *Voices from the Middle, 14*(4), 7–14.

Allington, R. L. (2011a). What at-risk readers need. *Educational Leadership, 68*(6), 40–45.

Allington, R. L. (2011b, September). *What struggling readers need.* Keynote presentation at the 49th Annual Conference of the Florida Reading Association, Orlando, Florida.

Allington, R. L., & McGill-Franzen, A. (2003). Use students' summer setback months to raise minority student achievement. *Education Digest, 69*(3), 19–24.

Alvarez, M. C., & Risko, V. J. (2010). *What comes before matters in the end: Directions for reading comprehension instruction.* In S. Szabo, T. Morrison, L. Martin, M. Boggs, & L. Raine (Eds.), *Yearbook (Association of Literacy Educators and Researchers): Vol. 32. Building literacy communities* (pp. 32–46). Louisville, KY: Association of Literacy Educators and Researchers.

Alvermann, D. (2005). Literacy on the edge: How close are we to closing the literacy achievement gap? *Voices from the Middle, 13*(1), 8–15.

American Education Research Association. (2004). English Language Learners: Boosting academic achievement. Essential information for education. *Policy, 2*(1), 1–4.

Angelou, M. (1993, January 21). The inauguration: On the pulse of morning. *The New York Times.*

Annenberg Foundation. (2011). Teaching reading 3–5 workshop. Available at http://www.learner.org/workshops/teachreading3–5

Applegate, A. J., Applegate, M. D., McGeehan, C. M., Pinto, C. M., & Kong, A. (2009). The assessment of thoughtful literacy in NAEP: Why the states aren't measuring up. *The Reading Teacher, 62*(5), 372–381.

Artiles, A. J. (2003). Special education's changing identity: Paradoxes and dilemmas in view of culture and space. *Harvard Educational Review, 73*(2), 164–202.

Artiles, A. J., & Kozleski, E. (2007). Beyond convictions: Interrogating culture, history, and power in inclusive education. *Language Arts, 84,* 357–364.

Artiles, A., & Trent, S. C. (1994). Overrepresentation of minority students in special education: A continuing debate. *Journal of Special Education, 27(4),* 410–437.

Arts for Learning. (2010). *Arts for Learning: Young audiences of Oregon and Southwest Washington* (http://www.youtube.com/watch?v=AQu0oPaQgbs).

Asan, A. (2007). Concept mapping in science class: A case study of fifth grade students. *Educational Technology & Society, 10*(1), 186–195.

Ash, G. E., Kuhn, M. R., & Walpole, S. (2009). Analyzing "inconsistencies" in practice: Teachers' continued use of round robin reading. *Reading and Writing Quarterly, 25,* 87–103.

Au, K. (1993). *Literacy instruction in multicultural settings.* Fort Worth, TX: Harcourt Brace Jovanovich.

Au, K. (2000). A multicultural perspective on policies for improving literacy achievement: Equity and excellence. In M. L. Kamil, P. B. Mosenthal, P. D. Pearson, & R. Barr (Eds.), *Handbook of reading research* (Vol. 3, pp. 835–851). Mahwah, NJ: Erlbaum.

Au, K. (2006). *Multicultural issues and literacy achievement.* Mahwah, NJ: Erlbaum.

August, D. E., Carlo, M., Dressler, C., & Snow, C. (2005). The critical role of vocabulary development for English language learners. *Learning Disabilities Research and Practice, 20*(1), 50–57.

August, D. E., & Hakuta, K. E. (1997). *Improving schooling for language minority children: A research agenda.* Washington, DC: National Academy Press.

August, D. E., & Shanahan, T. (2006). *Developing literacy in second-language learners: Report of the National Literacy Panel on Language Minority Children and Youth.* Mahwah, NJ: Erlbaum.

Avalos, M. A., Plasencia, A., Chavez, C., & Rascon, J. (2007). Modified guided reading: Gateway to English as a second language and literacy learning. *The Reading Teacher, 61*(4), 318–329.

Baker, S. K., Simmons, D. C., & Kame'enui, E. J. (1998). Vocabulary acquisition: Instruction and curricular basics and implications. In D. C. Simmons & E. J. Kame'enui (Eds.), *What reading research tells us about children with diverse learning needs: Bases and basics* (pp. 219–238). Mahwah, NJ: Erlbaum.

Baldwin, J. (1955). *Notes of a native son.* Boston, MA: Beacon.

Barone, D., Mallette, M., & Xu, S. (2005). *Teaching early literacy development: Development, assessment, and instruction.* New York: Guilford Press.

Bass, J. A. F., Dasinger, S., Elish-Piper, L., Matthews, M. W., & Risko, V. J. (2008). *A declaration of readers' rights. Renewing our commitment to students.* Boston, MA: Pearson/Allyn & Bacon.

Bauer, E. B., & Arazi, J. (2011). Promoting literacy development for beginning English learners. *The Reading Teacher, 64*(5), 383–386.

Bauer, E. B., & Manyak, P. C. (2008). Creating language-rich instruction for English-language learners. *The Reading Teacher, 62*(2), 176–178.

Beck. I. L., & McKeown, M. G. (2001). Text talk: Capturing the benefits of read-aloud experiences for young children. *The Reading Teacher, 55*(1), 10–20.

Beck, I. L., & McKeown, M. G. (2005). *Text talk: Levels A & B.* New York: Scholastic.

Beck, I. L., & McKeown, M. G. (2007). Increasing young, low-income children's oral vocabulary repertoires through rich and focused instruction. *The Elementary School Journal, 107,* 251–171.

Beck, I. L., McKeown, M. G., & Kucan, L. (2002) *Bringing words to life: Robust vocabulary instruction.* New York: Guilford Press.

Beck, I. L., McKeown, M. G., & Kucan, L. (2008). *Creating robust vocabulary: Frequently asked questions and extended examples.* New York: Guilford Press.

Beck, I. L., Perfetti, C. A., & McKeown, M. G. (1982). Effects of long-term vocabulary instruction on lexical access and reading comprehension. *Journal of Educational Psychology, 74,* 506–521.

Beed, P. L., Hawkins, E. M., & Roller, C. M. (1991). Moving learners toward independence: The power of scaffolded instruction. *The Reading Teacher, 44*(9), 648–655.

Bennett, W. J. (Ed.). (1995). *The children's book of virtues.* New York: Simon & Schuster.

Berninger, V. W., Nielsen, K. H., Abbott, R. D., Wijsman, E., & Raskind, W. (2008). Gender differences in severity of writing and reading disabilities. *Journal of School Psychology, 46*(2), 151–172.

Biemiller, A. (2001). Teaching vocabulary: Early, direct, and sequential. *American Educator, 25*(1), 24–28.

Blachowicz, C. L. Z., & Fisher, P. J. L. (2000). Vocabulary instruction. In R. Barr, M. L., Kamil, P. B. Mosenthal, & P. D. Pearson (Eds.), *Handbook of reading research,* (Vol. 3, pp. 503–523). Mahwah, NJ: Erlbaum.

Blachowicz, C. L. Z., & Ogle, D. (2008). *Reading comprehension: Strategies for independent learners* (2nd ed.). New York: Guilford Press.

Black, P., & William, D. (1998). Assessment and classroom learning. *Assessment in Education, 5,* 7–71.

Block, C. C., Whiteley, C. S., Parris, S. R., Reed, K. L., & Cleveland, M. D. (2009). Instructional approaches that significantly increase reading comprehension. *Journal of Educational Psychology, 101*(2), 262–281.

Bloome, D., & Dail, A. R. K. (1997). Toward (re)defining miscue analysis: Reading as a social and cultural process. *Language Arts, 74*(8), 610–617.

Bourdieu, P. (1986). The forms of capital. In J. G. Richardson (Ed.), *Handbook of theory and research for the sociology of education* (pp. 241–258). New York: Greenwood.

Brabham, E. G., & Villaume, S. K. (2002). Leveled text: The good news and the bad news. *The Reading Teacher, 55*(5), 438–440.

Bracey, G. W. (2001). The 11th Bracey report on the condition of public education. *Phi Delta Kappan, 83*(2), 157–169.

Bransford, J. D., Brown, A. L., & Cocking, R. R. (Eds). (1999). *How people learn: Brain, mind, experience, and school.* Washington, DC: National Academy Press.

Bransford, J. D., Vye, N. Y., Kinzer, C., & Risko, V. J. (1990). Teaching thinking and content knowledge toward an integrated approach. In B. Jones (Ed.), *Teaching thinking* (pp. 381–413). Hillsdale, NJ: Erlbaum.

Burgess, S. R., Hecht, S. A., & Lonigan, C. J. (2002). Relations of the home literacy environment (HLE) to the development of reading-related abilities: A one-year longitudinal study. *Reading Research Quarterly, 37*, 408–426.

Bursuck, B., & Blanks, B. (2010). Evidence-based early reading practices within a Response to Intervention system. *Psychology in the Schools, 47*(5), 421–431.

Bus, A. G., van IJzendoorn, M. H., & Pelligrini, A. D. (1995). Joint book reading makes for success in learning to read: A meta-analysis on intergenerational transmission of literacy. *Review of Educational Research, 65*, 1–20.

Camburn, E., & Wong, S. (2011). Two decades of generalizable evidence on U.S. instruction from national surveys. *Teachers College Record, 113*(3), 561–610.

Carrier, K. A. (2006). Improving comprehension and assessment of English language learners using MMIO. *Clearing House, 79*(3), 131–136.

Cech, S. J. (2008). Test industry split over "formative" assessment. *Education Week, 28*, 1–15.

Cecil, N. L. (1988). Black dialect and academic success A study of teacher expectations. *Reading Improvement, 25*(1), 34–38.

Celebration Press/Pearson Learning Group. (2005). *Developmental reading assessment* (2nd ed.). Lebanon, IN: Author.

Chapman, J. W., Tunmer, W. E., & Prochnow, J. E. (2000). Early reading-related skills and performance, reading self-concept, and the development of academic self-concept: A longitudinal study. *Journal of Educational Psychology, 92*(4), 703–708.

Chard, D. J., & Kame'enui, E. J. (2000). Struggling first-grade readers: The frequency and progress of their reading. *Journal of Special Education, 34*(1), 28–37.

Chard, D. J., Stoolmiller, M., Harn, B., Wanzek, J., Vaughn, S., Linan-Thompson, S., & Kame'enui, E. J. (2008). Predicting reading success in a multilevel schoolwide reading model: A retrospective analysis. *Journal of Learning Disabilities, 41*(2), 174–188.

Charity, A. H., Scarborough, H. S., & Griffin, D. M. (2004). Familiarity with "school English" in African-American children and its relation to early reading achievement. *Child Development, 75*, 1340–1356.

Chocolate and Child Labor PSA. (2007). Available at www.yourube.com/watch?v=jzOskNU-GdM

Christian, B., & Bloome, D. (2004). Learning to read is who you are. *Reading & Writing Quarterly, 20*, 365–384.

Clay, M. M. (1985). *The early detection of reading difficulties* (3rd ed.). Portsmouth, NH: Heinemann.

Clay, M. M. (1991). *Becoming literate: The construction of inner control.* Portsmouth, NH: Heinemann.

Clay, M. M. (1993a). *An observational survey of early literacy achievement.* Portsmouth, NH: Heinemann.

Clay, M. M. (1993b). *Reading Recovery: A guidebook for teachers in training.* Portsmouth, NH: Heinemann.

Clay, M. M. (2000). *Running records for classroom teachers*. North Shores, New Zealand: Pearson/Heinemann.

Cognition and Technology Group (CTG) at Vanderbilt. (1990, August–September). Anchored instruction and its relationship to situated cognition. *Educational Researcher, 19*, 2–10.

Cognition and Technology Group (CTG) at Vanderbilt. (1992a). An anchored instruction approach to cognitive skills acquisition and intelligent tutoring. In J. W. Regian & V. J. Shute (Eds.), *Cognitive approaches to automated instruction* (pp. 135–170). Hillsdale, NJ: Erlbaum.

Cognition and Technology Group (CTG) at Vanderbilt. (1992b). Anchored instruction in science and mathematics: Theoretical basis, developmental projects, and initial research findings. In R. Duschl & R. Hamilton (Eds.), *Philosophy of science, cognitive psychology, and educational theory and practice* (pp. 244–273). Albany, NY: State University of New York Press.

Cognition and Technology Group (CTG) at Vanderbilt. (2003). Connecting learning theory and instructional practice: Leveraging some powerful affordances of technology. In H. F. O'Neil, Jr., & R. S. Perez (Eds.), *Technology applications in education* (pp. 173–209). Mahwah, NJ: Erlbaum.

Cole, A. D. (2006). Scaffolding beginning readers: Micro and macro cues teachers use during student oral reading. *The Reading Teacher, 59*(5), 450–459.

Collins, K. M. (2011). "My mom says I'm really creative!": Dis/ability, positioning, and resistance in multimodal instructional contexts. *Language Arts, 68*(6), 409–418.

Compton-Lilly, C. (2000). Staying on children: Challenging stereotypes about urban parents. *Language Arts, 77*, 420–427.

Compton-Lilly, C. (2006). Identity, childhood culture, and literacy learning: A case study. *Journal of Early Childhood Literacy, 6*(1), 35–76.

Compton-Lilly, C. (2007). *Re-reading families: The literate lives of urban children, the intermediate years*. New York: Teachers College Press.

Compton-Lilly, C. (2009). What can new literacy studies offer to the teaching of struggling readers? *The Reading Teacher, 63*(1), 88–90.

Connor, C. M., & Craig, H. K. (2006). African American preschoolers' language, emergent literacy skills, and use of African American English: A complex relation. *Journal of Speech, Language, and Hearing Research, 49*, 771–792.

Cooke, N. L., Kretlow, A. G., & Helf, S. (2010). Supplemental reading help for kindergarten students: How early should you start? *Preventing School Failure, 54*(3), 137–144.

Cooper, C. E., Crosnoe, M., & Pituch, K. (2010). Poverty, race, and parental involvement during the transition to elementary school. *Journal of Family Issues, 31*(7), 859–883.

Cope, B., & Kalantzis, M. (2000). *Multiliteracies: Literacy learning and the design of social futures*. South Yarra, Victoria, Australia: Macmillan.

Coyne, M. D., McCoach, B., & Kapp, S. (2007). Vocabulary intervention for kindergarten students comparing extended instruction to embedded instruction and incidental exposure. *Learning Disabilities Quarterly, 30*, 74–88.

Coyne, M. D., Simmons, D. C., & Kame'enui, E. J. (2004). Vocabulary instruction for young children at risk of experiencing reading difficulties: Teaching word meanings during shared storybook readings. In J. F. Baumann & E. J. Kame'enui (Eds.), *Vocabulary instruction: Research to practice* (pp. 41–58). New York: Guilford Press.

Craig, H. K., & Washington, J. A. (2004). Grade-related changes in the production of African American English. *Journal of Speech, Language, and Hearing Research, 47,* 450–463.

Cummins, J. (2003). Reading and the bilingual student: Fact and friction. In G. Garcia (Ed.), *English learners: reaching the highest level of English literacy* (pp. 2–33). Newark, DE: International Reading Association.

Cummins, J. (2007). Pedagogies for the poor? Realigning reading instruction for low-income students with scientifically based reading research. *Educational Researcher, 36*(9), 564–572.

Cunningham, P. (1990). The names test: A quick assessment of decoding ability. *The Reading Teacher, 44*(2), 124–129.

Dalton, B., & Grisham, D. L. (2011). eVoc strategies: 10 ways to use technology to build vocabulary. *The Reading Teacher, 64*(5), 306–317.

Darling-Hammond, L. (1987). Teacher quality and equality. In J. Goodlad & P. Keating (Eds.), *Access to knowledge: An agenda for our nation's schools* (pp. 237–258). New York: College Entrance Examination Board.

Delpit, L. (1992). Education in a multicultural society: Our future's great challenge. *Journal of Negro Education, 61,* 237–249.

Delpit, L. (1995). *Other people's children: Cultural conflict in the classroom.* New York: New Press.

Delpit, L. (2006). Lessons from teachers. *Journal of Teacher Education, 57*(3), 220–231.

Delpit, L., & Dowdy, J. K. (2002). *The skin that we speak: Thoughts on language and culture in the classroom.* New York: New Press.

Dewey, J. (1910). *How we think.* Lexington, MA: D. C. Heath.

Dewey, J. (1933). *How we think. A restatement of the relation of reflective thinking to the educative process* (Rev. ed.), Boston, MA: D. C. Heath.

Drummond, K. V., & Stipek, D. (2004). Low-income parents' beliefs about their role in children's academic learning. *The Elementary School Journal, 101*(3), 197–213.

Dudley-Marling, C. (2007). Return of the deficit. *Journal of Educational Controversy, 2*(1). Retrieved from http://www.wce.wwu.edu/Resources/CEP/eJournal/v002n001/a004.shtml

Dudley-Marling, C. (2009). Home-school literacy connections: The perceptions of African American and immigrant ESL parents in two urban communities. *Teachers College Record, 111*(7), 1713–1752.

Dudley-Marling, C., & Lucas, K. (2009). Pathologizing the language and culture of poor children. *Language Arts, 86*(5), 362–370.

Duke, N. K. (2000). 3.6 minutes per day: The scarcity of informational texts in first grade. *Reading Research Quarterly, 35*(2), 202–224.

Duke, N. K., & Bennett-Armistead, V. S. (2003). *Reading and writing informational text in the primary grades: Research-based practices.* New York: Scholastic.

Duke, N. K., & Billman, A. K. (2009). Informational text difficulty for beginning readers. In E. H. Hiebert (Ed.), *Finding the right texts: What works for beginning and struggling readers* (pp. 109–128). New York: Guilford Press.

Dworin, J. E. (2006). The family stories project: Using funds of knowledge for writing. *The Reading Teacher, 59*(6), 510–520.

Ebbers, S. M., & Denton, C. A. (2008). A root awakening: Vocabulary instruction for older students with reading difficulties. *Learning Disabilities Research & Practice, 21*(2), 90–102.

Ehri, L. C., Satlow, E., & Gaskins, I. W. (2009). Grapho-phonemic enrichment strengthens keyword analogy instruction for struggling readers. *Reading and Writing Quarterly: Overcoming Learning Difficulties, 25*, 162–191.

Entwisle, D. R., Alexander, K. L., & Olson, L. S. (2007). Early schooling: The handicap of being poor and male. *Sociology of Education, 80*(2), 114–138.

Espinosa, L. (2005). Curriculum and assessment considerations for young children from culturally, linguistically, and economically diverse backgrounds. *Psychology in the Schools, 42*(8), 837–853.

Espinosa, L., & Laffey, J. (2003). Urban primary teacher perceptions and student performance: Congruent or divergent? *Journal of Children and Poverty, 9*(2), 23–40.

Fan, X., & Chen, M. (2001). Parental involvement and students' academic achievement: A meta-analysis. *Educational Psychology Review, 13*(1), 1–22.

Fien, H., Santoro, L., Baker, S. K., Park, Y., Chard, D. J., Williams, S., & Haria, P. (2011). Enhancing teacher read alouds with small-group vocabulary instruction for students with low vocabulary in first-grade classrooms. *School Psychology Review, 40*(2), 307–318.

Fiene, J., & McMahon, S. (2007). Assessing comprehension: A classroom-based process. *The Reading Teacher, 60*(5), 406–417.

Fingon, J., Frank, C., & Kawell, S. (2010). Young readers camp: Developing a university model for supporting struggling readers and their families. *The California Reader, 43*(4), 36–41.

Fitton, L., & Gredler, G. R. (1996). Parental involvement in reading remediation with young children. *Psychology in the Schools, 33*, 325–32.

Fitzgerald, J. (1995). English-as-a-second-language learners' cognitive reading processes: A review of research in the United States. *Review of Educational Research, 65*, 145–190.

Ford, D. (1998). The underrepresentation of minority students in gifted education: Problems and promises in recruitment and retention. *The Journal of Special Education, 32*, 4–14.

Gambrell, L. B., Palmer, B. M., Coding, R. M., & Mazzoni, S. A. (1995). *Assessing motivation to read* (NRRC Instructional Resource No. 14). Athens, GA & College Park, MD: National Reading Research Center.

Ganske, K. (2006). *Word sorts and more: Sound, pattern, and meaning explorations (K–3)*. New York: Guilford Press.

Ganske, K., Monroe, J. K., & Strickland, D. (2003). Questions teachers ask about struggling readers and writers. *The Reading Teacher, 57*(2), 118–128.

Garas-York, K. (2010). Overlapping student environments: An examination of the home school connection and its impact on achievement. *Education and Urban Society, 42*(4), 430–449.

Gaskins, I. W. (2005). *Success with struggling readers: The Benchmark School approach.* New York: Guilford Press.

Gaskins, I. W. (2011). Interventions to develop decoding proficiencies. In A. McGill-Franzen & R. L Allington (Eds.), *Handbook of reading disability research* (pp. 289–306). New York: Routledge.

Gaskins, I. W., & Labbo, L. (2007). Diverse perspectives on helping young children build important foundational language and print skills. *Reading Research Quarterly, 42,* 338–351.

Gee, J. (2003). *What video games have to teach us about learning and literacy.* New York: Palgrave Macmillan.

Gersten, R., & Baker, S. (2000). What we know about effective instructional practices for English-language learners. *Exceptional Children, 66,* 454–471.

Gonzalez, J. E., Goetz, E. T., Payne, T., Taylor, A. B., Kim, M., & McCormick, A. S. (2011). An evaluation of Early Reading First (ERF) preschool enrichment on language and literacy skills. *Reading & Writing, 24*(3), 253–284.

Goodman, K. S. (1973). Miscues: Windows on the reading process. In K. S. Goodman (Ed.), *Miscue analysis: Applications to reading instruction* (pp. 3–14). Urbana, IL: Eric Clearinghouse on Reading and Communication Skills and the National Council of Teachers of English.

Goodman, K. S. (1996). *Ken Goodman on reading: A common-sense look at the nature of language and the science of reading.* Portsmouth, NH: Heinemann.

Goodman, Y. (1996). Revaluing readers while readers revalue themselves: Retrospective miscue analysis. *The Reading Teacher, 49,* 600–609.

Goodman, Y., Watson, D., & Burke, C. (1987). *Reading miscue analysis: Alternative procedures.* New York: Richard Owens.

Gormley, K. A., & McDermott, P. (2011). Traditions of diagnosis. In A. McGill-Franzen & R. L. Allington (Eds.), *Handbook of reading disability research* (pp. 162–172). New York: Routledge.

Gowin, D. B., & Alvarez, M. C. (2005). *The art of educating with V diagrams.* New York: Cambridge University Press.

Graves, M. F. (2000). A vocabulary program to complement and bolster a middle-grade comprehension program. In B. M. Taylor, M. F. Graves, & P. Van Den Broek (2001), *Reading for meaning* (pp. 116–135). Newark, DE: International Reading Association.

Graves, M. F. (2004). *Teaching reading in the 21st century.* New York: Allyn & Bacon.

Graves, M. F., & Philippot, R. A. (2002). High-interest, easy reading: An important resource for struggling readers. *Preventing School Failure, 46*(4), 179–182.

Greenleaf, C. L., Schoenbach, R., Cziko, C., & Mueller, F. L. (2001). Apprenticing adolescent readers to academic literacy. *Harvard Educational Review, 71,* 79–129.

Griffin, S., & Case, R. (1997). Rethinking the primary school math curriculum: An approach based on cognitive science. *Issues in Education, 3*(1), 1–49.

Griffiths, A. J., VanDerHeyden, A. M., Skokut, M., & Lilles, E. 2009). Progress monitoring in oral reading fluency within the context of RTI. *School Psychology Quarterly, 24*(1), 13–23.

Gustafson, S., Faith, L., Svensson, I., Tjus, T., & Heimann, M. (2011). Effects of three interventions on the reading skills of children with reading disabilities in grade 2. *Journal of Learning Disabilities, 44*(2), 123–135.

Guthrie, J. T. (2004). Teaching for literacy engagement. *Journal of Literacy Research, 36*, 1–30.

Guthrie, J. T., McGough, K., Bennett, L., & Rice, M. E. (1996). Concept-oriented reading instruction: An integrated curriculum to develop motivations and strategies for reading. In L. Baker, P. Afflerbach, & D. Reinking (Eds.), *Developing engaged readers in school and home communities* (pp. 165–190). Hillsdale, NJ: Erlbaum.

Guthrie, J., & Wigfield, A. (2000). Engagement and motivation in reading. In M. Kamil, P. B. Mosenthal, P. D. Pearson, & R. Barr (Eds.), *Handbook of reading research* (Vol. 3, pp. 403–422). Mahwah, NJ: Erlbaum.

Gutiérrez, K., Baquedano-López, P., & Álvarez, H. (2001). Literacy as hybridity: Moving beyond bilingualism in urban classrooms. In M. de la Luz Reyes & J. Halcón (Eds.), *The best for our children: Critical perspectives on literacy for Latino students* (pp. 122–141). New York: Teachers College Press.

Gutiérrez, K., & Lee, C. D. (2009). Informal learning with children from diverse backgrounds. In L. M. Morrow, R. Rueda, & D. Lapp (Eds.), *Handbook of research on literacy instruction: Issues of diversity, policy, and equity* (pp. 216–232). New York: Guilford Press.

Hall, L. A., Burns, L. D., & Edwards, E. C. (2011). *Empowering struggling readers: Practices for the middle grades.* New York: Guilford Press.

Harmon, J. M., Wood, K. D., & Kiser, K. (2009). Promoting vocabulary learning with the interactive word wall. *Middle School Journal, 40*(3), 58–63.

Harrison, K. (2003). *A wrinkle in time* [motion picture]. Burbank, CA: Disney.

Harste, J. C. (2009). Reading as identity. *Journal of Reading Education, 34*(3), 5–7.

Hart, B., & Risley, T. R. (1995). *Meaningful differences in the everyday experiences of young American children.* Baltimore: Brookes.

Hart, B., & Risley, T. R. (2003). The early catastrophe: The 30 million word gap. *American Educator, 27*(1), 4–9.

Heller, J. I., & Reif, F. (1984). Prescribing effective human problem solving processes: Problem description in physics. *Cognition and Instruction, 1*, 177–216.

Henderson, A. T., & Mapp, K. L. (2002). *A new wave of evidence: The impact of school, family, and community connections on student achievement.* Austin, TX: Southwest Educational Development Laboratory, National Center for Family and Community Connections with Schools.

Hibbing, A. N., & Rankin-Erickson, J. L. (2003). A picture is worth a thousand words: Using visual images to improve comprehension for middle school struggling readers. *The Reading Teacher, 56*(8), 758–770.

Hiebert, E. H. (Ed.). (2009). *Reading more, reading better: Solving problems in the teaching of literacy.* New York: Guilford.

Hiebert, E. H. (2011, August 3). *Is reading in kindergarten the means for ensuring college and career readiness?* [Web log post]. Retrieved from http://textproject.org/frankly-freddy/

Hiebert, E. H., & Martin, L. A. (2009). Repetition of words: The forgotten variable in texts for beginning and struggling readers. In E. H. Hiebert & M. Sailors (Eds.), *Finding the right texts: What works for beginning and struggling readers* (pp. 47–69). New York: Guilford Press.

Hiebert, E. H., & Sailors, M. (Eds.). (2009). *Finding the right texts: What works for beginning and struggling readers.* New York: Guilford Press.

Hollins, E. R. (1996). *Culture in school learning: Revealing the deep meaning.* Mahwah, NJ: Erlbaum.

Hughes, L. (1990). *Selected poems of Langston Hughes.* New York: Vintage Books.

Hurley, S. R., & Blake, S. (2000). Assessment in the content areas for acquiring English. In S. R. Hurley & J. V. Tinahero (Eds.), *Literacy assessment of second language learners* (pp. 84–103). Boston, MA: Allyn & Bacon.

Iaquinta, A. (2006). Guided reading: A research-based response to the challenges of early reading instruction. *Early Childhood Education Journal, 33*(6), 413–418.

Iddings, A. C. D., Risko, V. J., & Rampulla, M. P. (2009). When you don't speak their language: Guiding English-language learners through conversations about text. *The Reading Teacher, 63*(1), 52–61.

Individuals with Disabilities Education Improvement Act (IDEIA) of 2004. Pub. L. No. 108-446, 118 Stat. 2647 (2004).

Ingersoll, R. M. (2002). *Teacher quality and educational inequality.* Seattle: University of Washington, Center for the Study of Teaching and Policy.

International Reading Association (IRA). (2002). *Family-school partnerships: Essential elements of literacy instruction in the United States.* A position statement of the International Reading Association. Newark, DE: Author.

International Reading Association (IRA). (2010). *Standards for reading professionals—revised 2010.* Newark, DE: Author.

Ivey, G. (1999). A multicase study in the middle school: Complexities among young adolescent readers. *Reading Research Quarterly, 34*(2), 172–192.

Jalongo, M., & Sobolak, M. (2011). Supporting young children's vocabulary growth: The challenges, the benefits, and evidence-based strategies. *Early Childhood Education Journal, 38*(6), 421–429.

Jenkins, J. R., Peyton, J. A., Sanders, E. A., & Vadasy, P. F. (2004). Effects of reading decodable texts in supplemental first grade tutoring. *Scientific Studies of Reading, 8*(1), 53–85.

Jenkins, S. (2009). How to maintain school reading success: Five recommendations from a struggling male reader. *The Reading Teacher, 63*(2), 159–162.

Jewett, P. C., Wilson, J. L., & Vanderburg, M. A. (2011). The unifying power of a whole-school read. *Journal of Adolescent & Adult Literacy, 54*(6), 415–424.

Johnson, A. S. (2007). An ethics of access: Using life history to trace preservice teachers' initial viewpoints on teaching for equity. *Journal of Teacher Education, 58*(4), 299–314.

Johnson, A. S. (2010). The Jones family culture of literacy. *The Reading Teacher*, *64*(1), 33–43.

Johnson, S. (1977). *Samuel Johnson: Selected poetry and prose* (F. Brady & W. K. Wimsatt, Eds.). Berkeley: University of California Press.

Johnson-Laird, P. N. (1983). *Mental models: Towards a cognitive science of language, inference, and consciousness.* Cambridge, UK: Cambridge University Press.

Johnston, P. (1997). *Knowing literacy: Constructive literacy assessment.* York, ME: Stenhouse.

Johnston, P., & Costello, P. (2005). Principles for literacy assessment. *Reading Research Quarterly, 40*(2), 256–267.

Juel, C., & Minden-Cupp, C. (2000). Learning to read words: Linguistic units and instructional strategies. *Reading Research Quarterly, 35*(4), 458–492.

Kapinus, B. A., Collier, G. V., & Kruglanski, H. (1994). The Maryland school performance assessment program: A new view of assessment. In S. W. Valencia, E. H. Hiebert, & P. P. Afflerbach (Eds.), *Authentic reading assessment: Practices and possibilities.* Newark, DE: International Reading Association.

Karolyn, L. A., & Gonzalez, G. C. (2011). Early care and education for children in immigrant families. *The Future of Children, 21*(1), 103–122.

Kay, A. M., Neher, A., & Lush, L. H. (2010). Writing a relationship: Home-school journals. *Language Arts, 87*(6), 417–426.

Kea, C. D., & Utley, C. A. (1998). To teach me is to know me. *Journal of Special Education, 32*(1), 44–7.

Kelly, S., & Turner, J. (2009). Rethinking the effects of classroom activity structure on the engagement of low-achieving students. *Teachers College Record, 111,* 1665–1692.

Kenner, C. (2004). *Becoming biliterate: An microethnographic perspective.* Mahwah, NJ: Erlbaum.

Kidd, J. K., Sanchez, S. Y., & Thorp, E. K. (2004). Gathering family stories: Facilitating preservice teachers' cultural awareness and responsiveness. *Action in Teacher Education, 26*(1), 64–73.

Kieffer, M. J. (2008). Catching up or falling behind? Initial English proficiency, concentrated poverty, and the reading growth of language minority learners in the United States. *Journal of Educational Psychology, 100*(4), 851–868.

Kieffer, M. J., & Lesaux, N. K. (2007). Breaking down words to build meaning: Morphology, vocabulary, and reading comprehension in the urban classroom. *The Reading Teacher, 61,* 134–144.

Kieffer, M. J., & Lesaux, N. K. (2010). Morphing into adolescents: Active word learning for English-language learners and their classmates in middle school. *Journal of Adolescent & Adult Literacy, 54*(1), 47–56.

King, M. L. (1986). *A testament of hope: The essential writings and speeches of Martin Luther King, Jr.* (J. M. Washington, Ed.). New York: HarperCollins.

Kirby, J. R., & Hogan, B. (2008). Family literacy environment and early literacy development. *Exceptionality Education Canada, 18*(3), 112–130.

Klingner, J., & Vaughn, S. (2004). Specific strategies for struggling second-language readers. In T. Jetton & J. Dole (Eds.), *Adolescent literacy research and practice* (pp. 183–209). New York: Guilford Press.

Labbo, L. D. (2007). The golden rule should rule: Modest revelations on preservice teachers' explorations into cultural identity, prejudice, and empathy. *Journal of Reading Education, 33*(1), 40–44.

Labov, W. (2003). When ordinary children fail to read. *Reading Research Quarterly, 38*(1), 128–131.

Ladson-Billings, G. (2001). *Crossing over to Canaan: The journey of new teachers in diverse classrooms.* San Francisco: Jossey-Bass.

Ladson-Billings, G. (2006). Yes, but how do we do it? Practicing culturally relevant pedagogy. In J. Landsman & C. W. Lewis (Eds.), *White teachers/diverse classrooms: A guide to inclusive schools, promoting high expectations and eliminating racism* (pp. 29–42). Sterling, VA: Stylus.

Landis, D., Kalieva, R., Abitova, S., Izmukhanbetova, S., & Musaeva, Z. (2006). Learning through ethnographic dialogues. *Language Arts, 83*, 192–202.

Lankshear, C., & Knobel, M. (2003). *New literacies: Changing knowledge and classroom learning.* Buckingham, UK: Open University Press.

Lantolf, J. P. (2000). Second language learning as a mediated process. *Language Teaching, 33*(2), 79–86.

Lau-Tsze. (2004). *The speculations on metaphysics, polity and morality of the old philosopher, Lau Tsze* (J. Chalmers, Trans.). Montana: Kessinger. (Original translation of work published 1868)

Lee, C. D. (2005). Culture and language: Bi-dialectal issues in literacy. In J. Flood & P. L. Anders (Eds.), *Literacy development of students in urban schools: Research and policy* (pp. 241–274). Newark, DE: International Reading Association.

Lee, C. D. (2008). The centrality of culture to the scientific study of learning and development: How an ecological framework in education research facilitates civic responsibility. *Educational Researcher, 37*(5), 267–279.

Lee, C. D., Rosenfeld, E., Mendenhall, R., Rivers, A., & Tynes, B. (2004). Cultural modeling as a frame for narrative analysis. In C. Dauite & C. Lightfoot (Eds.), *Narrative analysis: Studying the development of individuals in society* (pp. 39–62). Thousand Oaks, CA: Sage.

Lee, J., Grigg, W. S., & Donahue, P. L. (2007). *Nation's report card: Reading* (NCES 2007-496). Washington, DC: U.S. Department of Education, Institute of Education Sciences, National Center for Education Statistics.

Lemke, J. L. (1990). *Talking science: Language, learning, and values.* Norwood: Ablex.

Lenski, S. D., Ehlers-Zavala, F., Daniel, M. C., & Sun-Irminger, X. (2006). Assessing English-language learners in mainstream classrooms. *The Reading Teacher, 60*(1), 24–35.

Lesaux, N. K., & Kieffer, M. J. (2010). Exploring sources of reading comprehension difficulties among language minority learners and their classmates in early adolescence. *American Educational Research Journal, 47*, 596–632.

Lesaux, N. K., Kieffer, M. J., Faller, S., & Kelley, J. G. (2010). The effectiveness and ease of implementation of an academic vocabulary intervention for linguistically diverse students in urban middle schools. *Reading Research Quarterly, 45*(2), 196–228.

Leslie, L., & Caldwell, J. (2006). *Qualitative Reading Inventory—4.* Boston, MA: Allyn & Bacon.

López-Robertson, J., Long, S., & Turner-Nash, K. (2010). First steps in constructing counter narratives of young children and their families. *Language Arts, 88*(2), 93–103.

Love, M. S. (2004/2005). Multimodality of learning through anchored instruction. *Journal of Adolescent & Adult Literacy, 48*(4), 300–310.

Lovelace, S., & Stewart, S. R. (2009). Effects of robust vocabulary instruction and multicultural text on the development of word knowledge among African American children. *American Journal of Speech-Language Pathology, 18*(2), 168–179.

Maderazo, C., Martens, P., Croce, K., Martens, R., Doyle, M., Aghalarov, S., & Noble, R. (2010). Beyond picture walks: Revaluing picture books as written and pictorial texts. *Language Arts, 87*(6), 437–446.

Mancilla-Martinez, J., & Lesaux, N. K. (2010). Predictors of reading comprehension for struggling readers: The case of Spanish-language minority learners. *Journal of Educational Psychology, 102*(3), 701–711.

Manjula, P., Saraswathi, G., Prakash, P., & Ashalatha, K. V. (2009). Involvement of parents in the education of children with reading and writing difficulties: Impact of an intervention. *Educational Research and Review, 4*(4), 208–212.

Martin, L. E., & Kragler, S. (2011). Becoming a self-regulated reader: A study of primary-grade students' reading strategies. *Literacy Research and Instruction, 50,* 89–104.

Martin, M., Fergus, E., & Noguera, P. (2010). Responding to the needs of the whole child: A case study of a high-performing elementary school for immigrant children. *Reading & Writing Quarterly, 26,* 195–222.

Mathes, P. G., Denton, C. A., Fletcher, J. M., Anthony, J. L., Francis, D. J., & Schatschneider, C. (2005). The effects of theoretically different instruction and student characteristics on the skills of struggling readers. *Reading Research Quarterly, 40*(2), 148–182.

Mathes, P. G., Pollard-Durodola, S. D., Cárdenas-Hagan, E., Linan-Thompson, S., & Vaughn, S. (2007). Teaching struggling readers who are native Spanish speakers: What do we know? *Language, Speech, and Hearing Services in Schools, 38,* 260–271.

May, L. (2011). Animating talk and texts: Culturally relevant teacher read-alouds of informational texts. *Journal of Literacy Research, 48*(1), 3–38.

McAllister, D. (1996). *Retelling assessment form* [unpublished document]. Nashville, TN: Vanderbilt University.

McCarthey, S. J., & Moje, E. (2002). "Conversations": Identity matters. *Reading Research Quarterly, 37*(2), 228–253.

McCarty, T. L., & Romero-Little, M. E. (2005, April). Accountable to whom? NCLB, English-only, and Native American learners. Paper presented at the annual meeting of the American Educational Research Association, Montreal, Canada.

McDermott, R. (2004). Putting literacy in its place. *Journal of Education, 184*(1), 11–20.

McDermott, R., Goldman, S., & Varenne, H. (2006). The cultural work of learning disabilities. *Educational Researcher, 35*(6), 12–17.

McGee, L., & Richgels, D. (2004). *Literacy beginnings: Supporting young readers and writers* (4th ed.). New York: Allyn & Bacon.

McIntosh, A. S., Graves, A., & Gersten, R. (2007). The effects of response to intervention on literacy development in multiple-language settings. *Learning Disability Quarterly, 30*(3), 197–212.

McIntyre, E., Hulan, N., & Layne, V. (2011). *Reading instruction for diverse classrooms: Research-based, culturally responsive practice*. New York: Guilford Press.

McIntyre, E., Hulan, N., & Maher, M. (2010). The relationship between literacy learning and cultural differences: A study of teachers' dispositions. *Journal of Reading Education, 35*(3), 19–25.

McIntyre, E., Rightmyer, E., Powell, R., Powers, S., & Petrosko, J. (2006). How much should young children read? A study of the relationship between development and instruction. *Literacy Teaching and Learning, 11*(1), 51–72.

McKenna, M. C., Kear, D. J., & Ellsworth, R. A. (1995). Children's attitudes toward reading: A national survey. *Reading Research Quarterly, 30*, 934–956.

McKeown, M. G., Beck, I. L., Omanson, R. C., & Perfetti, C. A. (1983). The effects of long-term vocabulary instruction on reading comprehension: A replication. *Journal of Reading Behavior, 15*, 3–18.

McKeown, M. G., Beck, I. L., Omanson, R. C., & Pople, M. T. (1985). Some effects on the nature and frequency of vocabulary instruction on the knowledge and use of words. *Reading Research Quarterly, 20*, 522–535.

McLarty, K., Goodman, J., Risko, V. J., Kinzer, C., Vye, N., Rowe, D., & Carson, J. (1990). Implementing anchored instruction: Guiding principles for curriculum development. In S. McCormick & J. Zutell (Eds.), *Yearbook of the National Reading Conference: Vol. 39. Literacy, theory and research* (pp. 109–120). Chicago: National Reading Conference.

McLoyd, V. C., & Purtell, K. M. (2008). How poverty and income affect children's cognitive functioning and school achievement. In S. Neuman (Ed.), *Educating the other America* (pp. 52–73). Baltimore: Brookes.

Meadows, D. (2003). Digital storytelling: Research-based practice in new media. *Visual Communication, 2*(2), 189–193.

Meece, J. L., Glienke, B. B., & Burg, S. (2006). Gender and motivation. *Journal of School Psychology, 44*(5), 351–373.

Mesmer, H. A. E., & Cumming, S. (2009). Text-reader matching: Meeting the needs of struggling readers. In E. H. Hiebert & M. Sailors (Eds.), *Finding the right texts: What works for beginning and struggling readers* (pp. 149–176). New York: Guilford Press.

Meyer, B. J. F., & Wijekumar, K. (2007). A web-based tutoring system for the structure strategy: Theoretical background, design, and findings. In D. S. McNamara (Ed.), *Reading comprehension strategies: Theories, interventions, and technologies* (pp. 347–375). Mahwah, NJ: Erlbaum.

Mills, K. A. (2010). Shrek meets Vygotsky: Rethinking adolescents' multimodal literacy practices in schools. *Journal of Adolescent & Adult Literacy, 54*(1), 35–45.

Mills, K. A., & Chandra, V. (2011). Microblogging as a literacy practice for educational communities. *Journal of Adolescent & Adult Literacy, 55*(1), 35–45.

Milner, H. R., IV. (2011). Culturally relevant pedagogy in a diverse urban classroom. *Urban Review, 43,* 66–89.

Mol, S. E., & Bus, A. G. (2011). To read or not to read: A meta-analysis of print exposure from infancy to early adulthood. *Psychological Bulletin, 137*(2), 267–296.

Moll, L. C. (1997). The creation of mediating settings. *Mind, Culture, and Activity, 4*(3), 192–199.

Moll, L. C. (2003, February 6). *Biliteracy development in "marked" children: Sociocultural considerations.* Maycie K. Southall Distinguished Lecture given at Vanderbilt University, Peabody College, Department of Teaching and Learning, Nashville, TN.

Moll, L. C., Amanti, C., Neff, D., & Gonzalez, N. (1992). Funds of knowledge for teaching: Using a qualitative approach to connect homes and classrooms. *Theory into Practice, 31*(2), 132–141.

Moll L. C., & Greenberg, J. (1990). Creating zones of possibilities: Combining social contexts for instruction. In. L. C. Moll (Ed.), *Vygotsky and education* (pp. 319–348). Cambridge, UK: Cambridge University Press.

Moll, L. C., Saez, R., & Dworin, J. E. (2001). Exploring biliteracy: Two student case examples of writing as a social practice. *The Elementary School Journal, 101,* 435–449.

Moll, L. C., Velez Ibanez, C., & Greenberg, J. (1990). *Community knowledge and classroom practices: Combining reports for literacy instruction.* Arlington, VA: Development Associates.

Morris, D. (1992). Concept of word: A pivotal understanding in the learning to read process. In S. Templeton & D. Bear (Eds.), *Development of orthographic knowledge and the foundations of literacy* (pp. 53–78). Hillsdale, NJ: Erlbaum.

Morris, D. (2011). Interventions to develop phonological and orthographic systems. In A. McGill-Franzen & R. L. Allington (Eds.), *Handbook of reading disability research* (pp. 279–288). New York: Routledge.

Morrison, K. A., Robbins, H. H., & Rose, D. G. (2008). Operationalizing culturally relevant pedagogy: A synthesis of classroom-based research. *Equity & Excellence in Education, 41*(4), 433–452.

Morrow, L. M. (1988). Young children's responses to one-to-one story readings in school settings. *Reading Research Quarterly, 23,* 89–107.

Morrow, L. M., Tracey, D. H., Woo, D. G., & Pressley, M. (1999). Characteristics of exemplary first-grade reading instruction. *The Reading Teacher, 52,* 462–476.

Mueller, P. (2001). *Lifers: Learning from at-risk adolescent readers.* Portsmouth, NH: Heinemann.

Nagy, W. E. (1988). *Teaching vocabulary to improve reading comprehension.* Newark, DE: International Reading Association.

Nagy, W. E. (2005). Why vocabulary instruction needs to be long-term and comprehensive. In E. H. Hiebert & M. L. Kamil (Eds.), *Teaching and learning vocabulary: Bringing research to practice* (pp. 20–44). Mahwah, NJ: Erlbaum.

Nagy, W. E., Garcia, G. E., & Durgunoglu, A. Y. (1993). Spanish-English bilingual students' use of cognates in English reading. *Journal of Reading Behavior, 25*(3), 241–259.

Nagy, W. E., & Scott, J. A. (2000). Vocabulary processes. In M. L. Kamil, P. B. Mosenthal, P. D. Pearson, & R. Barr (Eds.), *Handbook of reading research* (Vol. 3, pp. 269–284). Mahwah, NJ: Erlbaum.

Nation, P. (2003). Effective ways of building vocabulary knowledge. *ESL Magazine, 6*(4), 14–15.

National Comprehensive Center for Teacher Quality & Public Agenda. (2008). *Lessons learned: New teachers talk about their jobs, challenges, and long-range plans: Issue No. 3. Teaching in Changing Times.* Washington, DC: National Comprehensive Center for Teacher Quality.

National Endowment for the Arts. (2007). Annual report. Available at http://www.nea.gov/about/07Annual/AR2007.pdf

National Institute of Child Health and Human Development. (2000). *Teaching children to read: An evidence-based assessment of the scientific research literature on reading and its implications for reading instruction.* (Report of the National Reading Panel; NIH Publication No. 00-4769). Washington, DC: U.S. Government Printing Office.

National Research Council. (2001). *Classroom assessment and the national science education standards.* Washington, DC: National Academy Press.

Newman, F. M., Marks, H. M., & Gamoran, A. (1995, Spring). Authentic pedagogy: Standards that boost study performance. *Issues in Restructuring Schools,* No. 8. Madison, WI: University of Wisconsin, Center on Organization and Restructuring of Schools.

Nieto, S. (2000). *Affirming diversity: The sociopolitical context of multicultural education* (3rd ed.). New York: Longman.

No Child Left Behind Act of 2001 (NCLB). Pub. L. No. 107-110, 115 Stat. 1425 (2002). Retrieved from http:///www. 2.ed.gov/policy/elsec/leg/esea02/107-110.pdf

Nocon, H., & Cole, M. (2009). Relating diversity and literacy theory. In L. M. Morrow, R. Rueda, & D. Lapp (Eds.), *Handbook of research on literacy and diversity* (pp. 13–31). New York: Guilford Press.

Noll, E., & Watkins, R. (2003). The impact of homelessness on children's early literacy experiences. *The Reading Teacher, 57*(4), 362–371.

Ogle, D., & Correa-Kovtun, A. (2010). Supporting English-language learners and struggling readers in content literacy with the "Partner Reading and Content, Too" routine. *The Reading Teacher, 63*(7), 532–542.

Ohler, J. (2006). The world of digital storytelling. *Educational Leadership, 63*(4), 44–47.

Oldfather, P. (1995). Commentary: What's needed to maintain and extend motivation for literacy in the middle grades. *Journal of Reading, 38*(6), 420–422.

Opitz, M. F., & Rasinski, T. V. (1998). *Good-bye round robin.* Portsmouth, NH: Heinemann.

Ordonez-Jasis, R., & Ortiz, R. W. (2006). Reading their worlds: Working with diverse families to enhance children's early literacy development. *Young Children, 61*(1), 42–44.

Orellana, M. F., & Reynolds, J. F. (2008). Cultural modeling: Leveraging bilingual skills for school paraphrasing tasks. *Reading Research Quarterly, 43*(1), 48–65.

Orellana M. F., Reynolds, J., Dorner, L., & Meza, M. (2003). In other words: Translating or "para-phrasing" as a family literacy practice in immigrant households. *Reading Research Quarterly, 38*, 12–34.

Orellana, M. F., Reynolds, J., & Martinez, D. C. (2011). Cultural modeling: Building on cultural strengths as an alternative to remedial reading approaches. In A. McGll-Franzen & R. L. Allington (Eds.), *Handbook of reading disability research* (pp. 273–278). New York: Routledge.

Oswald, D. P., Coutinho, M. J., Best, A. M., & Singh, N. (1999). Ethnic representation in special education: The influence of school-related economic and demographic variables. *Journal of Special Education, 32*(4), 194–206.

Páez, M. M., Bock, K. P., & Pizzo, L. (2011). Supporting the language and early literacy skills of English language learners: Effective practices and future directions. In S. B. Neumann & D. K. Dickinson (Eds.), *Handbook of early literacy research, Volume 3.* (pp. 136–152).

Páez, M. M., Tabors, P. O., & Lopez, M. (2007). Dual language and literacy development of Spanish-speaking preschool children. *Journal of Applied Developmental Psychology, 28*(2), 85–102.

Palumbo, A., & Sanacore, J. (2009). Helping struggling middle school literacy learners achieve success. *ClearingHouse, 82*(6), 275–280.

Pappas, C. C., Varelas, M., Barry, A., & Rife, A. (2003). Dialogic inquiry around information text: The role of intertextuality in constructing scientific understandings in urban primary classrooms. *Linguistics and Education, 13*(4), 435–482.

Paris, S. (2005). Reinterpreting the development of reading skills. *Reading Research Quarterly, 40*(2), 184–202.

Parrish, T. (2002). Racial disparities in the identification, funding, and provision of special education. In D. J. Losen, & G. Orfield (Eds.), *Racial inequity in special education* (pp. 15–37). Cambridge, MA: Harvard Education Press.

Pease-Alvarez, L. (2006). Finding my focus. *Negotiating pedagogy in context.* Retrieved from http://www.cfkeep.org/html/stitch.php?s=69609704026589&id=75966125797449

Pellegrino, J. W., Chudowsky, N., & Glaser, R. (2001). *Knowing what students know: The science and design of educational assessment.* Washington, DC: National Academy Press.

Perez, B. (Ed.). (2004). *Sociocultural contexts of language and literacy* (2nd ed.). Mahwah, NJ: Erlbaum.

Peverini, S. (2009). The value of teacher expertise and good judgment: Recent inspiring reading about assessment. *Language Arts, 86*(5), 398–402.

Pickering, C., & Painter, J. (2005). Using Shrek and Bart Simpson to build respectful learning communities. In B. Comber & B. Kamler (Eds.), *Turn-around pedagogies: Literacy interventions for at-risk students* (pp. 77–92). Newtown, NSW, Australia: Primary English Teaching Association.

Pinnell, G. S., & Fountas, I. C. (2004). *Word study lessons: Letters, words, and how they work: Grade 3.* Portsman, NH: Heinemann.

Planty, M., Hussar, W., Snyder, T., Kena, G., KewalRamani, A., Kemp, J., Bianco, K., & Dinkes, R. (2009). *The condition of education 2009* (NCES 2009-081).

Washington, DC: U.S. Department of Education, Institute of Education Sciences, National Center for Education Statistics.

Popham, W. J. (2008). *Transformative assessment*. Alexandria, VA: Association for Supervision and Curriculum Development.

Portes, P., & Salas, S. (2009). Poverty and its relation to development and literacy. In L. M. Morrow, R. Rueda, & D. Lapp (Eds.), *Handbook on research and diversity* (pp. 97–113). New York: Guilford Press.

Proctor, P., August, D., Carlo, M., & Snow, C. (2005). Native Spanish-speaking children reading in English: Toward a model of comprehension. *Journal of Educational Psychology, 97*(2), 246–256.

Purcell-Gates, V., Duke, N. K., & Martineau, J. A. (2007). Learning to read and write genre-specific text: Roles of authentic experience and explicit teaching. *Reading Research Quarterly, 42*(1), 8–45.

Ramey, L., & Ramey, C. T. (1998). The transition to school: Opportunities and challenges for children, families, educators, and communities. *The Elementary School Journal, 98*(4), 311–327.

RAND Reading Study Group. (2002). *Reading for understanding: Toward an R & D program in reading comprehension*. Santa Monica, CA: RAND Corporation.

Rasinski, T. V. (2004). *Assessing reading fluency*. Honolulu: Pacific Resources for Education and Learning. Retrieved from http://www.prel.org/products/re_/assessing-fluency.htm

Rasinski, T. V. (2005). *Daily word ladders: Grades 4–6*. New York: Teaching Resources.

Rasinksi, T. V. (2011). *Understanding (and teaching) real fluency!* Presentation at the Morgridge International Reading Center Inaugural Lecture Series, Morgridge International Reading Center, OCF, Orlando, FL.

Richgels, D. (2001). Invented spelling, phonemic awareness, and reading and writing instruction. In S. Neuman & Y. D. Dickinson (Eds.), *Handbook of early literacy research* (pp. 142–155). New York: Guilford Press.

Riley, D. W. (1995). *The complete Kwanzaa: Celebrating our cultural harvest*. New York: HarperCollins.

Rinaldi, C., & Samson, J. (2008). English language learners and response to intervention: Referral recommendations. *Teaching Exceptional Children, 40*(5), 6–14.

Risko, V. J. (2011). Celebrating teachers: Teaching with humanity. *Reading Today, 29*(1), 4–5.

Risko, V. J., & Walker-Dalhouse, D. (2007). Tapping students' cultural funds of knowledge to address the achievement gap. *The Reading Teacher, 61*(1), 98–100.

Risko, V. J., & Walker-Dalhouse, D. (2009). Parents and teachers: Talking with or past each other—or not talking at all? *The Reading Teacher, 62*(5), 442–444.

Risko, V. J., & Walker-Dalhouse, D. (2010). Making the most of assessment to inform instruction. *The Reading Teacher, 63*(5), 420–422.

Risko, V., Walker-Dalhouse, D., & Arragones, A. (2011). The promise of an alternate perspective: Viewing struggling readers through a socio-cultural research lens. *Association of Literacy Educators and Researchers Yearbook, 33*, 187–203.

Risko, V. J., Walker-Dalhouse, D., Bridges, E. S., & Wilson, A. (2011). Drawing on text features for reading and comprehension and composing. *The Reading Teacher, 64*(5), 376–378.

Roderick, M., & Camburn, E. (1999). Risk and recovery from course failure in the early years of high school. *American Educational Research Journal, 36*(2), 303–343.

Rogoff, B. (2003). *The cultural nature of human development.* Oxford, UK: Oxford University Press.

Rohr, J., & He, Y. (2010). Preservice teachers and parents using a reading course to change perceptions and practice. *Educational Studies, 36*(1), 35–45.

Rojas-Drummond, S. M., Albarran, C. D., & Littleton, K. S. (2008). Collaboration, creativity and the co-construction of oral and written texts. *Thinking Skills and Creativity, 3*(3), 177–191.

Rupley, W. H., Blair, T. R., & Nichols, W. D. (2009). Effective reading instruction for struggling readers: The role of direct/explicit teaching. *Reading and Writing Quarterly, 25*, 125–138.

Sadik, A. (2008). Digital storytelling: A meaningful technology-integrated approach for engaged student learning. *Education Technology Research Development, 56*(4), 487–506.

Samuels, S. J., & Farstup, A. E. (Eds.). (2006). *What research has to say about fluency instruction.* Newark, DE: International Reading Association.

Sanacore, J. (2000). Promoting effective literacy learning in minority students by focusing on teacher workshops and reflective practice: A comprehensive project supported by the Annenberg Foundation. *Reading Psychology: An International Quarterly, 21*, 233–255.

Sanacore, J. (2004). Genuine caring and literacy learning for African American children. *The Reading Teacher, 57*(8), 744–753.

Santa, C., & Hoien, T. (1999). An assessment of Early Steps: A program for early intervention of reading problems. *Reading Research Quarterly, 34*(1), 54–79.

Scanlon, D. M., Gelzheiser, L. M., Vellutino, F. R., Schatschneider, C., & Sweeney, J. M. (2010). Reducing the incidence of early reading difficulties: Professional development for classroom teachers versus direct interventions for children. In P. H. Johnston (Ed.), *RTI in literacy: Responsive and comprehensive* (pp. 237–291). Newark, DE: International Reading Association.

Scanlon, D. M., Vellutino, F. R., Small, S. G., Fanuele, D. P., & Sweeney, J. M. (2005). Severe reading difficulties—can they be prevented? A comparison of prevention and intervention approaches. *Exceptionality, 13*(4), 209–227.

Schmidt, P. R. (1998). The ABC's of cultural understanding and communication. *Equity and Excellence in Education, 31*(2), 28–38.

Scott, J. A., Jamieson-Noel, D., & Asselin, M. (2003). Vocabulary instruction throughout the day in 23 Canadian upper-elementary classrooms. *The Elementary School Journal, 103*, 269–268.

Senechal, M., & Cornell, E. H. (1993). Vocabulary acquisition through shared reading experiences. *Reading Research Quarterly, 25*(4), 361–374.

Shanahan, T., & Barr, R. (1995). Reading recovery: An independent evaluation of the effects of an early instructional intervention for at-risk learners. *Reading Research Quarterly, 30*(4), 958–996.

Sharp, D. L. M., Bransford, J. D., Goldman, S. R., Risko, V. J., Kinzer, C. K., & Vye, N. J. (1995). Dynamic visual support for story comprehension and mental model building by young, at-risk children. *Educational Technology Research and Development, 43*(4), 25–41.

Shaywitz, S. E., Shaywitz, B. A., Fletcher, J. M., & Escobar, M. D. (1990). Prevalence of reading disability in boys and girls: Results of the Connecticut Longitudinal Study. *Journal of the American Medical Association, 264,* 998–1002.

Shields, P. H., Gordon, J. G., & Dupree, D. (1983). Influence of parent practices upon the reading achievement of good and poor readers. *Journal of Negro Education, 52*(4), 436–445.

Silva, E. (2008). *Measuring skills for the 21st century.* Washington, DC: Education Sector. Retrieved from http://www.educationsector.org/publications/measuring -skills-21st-century.

Silverman, R., & Crandell, J. D. (2010). Vocabulary practices in prekindergarten and kindergarten classrooms. *Reading Research Quarterly, 45*(3), 318–340.

Smith, J. A., & Read, S. (2009). *Early literacy instruction: Teaching reading and writing in today's primary grades* (2nd ed.). New York: Allyn & Bacon.

Smolkin, L. B., & Donovan, C. A. (2003). Supporting comprehension acquisition for emerging and struggling readers: The interactive information book read-aloud. *Exceptionality, 11,* 25–38.

Snow, C. E. (1993). Families as social contexts for literacy development. In C. Daiute (Ed.), *The development of literacy through social interaction* (pp. 11–24). San Francisco: Jossey-Bass.

Snow, C. E., Barnes, W. S., Chandler, J., Goodman, I. F., & Hemphill, L. (1991). *Unfulfilled expectations: Home and school influences on literacy.* Cambridge, MA: Harvard University Press.

Snow, C. E., Burns, M. S., & Griffin, P. (1998). *Preventing reading difficulties in young children.* Washington, DC: National Academy Press.

Sobolak, M. J. (2011). Modifying robust vocabulary instruction for the benefit of low socioeconomic students. *Reading Improvement, 48*(1), 14–23.

Sokolinski, S. (2010). LIFE Support: A family literacy program for struggling first-grade readers and their families. *Illinois Reading Council Journal, 36*(2), 3–12.

Spencer, T. G. (2009). Complicating what it means to "struggle": One young child's experience with a mandated literacy initiative. *Contemporary Issues in Early Childhood, 10*(3), 218–231.

Stahl, S. (1992). Saying the "p" word: Nine guidelines for exemplary phonics instruction. *The Reading Teacher, 45*(8), 618–625.

Stichter, J. P., Stormont, M., & Lewis, T. J. (2009). Instructional practices and behavior during reading: A descriptive summary and comparison of practices in Title One and non-title elementary schools. *Psychology in the Schools, 46*(2), 172–183.

Stornaiuolo, A., Hull, G., & Nelson, M. (2009). Mobile texts and migrant audiences: Rethinking literacy and assessment in a new media age. *Language Arts, 86*(5), 382–392.

Stuhlman, M. W., & Pianta, R. C. (2009). Profiles of educational quality in first grade. *The Elementary School Journal, 109*(4), 323–342.

Taboada, A. (2009). English-language learners, vocabulary, and reading comprehension: What we know and what we need to know. *College Reading Association Yearbook, 30*, 307–322.

Tabors, P. O., Paez, M., & Lopez, M. M. (2003). Dual language abilities of Spanish-English bilingual four-year olds: Initial findings from the Early Childhood Study of Language and Literacy Development of Spanish-speaking children. *NABE Journal of Research and Practice, 1*, 70–91. Retrieved from http://www.uc.edu/njrp/

Tadesse, S., Hoot, J., & Watson-Thompson, O. (2009). Exploring the special needs of African refugee children in U.S. schools. *Childhood Education, 85*(6), 352–356.

Takanishi, R. (2006). Leveling the playing field: Supporting immigrant children from birth to eight. *The Future of Children, 14*, 61–79.

Tatum, A. (2008). Toward a more anatomically complete model of literacy instruction: A focus on African American male adolescents and texts. *Harvard Educational Review, 78*(1), 155–180.

Taylor, B. M., Pearson, P. D., Clark, K., & Walpole, S. (2000). Effective schools and accomplished teachers: Lessons about primary grade reading instruction in low-income schools. *The Elementary School Journal, 101*, 121–166.

Taylor, B. M., Pressley, M. P., & Pearson, P. D. (2000). *Research supported characteristics of teachers and schools that promote reading achievement*. Washington, DC: National Education Association.

Taylor, D. B., Mraz, M., Nichols, W. D., Rickelman, R. J., & Wood, K. D. (2009). Using explicit instruction to promote vocabulary learning for struggling readers. *Reading and Writing Quarterly, 25* (2/3), 205–220.

Taylor, R. W. (2010). The role of teacher education programs in creating culturally responsive teachers: A moral imperative for ensuring the academic success of diverse student populations. *Multicultural Education, 17*(3), 24–28.

Tellez, K., & Waxman, H. C. (2006). A meta-synthesis of qualitative research on effective teaching practices for English language learners. In J. M. Norris & L. Ortega (Eds.), *Synthesizing research on language learning and teaching* (pp. 245–277). Philadelphia: John Benjamins Publishing.

Thayer-Bacon, B. (1993). Caring and its relationship to critical thinking. *Educational Theory, 47*, 239–260.

Thayer-Bacon, B., & Bacon, C. (1997). The nurturing of a relational epistemology. *Educational Theory, 47*, 239–260.

Tiedt, I. M. (2000). *Teaching with picture books in the middle school*. Newark, DE: International Reading Association.

Tierney, R. (1998). Literacy assessment reform: Shifting beliefs, principled possibilities, and emerging practices. *The Reading Teacher, 51*(5), 374–390.

Tinajero, J. (2004). *Comprehension instruction for English language learners.* Washington, DC: Hampton-Brown.

Tompkins, G. E. (2006). *Literacy for the 21st century* (4th ed.). Upper Saddle River, NJ: Pearson.

Torres-Guzman, M. E. (1992). Stories of hope in the midst of despair: Culturally responsive education for Latino students in an alternative high school in New York City. In M. Saravia-Shore & S. F. Arvizu (Eds.), *Cross-cultural literacy: Ethnographies of communication in multi-ethnic classrooms* (pp. 477–490). New York: Garland.

Triplett, C. F. (2007). The social construction of "struggle": Influences of school literacy contexts, curriculum, and relationships. *Journal of Literacy Research, 39(1),* 95–126.

Turbill, J. (2001). A researcher goes to school: Using technology in the kindergarten literacy curriculum. *Journal of Early Childhood Literacy, 1,* 255–279.

Uludag, A. (2008). Elementary preservice teachers' opinions about parental involvement in elementary children's education. *Teaching and Teacher Education, 24,* 807–817.

Uribe, M., & Nathenson-Mejia, S. (2008). *Literacy essentials for English language learners.* New York: Teachers College Press.

U.S. Department of Education (1994). No Child Left Behind Act 2001. (Pub. 1, No. 107-110). http://www. 2.ed.gov/policy/elsec/leg/esea02/107-110.pdf

Valencia, R., & Black, M. (2002). "Mexican Americans don't value education!": On the basis of myth, mythmaking and debunking. *Journal of Latinos and Education, 1*(2), 81–103.

Valencia, S. W. (2011). Reader profiles and reading disabilities. In A. McGill-Franzen & R. L Allington (Eds.), *Handbook of reading disability research* (pp. 25–35). New York: Routledge.

Van Sluys, K., & Reinier, R. (2006). "Seeing the possibilities": Learning from, with, and about multilingual classroom communities. *Language Arts, 83*(4), 321–331.

Vander Zanden, S., & Wohlwend, K. E. (2011). Paying attention to procedural texts: Critically reading school routines as embodied achievement. *Language Arts, 88*(5), 337–345.

Vellutino, F. R., & Scanlon, D. M. (2002). The interactive strategies approach to reading intervention. *Contemporary Educational Psychology, 27,* 573–635.

Vellutino, F. R., Scanlon, D. M., Sipay, E. R., Small, S. G., Pratt, A., Chen, R., & Denckla, M. B. (1996). Cognitive profiles of difficult-to-remediate and readily remeidated poor readers: Early intervention as a vehicle for distinguishing between cognitive and experiential deficits as basic causes of specific reading disability. *Journal of Educational Psychology, 88,* 601–638.

*Vision: Quote/Unquote.* (2002). Bedford, MA: Applewood Books.

Vygotsky, L. (1978). Interaction between learning and development. In *Mind and society* (pp. 79–91). Cambridge, MA: Harvard University Press.

Walker-Dalhouse, D., & Dalhouse, A. D. (2006). Investigating White preservice teachers' beliefs about teaching in culturally diverse classrooms. *The Negro Educational Review, 57*(1–2), 69–84.

Walmsley, S. A. (2006). Getting the big idea: A neglected goal for reading comprehension. *The Reading Teacher, 60*(3), 281–285.

Whitin, P. E. (2009). "Tech-to-stretch": Expanding possibilities for literature response. *The Reading Teacher, 62*(5), 408–418.

Wigfield, A., & Guthrie, J. T. (1997). Relations of children's motivation for reading to the amount and breadth of their reading. *Journal of Educational Psychology, 89*, 420–432.

Williams, C., & Lundstrom, R. P. (2007). Strategy instruction during word study and interactive writing activities. *The Reading Teacher, 61*(3), 204–212.

Willingham, D. T. (2009). *Why don't students like school? A cognitive scientist answers questions about how the mind words and what it means for the classroom.* San Francisco: Jossey-Bass.

Willingham, D. T. (2010). Teaching content is teaching reading. Available at http://www.youtube.com/watch?v=RiP-ijdxqEc

Wixson, K. K., & Valencia, S. W. (2011). Assessment in RTI: What teachers and specialists need to know. *The Reading Teacher, 64*(6), 466–469.

Wolf, M. (2007). *Proust and the squid: The story and science of the reading brain.* New York: HarperCollins.

Wolfram, W., Adger, C. T., & Christian, D. (1999). *Dialects in schools and communities.* Mahwah, NJ: Erlbaum.

Wolk, S. (2009). Reading for a better world: Teaching for social responsibility with young adult literature. *Journal of Adolescent & Adult Literacy, 52*(8), 664–673.

Woods, K. D., Harmon, J. M., & Hedrick, W. B. (2004). Teaching vocabulary to diverse learners: Recommendations from the research. *Middle School Journal, 35*(5), 57–63.

Yopp, R. H., & Yopp, H. K. (2000). Sharing informational text with young children. *The Reading Teacher, 53*(5), 410–423.

Young, C., & Rasinski, T. (2009). Implementing Readers Theatre as an approach to classroom fluency instruction. *The Reading Teacher, 63*(1), 4–13.

Zentalla, A. C. (1997). *Growing up bilingual: Puerto Rican children in New York.* Oxford, UK: Blackwell.

## CHILDREN'S BOOKS CITED

Aardema, V. (1975). *Why mosquitoes buzz in people's ears.* New York: Scholastic.

Adler, D. A. (2003). *A picture book of Lewis and Clark.* New York: Holiday House.

Aiken, J. (1987). *The wolves of Willoughby Chase.* New York: Dell Yearling.

Avi. (1981). *Who stole the wizard of Oz?* New York: Knopf.

Bradman, T. (2007). *Give me shelter: Stories about children who seek asylum.* London: Frances Lincoln Children's Books.

Cha, D. (1996). *Dia's story cloth* [stitched by Chue & Nhia Thao Cha]. New York: Lee & Low.

Coates, J. L. (2010). *A hare in the elephant's trunk.* Markham, Ontario, Canada: Red Deer Press.

Davidson, M. (1986). *I have a dream: The story of Martin Luther King*. New York: Scholastic.

De Vicq de Cumptich, R. (2000). *Bembo's zoo*. New York: Henry Holt.

Elting, M., & Folsom, M. (2005). *Q is for duck: An alphabet guessing game*. Boston: Sandpiper.

Fleischman, P. (1997). *Seedfolks*. New York: Harper Collins.

Galdone, P. (1975). *The frog prince*. New York: Scholastic.

Hermes, P. (2001). *The starving time: Elizabeth's Jamestown colony*. New York: Scholastic.

Hoffman, M. (2002). *The color of home* (K. Littlewood, Illus.). New York: Phyllis Fogelman Books.

Hughes, L. (1990). *Selected poems of Langston Hughes*. New York: Vantage Classics, Vantage Books.

Kroll, S. (1996). *Lewis and Clark: Explorers of the American West*. New York: Holiday House.

L'Engle, M. (1973). *A wrinkle in time*. New York: Dell Yearling.

Levine, E. (2007). *Henry's freedom box: A true story from the Underground Railroad* (K. Nelson, Illus.). New York: Scholastic Press.

Lewis, C. S. (1995). *The lion, witch and the wardrobe* (R. Lawrie, Illus. & Ed.) [Graphic novel]. New York: HarperCollins.

Lombard, J. (2006). *Drita, my homegirl: A story of a refugee girl from Kosovo*. New York: Penguin.

Martin, B., Jr., Archambault, J., & Rand, T. (1997). *Knots on a counting rope*. New York: Macmillan.

Parks, R. (with Haskins, J.). (1992). *Rosa Parks: My story*. New York: Scholastic.

Pellegrino, M. (2009). *Journey of dreams*. London, UK: Frances Lincoln Children's Books.

Raschka, C. (2003). *Talk to me about the alphabet*. New York: Henry Holt.

Rey, H. A., & Rey, M. (1969). *Curious George*. Boston: Houghton Mifflin.

Sharmat, M. J. (2002). *Nate the great* (M. Smont, Illus.). New York: Delacorte.

Tan, S. (2007). *The arrival*. New York: Arthur Levine Books/Scholastic.

Taylor, M. D. (1990). *Mississippi bridge* (M. Ginsburg, Illus.). New York: Penguin Books.

Williams, K. L., &, Mohammad, K. (2007). *Four feet, Two sandals*. Grand Rapids, MI: Eerdmans Books for Young Readers.

Williams, M. (2001). *Brothers in hope: The story of the lost boys of Sudan* (G. Christie, Illus.). New York: Lee & Low.

Wood, J. (1991). *Moo Moo, Brown Cow* (R. Bonner, Illus.). New York: Harcourt.

# Index

Aardema, V., 40
*Aaron Shepard's RT Page*, 109
Abbott, R. D., 13–14
Abitova, S., 45
Abrego, M. H., 159
Adam (case), 97, 98–99, 104–106
Adger, C. T., 22
Adler, David A., 143
Afflerbach, P. P., 39, 54
African American English (AAE), 22
African Americans
  codeswitching by, 9, 24
  Colin (student), 1–4, 5, 7–8, 10–13, 16, 19,
     130–131, 134–139, 142–143, 164–165
  context of genuine caring and, 24
  dialectical differences, 22
  Kwanzaa principles, 25–26
  labeling students, 12
  Maria (student), 84–86, 93–96
  parent and family involvement, 157, 160
  Shakeela (student), 40, 55–56
  vocabulary development, 126
Aghalarov, S., 149
Aiken, J., 58–59, 60–62
Albarran, C. D., 150
Alexander, K. L., 14
Allen, J., 28, 36, 37, 111
  Allington, Richard L., ix, xi, 10, 14, 88, 92
Alvarez, H., 9
Alvarez, Marino C., 139–140, 144–145, 149
Alvermann, D., 23
Amanti, C., 22–23, 141
American Education Research Association
  (AERA), 119, 126
Analogies, 105–106
Analytical thinking, 76, 146–147
Anchors
  in anchored instruction, 68, 70–72, 133
  defined, 68
  teaching with, 72–78
  videos as, 72–82
Angelou, Maya, 26
Animated talking, 29–30
Annenberg Foundation, 101
Anthony, J. L., 89–90

Applegate, A. J., 63
Applegate, M. D., 63
Arazi, J., 95
Archambault, J., 151
Arragones, A., 19, 21
*The Arrival* (Tan), 27–28, 33
Artiles, A. J., xi, 12, 44
Asan, A., 144
Ash, G. E., 137
Ashalatha, K. V., 158
Asian Americans, Aslam (case), 40–41, 55,
  58–62
Aslam (case), 40–41, 55, 58–62
Asselin, M., 143
Assessment, 39–67
  case analyses, 40–41, 55–62
  comprehension, 46–47, 51–55
  conceptualizing, 41–44
  ecological perspective on, 42, 43
  features of useable reading, 43–44
  formative, 63–65
  importance of, 165–166
  of instructional goals and reading activities,
    139
  miscue analysis in, 47–48, 50
  multiple and ongoing, 88
  of multiple skills, 59–65
  preassessment of student beliefs, 36
  reading fluency, 51
  running records in, 48–50, 62, 135–136
  situated in authentic reading activities,
    46–59
  situated in doable activity, 66
  situated in multimodal representations,
    65–66
  situated in students' perspective, 44–46
  of student strengths and difficulties,
    134–138
  summative, 65
  as support for instruction, 42–43
  of text, 138–139
  of vocabulary development, 112
Au, K., 23, 44, 124
August, D. E., 22, 93, 94, 119, 125
Authentic texts

Authentic texts (*continued*)
    in anchored instruction, 70–71
    assessment situated in authentic reading
        activities, 46–59
    importance of, 10
    nature of, 10
Automaticity, 51
Avalos, M. A., 95
Avi, 69

Bacon, C., 23–24
Baker, S. K., 119, 121–123, 126
Baldwin, James, 19
Baquedano-López, P., 9
Barnes, W. S., 13, 157
Barone, D., 123
Barr, R., 14
Barry, A., 93
Bass, J. A. F., 4
Bauer, E. B., 24, 95
Beck, I. L., 116, 118, 125, 126, 128, 145
Beed, P. L., 105
*Bembo's Zoo* (de Vicq de Cumptich), 123
Bennett, L., 15
Bennett, W. J., 24
Bennett-Armistead, V. S., 147
Berninger, V. W., 13–14
Best, A. M., 12
Biemiller, A., 111, 118
Billman, A. K., 16
Biographies, 26
Blachowicz, C. L. Z., 10, 117
Black, M., 13
Black, P., 64
Blacks. *See* African Americans
Blair, T. R., 125
Blake, S., 64
Blanks, B., 88
Block, C. C., 90, 91
Blogging, 150
Bloome, D., 38, 42
Bock, K. P., 93
Bourdieu, P., 22
Brabham, E. G., 15, 16
Bracey, G. W., 39
Bradman, T., 34
Bransford, John D., 5, 10, 48, 70, 71, 73, 78, 142,
        143
Bridges, E. S., 132, 143, 149
*Brothers in Hope* (Williams), 33–34
Brown, A. L., 5, 10, 48, 78, 142, 143
Burg, S., 14
Burgess, S. R., 157
Burke, C., 47
Burns, L. D., 127
Burns, M. S., 156

Bursuck, B., 88
Bus, A. G., 93, 157

Caldwell, J., 85
Camburn, E., 70, 72
Cárdenas-Hagan, E., 93, 94
Caring, 23–24
Carlo, M., 119, 125
Carrier, K. A., 66
Carson, J., 71
Carver, George Washington, 26
Case, R., 4
Cases
    Adam (student), 97, 98–99, 104–106
    Aslam (student), 40–41, 55, 58–62
    Catherine (student), 111–116, 119–121, 127
    Christine (teacher), 20–21, 24–26
    Colin (student), 1–4, 5, 7–8, 10–13, 16, 19,
        130–131, 134–139, 142–143, 164–165
    Erin (teacher), 21, 27–28
    Mr. Hall (teacher), 29
    Jenny (student), 41, 55, 56–58
    Jeremy (student), 97, 99–100, 106–109
    Kayla (student), 6
    Lenia (student), 69, 72, 81–82
    Maria (student), 85–86, 93–96
    Meg (student), 76–78
    Mr. Nelson (teacher), 73–82
    Seth (teacher), 21, 27
    Shakeela (student), 40, 55–56
    William (student), 152–155
Catherine (case), 111–116, 119–121, 127
Cech, S. J., 64
Cecil, N. L., 22
Celebration Press, 51
Central concepts, 140–141
Cha, D., 34
Chandler, J., 13, 157
Chandra, V., 150
Chapman, J. W., 14
Chard, D. J., 89, 90, 121–123
Charity, A. H., 22
Chavez, C., 95
Chen, M., 152
Chen, R., 101
*The Children's Book of Virtues* (Bennett), 24
Chocolate and Child Labor PSA, 68, 73
Christian, B., 38
Christian, D., 22
Christine (case), 20–21, 24–26
Chudowsky, N., 43
Clark, K., 10
Clay, Marie M., 43, 48–49, 55, 58–59, 91, 100,
        107
Cleveland, M. D., 90, 91
Coates, J. L., 33, 35

Cocking, R. R., 5, 10, 48, 78, 142, 143
Codeswitching, 9, 24, 27
Coding, R. M., 112
Cognition and Technology Group (CTG) at
    Vanderbilt University, 70, 75, 76
Cole, A. D., 105
Cole, M., 4, 11
Colin (case), 1–4, 5, 7–8, 10–13, 16, 19, 130–131,
    134–139, 142–143, 164–165
Collier, G. V., 54
Collins, K. M., xi
*The Color of Home* (Hoffman), 34
Comic Creator on the Read-Write-Think
    website, 150
Comic strips, 150
Common Core Standards, 31–32, 133
Common text, 1
Comprehension, 129–151
    of anchors, 72
    assessment of, 46–47, 51–55
    difficulties students experience, 131–132
    guided instruction in, 130–139
    maximizing benefits of guided text
        instruction, 139–143
    reading to deepen, 143–150
Comprehension assessments, 46–47, 51–55
Compton-Lilly, C., 11–12, 13, 19, 45, 161
Concept maps, 144–145
Conceptual instruction
    assessment and, 41–44
    connecting concepts across curriculum, 75,
        79–80
    early literacy, 89–91
    guided instruction in comprehension, 130–139
    involving parents and family, 155–158
    nature of, 17, 165
    videos in, 72–82
    vocabulary development, 100–103, 116–129
Conditional knowledge, 75, 79
Connor, C. M., 22
Constructivist perspective, 4
Context for learning, 23–26
Conversations, 45
Cooke, N. L., 88–89
Cooper, C. E., 158
Cope, B., 132, 143, 147
Cornell, E. H., 119
Correa-Kovtun, A., 147
Costello, P., 43, 44
Coutinho, M. J., 12
Coyne, M. D., 123, 128
Craig, H. K., 22
Crandell, J. D., 121
Creativity, 17
Critical stance, in culturally relevant teaching,
    29–30

Croce, K., 149
Crosnoe, M., 158
Cross-checking, 49
Cross-curricular connections, 75, 79–80
Cultural and linguistic background
    capitalizing on, 4, 19–38
    creating context for learning, 23–26
    foundations for instruction, 23
    lack of culturally responsive instruction,
        10–12, 18
    teachers teaching students with
        backgrounds different from their
        own, 21, 27–28
Cultural capital, 22
Cultural competence, 28–30
Culturally responsive instruction
    cultural modeling, 30–35
    lack of, 10–12, 18
    need for, 11, 18, 132–133
    in reading, 28–30
    teacher preparation for diverse teaching,
        35–37
Cultural modeling, 30–35
    example of, 31–35
    nature of, 30–31
Cumming, S., 91
Cummins, J., 4, 102, 126, 131
Cunningham, P., 98
*Curious George* (Rey & Rey), 27
Curriculum-Based Reader's Theater, 127
Cziko, C., 117

Dail, A. R. K., 42
Dalhouse, A. D., 159
Dalton, B., 120
Daniel, M. C., 66
Darling-Hammond, L., 35
Dasinger, S., 4
Davidson, M., 121
Delpit, L., 9, 29
Denckla, M. B., 101
Denton, C. A., 89–90, 119
Developmental Reading Assessment, 51
De Vicq de Cumptich, R., 123
Devlin, Katie, 45
Dewey, John, 75, 111
*Dia's Story Cloth* (Cha), 34
Digital stories, 150
Dinkes, R., xi
Discussions, 133–134, 143
Diversity
    standards concerning, 23
    teacher preparation for diverse learning,
        35–37
Donahue, P. L., xi
Donovan, C. A., 93

Dorner, L., 94, 124
Dowdy, J. K., 9
Doyle, M., 149
Dressler, C., 119, 125
*Drita, My Homegirl* (Lombard), 34
Drummond, K. V., 157–158
Dudley-Marling, C., 119, 160
Duke, N. K., 10, 16, 91, 93, 147
Dupree, D., 153–154, 163
Durgunoglu, A. Y., 125
Dworin, J. E., 4, 11, 45
Dysfluent reading, 51

Early Childhood Study of Language and
    Literacy Development of Spanish-
    Speaking Children (ECS), 93
Early Reading First (ERF), 116
Early reading instruction, 84–96
    beneficial factors, 91–93
    conceptualizing early literacy instruction,
        89–91
    early literacy experiences and, 87–89,
        118–119, 156–157
    Maria (student), 84–86, 95–96
    socioeconomic status and, 87–88, 90, 93, 162
Ebbers, S. M., 119
EBD (emotional and behavioral disorder), 12
Ecological assessment, 42, 43
Edwards, E. C., 127
Ehlers-Zavala, F., 66
Ehri, L. C., 105, 106
Elementary and Secondary Education Act of
    1965, 116
Elish-Piper, L., 4
Ellsworth, R. A., 14
Elting, M., 123
Empowerment
    characteristics of instruction for, 17–18
    as goal of instruction, 17, 165–166
Engaged readers, nature of, 14
Engagement
    nature of engaged readers, 14
    reading difficulties and, 7, 18
English learners
    classroom teachers of, 21, 27–28
    vocabulary development of, 111, 117–119,
        124–127
Entwisle, D. R., 14
Equity, inattention to, 12–13
Erin (case), 21, 27–28
Escobar, M. D., 13
Espinosa, L., 96
Expertise
    building, 76–77
    production and deepening, 82
Expository writing skills, 11–12

Faith, L., 105
Faller, S., 140
Family story project, 45–46, 160–161
Fan, X., 152
Fanuele, D. P., 90
Farstrup, A. E., 51
Fergus, E., 159, 161–162
Fien, H., 121–123
Fiene, J., 64–65
Fingon, J., 162
Fisher, P. J. L., 117
Fitton, L., 162
Fitzgerald, J., 126
Fleischman, Paul, 71
Fletcher, J. M., 13, 89–90
Fluency, 51, 108–109
Folsom, M., 123
Ford, D., xi
Formative assessment, 63–65
Fountas, I. C., 109
*Four Feet, Two Sandals* (Williams &
    Mohammad), 34
Francis, D. J., 89–90
Frank, C., 162

Galdone, P., 55–56
Gambrell, L. B., 112
Gamoran, A., 45
Ganske, K., 15, 107, 158
Garas-York, K., 22
Garcia, G. E., 125
Gaskins, I. W., 104–107
Gates McGinitie Reading Test, 112
Gee, J., 140–141
Gelzheiser, L. M., 90
Gender differences, reading difficulties and,
    13–14
Genuine caring, 23–24
Gersten, R., 63, 126
*Give Me Shelter* (Bradman), 34
Glaser, R., 43
Glienke, B. B., 14
Goetz, E. T., 116
Goldman, S. R., 8–9, 70
Gonzalez, G. C., 87
Gonzalez, J. E., 116
Gonzalez, N., 22–23, 141
Goodman, I. F., 13, 157
Goodman, J., 71
Goodman, Kenneth S., 47
Goodman, Y., 46–48, 64
Gordon, J. G., 153–154, 163
Gormley, K. A., 44, 130, 166
Gowin, D. B., 144–145
Graphic novels, 27–28, 98, 142–143, 147–149
Graphic organizers, 118, 120–121, 122

Graphophonemic cues, 49, 50, 101, 102, 103, 105, 106–107, 109
Graves, A., 63
Graves, M. F., 15, 16, 117, 127
Gredler, G. R., 162
Greenberg, J., 4, 13, 157, 159
Greenleaf, C. L., 117
Griffin, D., 22
Griffin, P., 156
Griffin, S., 4
Griffiths, A. J., 88
Grigg, W. S., xi
Grisham, D. L., 120
Grouping arrangements, 81–82
Guided instruction, 129–151
    Colin (case), 130–131, 133–139
    comprehension difficulties of students, 131–132
    comprehension instruction as game changer, 132–134
    conceptualizing instruction, 130–139
    guided reading, 94–95
    importance of, 10
    instructional text discussions, 133–134
    maximizing benefits of, 139–143
    nature of, 10
    preparing for comprehension instruction, 134–139
    reading to deepen comprehension, 143–150
    text talk and productions, 134, 149–150
Gustafson, S., 105
Guthrie, J. T., 6, 7, 10, 15
Gutiérrez, K., 3, 4, 9

Hakuta, K. E., 22
Hall, L. A., 127
Hall, Mr. (case), 29
*A Hare in the Elephant's Trunk* (Coates), 33, 35
Haria, P., 121–123
Harmon, J. M., 123–124, 126
Harn, B., 89
Harrison, Kent, 68, 72–82
*Harry Potter* series, 73, 134, 147
Harste, Jerry C., 19, 38
Hart, B., 119
Haskins, J., 116
Hawkins, E. M., 105
He, Y., 159–161
Hecht, S. A., 157
Hedrick, W. B., 126
Heimann, M., 105
Helf, S., 88–89
Heller, J. I., 145
Hemphill, L., 13, 157
Henderson, A. T., 152
*Henry's Freedom Box* (Levine), 114–116

Hermann-Wilmarth, J., 28, 36, 37
Hermes, P., 143
Hibbing, A. N., 149
Hiebert, E. H., 15, 16, 54, 91
Hispanic Americans. *See* Latinos
Hoffman, M., 34
Hogan, B., 156, 157
Hoien, T., 100–101
Hollins, E. R., 23
Home language, 40–41
Hoot, J., 23
*How People Learn* (Bransford et al.), 78
*How We Think* (Dewey), 111
Hughes, Langston, 26, 116
Hulan, N., 36, 127
Hull, G., 65
Hurley, S. R., 64
Hussar, W., xi

Iaquinta, A., 95
*I Can* books, 41
Iddings, A. C. D., 9, 21, 27, 46
*I Have a Dream* (King), 121
Ijzendoorn, M. H. van, 157
Imagination, 17
Independence in reading, 164–166
Independent-level texts, 15–16
Individuals with Disabilities Education Improvement Act (IDEIA), 63, 88
Ingersoll, R. M., 35
Instructional-level texts, 15–16
Instructional sequence, cultural data sets and, 34–35
Interest, reading difficulties and, 7
International Reading Association (IRA), 12, 23, 159
Intervention Only (IO), 90
Interviews, with family members, 45
Investing in Innovation Fund, 71
*I See* books, 41
*The Island* (Lewis), 2, 138, 142
Ivey, G., 137
Izmukhanbetova, S., 45

Jalongo, M., 117
Jamieson-Noel, D., 143
Jenkins, J. R., 15
Jenkins, S., 155
Jenny (case), 41, 55, 56–58
Jeremy (case), 97, 99–100, 106–109
Jewett, P. C., 71
Johnson, A. S., 37, 157
Johnson, S., 25
Johnson-Laird, P. N., 74–75
Johnston, P., 43, 44, 46, 64
*Journey of Dreams* (Pellegrino), 33, 34–35

Juel, C., 107

Kalantzis, M., 132, 143, 147
Kalieva, R., 45
Kame'enui, E. J., 89, 90, 119, 128
Kapinus, B. A., 54
Kapp, S., 123
Karolyn, L. A., 87
Kawell, S., 162
Kay, A. M., 155
Kayla (case), 6
Kea, C. D., 36
Kear, D. J., 14
Kelley, J. G., 140
Kelly, S., 142
Kemp, J., xi
Kena, G., xi
Kenner, C., 24
KewalRamani, A., xi
Kidd, J. K., 160–161
Kieffer, M. J., 22, 117, 126–127, 140
Kim, M., 116
King, Martin Luther, 25, 26, 121
Kinzer, C. K., 70, 71, 73
Kirby, J. R., 156, 157
Kiser, K., 123–124
Klingner, J., 124
Knobel, M., 150
*Knots on the Counting Rope* (Martin et al.), 151
Knowledge acquisition, 17
Knowledge as tool, 77–78
Kong, A., 63
Kozleski, E., xi
Kragler, S., 101
Kretlow, A. G., 88–89
Kroll, Stephen, 143
Kruglanski, H., 54
Kucan, L., 118, 125, 145
Kuhn, M. R., 137
Kwanzaa principles, 25–26

Labbo, L. D., 37, 104
Labeling students, 3, 8–9, 12, 87–88
Labov, W., 37
Ladson-Billings, G., 28, 29
Laffey, J., 96
Landis, D., 45
Language development
    codeswitching, 9, 24, 27
    miscue analysis in, 47–48, 50
    teaching students with languages different
        from teacher, 27–28
    text selection and, 27–28
Lankshear, C., 150
Lantolf, J. P., 24
Latinos. *See also* English learners

codeswitching by, 27
early reading instruction for, 84–86, 93–96
labeling students, 12
Maria (student), 84–86, 95–96
parent and family involvement, 159
teaching students with languages different
    from teacher, 27
vocabulary development of English
    learners, 111, 124–127
Lau-Tsze, 24–25
Lawrie, Robert, 142
Layne, V., 127
Learners as competent (Gutiérrez & Lee), 4
Learning environments, 78–81
Learning Sciences Group at the University of
    Washington, 71
Learning with understanding, 76
Lee, C. D., 3, 4, 30–31
Lee, J., xi
Lemke, J. L., 140–141
L'Engle, Madeleine, 73–74
Lenia (case), 69, 72, 81–82
Lenski, S. D., 66
Lesaux, N. K., 95, 117, 124, 126–127, 140
Leslie, L., 85
Leveled texts, 15–16, 55
Levine, E., 114–116
Lewis, C. S., 2, 130, 138–141, 142–148
Lewis, T. J., 88
*Lewis and Clark* (Kroll), 143
Life history reviews, 157
Lilles, E., 88
Linan-Thompson, S., 89, 93, 94
*The Lion, the Witch, and the Wardrobe* (Lewis),
    138–139, 142–143
Literacy development, reasons for reading
    difficulties, 5–16
Literacy in Families Empowers (LIFE), 162–163
Littleton, K. S., 150
Lombard, J., 34
Long, S., 161
Lonigan, C. J., 157
Lopez, M. M., 93
López-Robertson, J., 161
Love, M. S., 71
Lovelace, S., 126
Lucas, K., 119
Lundstrom, R. P., 108
Lush, L. H., 155

Maderazo, C., 149
Maher, M., 36
Mallette, M., 123
Mancilla-Martinez, J., 95, 124
Mandela, Nelson, 26
Manjula, P., 158

Manyak, P. C., 24
Mapp, K. L., 152
Maria (case), 84–86, 95–96
Marks, H. M., 45
Martens, P., 149
Martens, R., 149
Martin, B., Jr., 151
Martin, L. A., 91
Martin, L. E., 101
Martin, M., 159, 161–162
Martineau, J. A., 10
Martinez, D. C., 3, 45–46, 94
Mathes, P. G., 89–90, 93, 94
Matthews, M. W., 4
May, L., 29–30
Mazzoni, S. A., 112
McAllister, Dena, 51, 53
McCarthey, S. J., 19
McCarthy, 11
McCarty, T. L., 102
McCoach, B., 123
McCormick, A. S., 116
McDermott, P., 44, 130, 166
McDermott, R., 8–9, 44
McGee, L., 121
McGeehan, C. M., 63
McGill-Franzen, A., 14
McGough, K., 15
McIntosh, A. S., 63
McIntyre, E., 36, 92, 93, 127
McKenna, M. C., 14
McKeown, M. G., 116, 118, 125, 126, 128, 145
McLarty, K., 71
McLoyd, V. C., 12
McMahon, S., 64–65
Meadows, D., 65
Meece, J. L., 14
Meg (case), 76–78
Mendenhall, R., 30–31
Mental models, 74–75
Mesmer, H. A. E., 91
Meyer, B. J. F., 147
Meza, M., 94, 124
Microblogging, 150
Mills, K. A., 143, 150
Milner, H. R., IV, 29
Minden-Cupp, C., 107
Miscue analysis, 47–48, 50
*Mississippi Bridge* (Taylor), 115
Modified Guided Reading, 95
Mohammad, K., 34
Moje, E., 19
Mol, S. E., 93
Moll, L. C., 4, 11, 13, 22–23, 141, 157, 159
Monroe, J. K., 15, 158
*Moo Moo Brown Cow* (Wood), 57

Morris, D., 100–101
Morrison, K. A., 29–30
Morrow, Emily, 150
Morrow, L. M., 10, 93
Motivation, issues of, 14
Movie trailers, 150
Mraz, M., 118
Mueller, F. L., 117
Mueller, P., 3, 4, 6
Multiple texts, 18, 32–34, 81–82
Musaeva, Z., 45

Nagy, W. E., 111, 125
Names Test (Cunningham), 98–99
*Narnia Remix Book Trailer*, 150
*Narnia* series (Lewis), 2–4, 5, 7, 8, 10–11, 73, 130, 134–148, 150
*Nate the Great* (Sharmat), 69
Nathenson-Mejia, S., 94
Nation, P., 126
National Comprehensive Center for Teacher Quality & Public Agenda, 36
National Endowment for the Arts, xi
National Institute of Child Health and Human Development (NICHD), 89, 116, 119
National Reading Panel (NRP), 116
National Research Council (NRC), 63
Native Americans
    labeling students, 12
    vocabulary development, 102
Neff, D., 22–23, 141
Neher, A., 155
Nelson, M., 65
Nelson, Mr. (case), 73–82
Newman, F. M., 45
Nichols, W. D., 118, 125
Nielsen, K. H., 13–14
Nieto, S., 3, 161
Noble, R., 149
No Child Left Behind Act of 2001 (NCLB), 116
Nocon, H., 4, 11
Noguera, P., 159, 161–162
Noll, E., 3
Nondominant students
    defined, 3
    as struggling readers, 3
*Notes of a Native Son* (Baldwin), 19

Ogle, D., 10, 147
Ohler, J., 65
Oldfather, P., 15
Olson, L. S., 14
Omanson, R. C., 126
Opitz, M. F., 137
Oral reading, assessment situated in authentic reading activities, 42, 46–59

Ordonez-Jasis, R., 13, 157
Orellana, M. F., 3, 24, 45–46, 94, 124
Organizational features of text, 147–149
Ortiz, R. W., 13, 157
Oswald, D. P., 12

Páez, M. M., 93
Painter, J., 45
Palmer, B. M., 112
Palumbo, A., 127
Pappas, C. C., 93
Parent and family involvement, 152–163
    conceptualizing, 155–158
    early literacy experiences and, 87–89,
        118–119, 156–157
    family stories in, 45–46, 160–161
    intervention programs, 158
    preservice teachers and, 159–162
    reading difficulties and, 13
    socioeconomic status and, 13, 87–88,
        157–158, 161
    student interviews with family members,
        45
    in text selection, 153–155
    universities and schools in, 161–162
    in vocabulary development, 118–119
    William (case), 152–155
Paris, S., 101
Park, Y., 121–123
Parks, Rosa, 116, 119–120
Parris, S. R., 90, 91
Parrish, T., 12
Paterson, Katherine, 129
Pattern recognition, 75
Payne, T., 116
Pearson, P. D., 10, 157
Pease-Alvarez, L., 10, 102
Pellegrino, J. W., 43
Pellegrino, M., 33, 34–35
Pelligrini, A. D., 157
Perez, B., 9
Perfetti, C. A., 126
Personal Museums (Winnipeg, Canada), 45
Perspective taking, 146–147
Perspective-taking, 80–81
Petrosko, J., 92, 93
Peverini, S., 64, 66
Peyton, J. A., 15
Philippot, R. A., 16
Phonemic awareness, 101
Phonics, 92, 94–95, 98, 102, 105, 109, 135
*Phonics and Word Study Lessons from Fountas &
    Pinnell*, 109
Pianta, R. C., 90
Pickering, C., 45
*A Picture Book of Lewis and Clark* (Adler), 143

Picture books, 96, 143, 149
Picture clues, 41
Pinnell, G. S., 109
Pinto, C. M., 63
Pituch, K., 158
Pixton Comics Website, 150
Pizzo, L., 93
Planty, M., xi
Plasencia, A., 95
Pluralism, inattention to, 12–13
Pollard-Durodola, S. D., 93, 94
Popham, W. J., 64
Pople, M. T., 126
Portes, P., 3, 5
Powell, R., 92, 93
Powers, S., 92, 93
Prakash, P., 158
Pratt, A., 101
Preservice teachers. *See* Teacher preparation
Pressley, M. P., 10, 157
Previewing text, 139–140, 141, 142–143
Prior knowledge
    activating and extending, 141
    connections between new concepts and,
        4–5
    in cultural modeling, 32
Proactive Reading, 89–90, 94
Problem solving, 79
Procedural knowledge, 75, 79
Prochnow, J. E., 14
Proctor, P., 119
Professional Development Only (PDO), 90
Prosody, 51, 109
Proverbs, 24–25, 26
Purcell-Gates, V., 10
Purtell, K. M., 12

*Q Is for Duck* (Elting & Folsom), 123
QRI, 85
Questions, generating, 74

Ramey, C. T., 13, 157
Ramey, L., 13, 157
Rampulla, M. P., 9, 21, 27, 46
Rand, T., 151
RAND Reading Study Group, 143
Rankin-Erickson, J. L., 149
Raschka, C., 123
Rascon, J., 95
Rasinski, Timothy V., 51, 107, 109, 137
Raskind, W., 13–14
Read, S., 91, 95
Read Aloud Curriculum, 123
Reader's Theater, 109, 127
*Reader's Theater Scripts and Plays*, 109
Reading aloud, 29–30, 93–94, 121–123, 131, 135

Reading difficulties, 5–16
    gender differences, 13–14
    identifying, 6–7
    inattention to equity and pluralism, 12–13
    interest and engagement, 7, 18
    issues of reading motivation, 14
    labeling students, 3, 8–9, 12, 87–88
    lack of appropriate and timely instruction,
        10
    lack of culturally responsive instruction,
        10–12, 18
    mindset for identifying problems, 8–9
    parent involvement and, 13
    predicting failure, 8–9
    skills and strategy development, 7–8, 17
    text correlations for student improvement,
        15–16
Reading First (RF), 116
Reading Recovery, 91, 100–101
Reading Workshop, 85–86, 125
Reed, K. L., 90, 91
Reif, F., 145
Reinier, R., 23
Repetitive texts, 15
Response to Intervention (RTI), 88
Responsive Reading, 89–90
Retellings, 51–57, 137
Rey, H. A., 27
Rey, M., 27
Reynolds, J. F., 3, 24, 45–46, 94, 124
Rice, M. E., 15
Richgels, D., 107, 121
Rickelman, R. J., 118
Rife, A., 93
Rightmyer, E., 92, 93
Riley, D. W., 25
Rinaldi, C., 89
Risko, Vicki J., 4, 9, 19, 21, 27, 30–31, 37, 39, 45,
    46, 53, 70, 71, 73, 132, 139–140, 143, 149,
    152, 155
Risley, T. R., 119
Rivers, A., 30–31
Robbins, H. H., 29–30
Roderick, M., 70
Rogoff, B., 11
Rohr, J., 159–161
Rojas-Drummond, S. M., 150
Roller, C. M., 105
Romero-Little, M. E., 102
*Rosa Parks* (Parks), 116
Rose, D. G., 29–30
Rosenfeld, E., 30–31
Rowe, D., 71
Rowling, J. K., 147
Rubin, R., 159
Running records, 48–50, 62, 135, 136

Rupley, W. H., 125

Sadik, A., 65–66
Saez, R., 4, 11
Sailors, M., 16
Salas, S., 3, 5
Samson, J., 89
Samuels, S. J., 51
Sanacore, J., 23, 24, 127
Sanchez, S. Y., 160–161
Sanders, E. A., 15
Santa, C., 100–101
Santoro, L., 121–123
Saraswathi, G., 158
Satlow, E., 105, 106
Scanlon, D. M., 90, 101
Scarborough, H. S., 22
Schatschneider, C., 89–90
Schmidt, P. R., 37
Schoenbach, R., 117
Scott, J. A., 111, 143
*Seedfolks* (Fleischman), 71
Self-concept about reading, 14
Self-efficacy, 14
Semantic cues, 49, 50, 101, 102, 103, 105
Senechal, M., 119
Seth (case), 21, 27
Shakeela (case), 40, 55–56
Shanahan, T., 14, 22, 93, 94
Sharmat, M. J., 69
Sharp, Diana L. M., 70
Shaywitz, B. A., 13
Shaywitz, S. E., 13
Shields, P. H., 153–154, 163
Sight vocabulary, 41
Silva, E., 65
Silverman, R., 121
Simmons, D. C., 119, 128
Singh, N., 12
Sipay, E. R., 101
Skill development, 7–8
Skokut, M., 88
SLD (specific learning disability), 12
Small, S. G., 90, 101
Smith, J. A., 91, 95
Smolkin, L. B., 93
Snow, C. E., 13, 119, 125, 156, 157
Snyder, T., xi
Sobolak, M. J., 111, 117, 118
Social justice, 24, 29
Sociocultural perspective, 4
Socioeconomic status
    early literacy experiences and, 87–88, 90,
        93, 162
    parent and family involvement and, 13,
        87–88, 157–158, 161

Socioeconomic status (*continued*)
    reading achievement and, 157, 162
    vocabulary development and, 113, 117–119,
        126
Sokolinski, S., 162–163
Spencer, T. G., 19
Stahl, S., 110
Standard American English (SAE), 22
Standards
    Common Core Standards, 31–32, 133
    diversity, 23
    importance of, 166
*Standards for Reading Professionals*—Revised
    2010, 23
*The Starving Time* (Hermes), 143
*Steck-Vaughn Elements of Reading Vocabulary*,
    118
Stewart, S. R., 126
Stichter, J. P., 88
Stipek, D., 157–158
Stoolmiller, M., 89
Stormont, M., 88
Stornaiuolo, A., 65
Storybook routines and practices, 94
Strategy development, 7–8
Strickland, D., 15, 158
Struggling readers. *See also* Reading difficulties
    helping students make connections, 4–5
    labeling, 3, 8–9, 12, 87–88
    nondominant students as, 3
    perspectives about early readers who
        struggle, 88–89
    reasons for reading difficulties, 5–16
Student perspective, assessment situated in,
    44–46
Stuhlman, M. W., 90
Success in reading, 164–166
Summative assessment, 65
Sun-Irminger, X., 66
Supplemental reading, 88–90
Sutterby, J. A., 159
Svensson, I., 105
Sweeney, J. M., 90
Syntactic cues, 49, 50, 101, 102, 103, 105

Tabaoda, A., 117
Tabors, P. O., 93
Tadesse, S., 23
Takanishi, R., 87
*Talk to Me About the Alphabet* (Raschka), 123
Tan, Shaun, 27–28, 33
Tatum, A., 55
Taylor, A. B., 116
Taylor, B. M., 10, 157
Taylor, D. B., 118
Taylor, M. D., 115

Taylor, R. W., 36
Teacher preparation
    for diverse learning, 35–37
    for parent and family involvement, 159–162
Teaching Reading 3-5 Workshop, Annenberg
    Foundation, 101
Tellez, K., 4
Texts
    authentic, 10
    common, 1
    correlations for student improvement,
        15–16
    independent/instructional-level, 15–16
    leveled, 15–16, 55
    matching to readers, 91–92
    multicultural, 29–30
    need for multiple, 18, 32–34, 81–82
    repetitive, 15
    selecting for language development, 27–28
Thayer-Bacon, B., 23–24
Think aloud procedure, 59, 60–61, 137
Thorp, E. K., 160–161
Tiedt, I. M., 149
Tierney, R., 48
Time spent reading, 10, 92–93
Tinajero, J., 125
Tius, T., 105
*To Kill a Mockingbird*, 73
Tompkins, G. E., 125
Torres-Guzman, M. E., 11, 12, 45
Toxic Avengers (New York City), 12, 45
Tracey, D. H., 10
Trent, S. C., 12
Triplett, C. F., 19, 87
Tunmer, W. E., 14
Turbill, J., 143
Turner, J., 142
Turner-Nash, K., 161
Tynes, B., 30–31

Uludag, A., 159
U.S. Department of Education, 161
University of Washington, Learning Sciences
    Group, 71
Uribe, M., 94
Utley, C. A., 36

Vadasy, P. F., 15
Valencia, R., 13
Valencia, S. W., xi, 54, 63
Vanderbilt University, Cognition and
    Technology Group (CTG), 70, 75, 76
Vanderburg, M. A., 71
VanDerHeyden, A. M., 88
Vander Zanden, S., 165
Van Sluys, K., 23

Varelas, M., 93
Varenne, H., 8–9
Vaughn, S., 89, 93, 94, 124
Velez Ibanez, C., 13, 157, 159
Vellutino, F. R., 90, 101
Villaume, S. K., 15, 16
Vision, 26
Visual cues, 49, 50, 118, 120–121, 122, 144–145
Vocabulary development, 59, 97–128
    Adam (student), 97, 98–99, 104–106
    balanced word identification instruction, 101–102
    Catherine (student), 111–116, 119–121, 127
    conceptualizing instruction, 100–103, 116–129
    of English learners, 111, 117–119, 124–127
    grade-level differences in, 119–121, 126–127
    guidelines for, 117
    importance of, 111
    instructional recommendations, 104–109
    Jeremy (student), 97, 99–100, 106–109
    major components of, 117
    as priority, 116–117
    robust practices in, 97, 104–109, 118, 126, 128
    sight vocabulary, 41
    socioeconomic status and, 113, 117–119, 126
Vye, N. J., 70, 71
Vye, N. Y., 73
Vygotsky, L., 75

Walker-Dalhouse, Doris, 19, 21, 30–31, 37, 39, 132, 143, 149, 152, 155, 159
Walmsley, S. A., 140
Walpole, S., 10, 137
Wanzek, J., 89
Washington, J. A., 22
Watkins, R., 3
Watson, D., 47
Watson-Thompson, O., 23
Waxman, H. C., 4
*What Really Matters for Struggling Readers* (Allington), 92
Whiteley, C. S., 90, 91
Whites
    Jenny (student), 41, 55, 56–58
    Lenia (student), 69, 72, 81–82
    vocabulary development, 111–116, 119–121, 127
Whole-part-whole strategies, 106, 109
*Who Stole the Wizard of Oz* (Avi), 69

*Why Mosquitoes Buzz in People's Ears* (Aardema), 40
Wigfield, A., 6, 14
Wijekumar, K., 147
Wijsman, E., 13–14
William, D., 64
William (case), 152–155
Williams, C., 108
Williams, K. L., 34
Williams, M., 33–34
Williams, S., 121–123
Willingham, Daniel T., 72, 145
Wilson, A., 132, 143, 149
Wilson, J. L., 71
Wixson, K. K., 63
Wohlwend, K. E., 165
Wolf, M., 5
Wolfram, W., 22
Wolk, S., 154
*The Wolves of Willoughby* (Aiken), 58–59, 60–62
Wong, S., 70, 72
Woo, D. G., 10
Wood, J., 57
Wood, K. D., 118, 123–124, 126
Word chunks, 106
Word ladders, 107
Wordle, 120–121, 122
Word learning and identification. *See* Vocabulary development
Word notebooks, 108, 114–115, 126
WordSift, 120–121
*Word Study: Partner Work with a Sort*, 107
*Word Study Lessons* (Pinnell & Fountas), 109
Word walls, 118, 123–124
*A Wrinkle in Time* (video), 68, 72–82
Writing
    gender differences in, 11–12
    in strategic learning, 108

Xu, S., 123

Yopp, H. K., 93
Yopp, R. H., 93
Young, C., 109
Young Audiences Arts for Learning Lessons project, 71
Young Audiences Arts for Learning program, 71
YouTube, 68, 71, 73, 107, 109, 142, 150

Zentalla, A. C., 9

# About the Authors

**Victoria J. Risko** is the 2011–2012 President of the International Reading Association and Professor Emerita, Vanderbilt University. She is a member of the Hall of Fame, International Reading Association. She is a former classroom teacher and reading specialist and for years has collaborated with classroom teachers and curriculum specialists to provide literacy instruction that makes a difference for students, especially students who experience reading difficulties. She is active as a professional development leader and made presentations at IRA World Congresses and European, national, and state conferences located in North America, Europe, Kazakhstan, Bermuda, Jamaica, West Africa, Botswana, Australia, New Zealand, the Philippines, Guatemala, and Costa Rica. Vicki is the recipient of research and outstanding teaching awards; author/co-author of numerous papers and chapters, and co-author of *Declaration of Readers' Rights* (2007) with JoAnn Bass, Sheryl Dasinger, Laurie Elish-Piper, and Mona Matthews and *Collaboration for Diverse Learners* (2001) (with Karen Bromley). Vicki has assumed multiple leadership roles in professional organizations, including her service as co-editor of the annual yearbook of the Literacy Research Association, President of the Association of Literacy Educators and Researchers, and President of the International Book Bank.

**Doris Walker-Dalhouse** is an Associate Professor in the Department of Educational Policy & Leadership at Marquette University and Professor Emerita, Minnesota State University Moorhead. She has served on the Board of Directors of the International Reading Association (IRA), the Literacy Research Association (formerly known as the National Literacy Conference [NRC], and in numerous leadership positions with IRA (President of the Red River Reading Council, Minnesota State Reading Association, and Co-Chair of the Response to Intervention Task Force). She is a former classroom teacher with experience teaching first-, second-, fourth-, fifth- and sixth-grade students, and has worked with elementary, middle, and high school students in reading clinics, high school students in the Upward Bound program, and college students in reading clinics, and developmental reading programs. She organized and operated a community-based reading clinic for Sudanese K-6 students funded by the Otto Bremer Foundation and the Fargo/Moorhead Foundation from 2006–2010, and continues to serve on the Board of Directors of the African Area Alliance. She has served as a national and international consultant and presenter. Doris is the recipient of the *Outstanding Faculty Research Award* at Minnesota State University Moorhead and an IRA *Celebrate Literacy Award* for her work in Minnesota.

Vicki and Doris were co-editors of the Research to Classroom column of *The Reading Teacher* from 2006 to 2011.